D0902610

Reading
in the
Classroom

Systems for
the Observation of
Teaching and Learning

edited by

Sharon Vaughn, Ph.D.

and

Kerri L. Briggs, Ph.D.

·P A U L·H·
BROOKES
PUBLISHING CO®

Baltimore • London • Sydney

Paul H. Brookes Publishing Co.
Post Office Box 10624
Baltimore, MD 21285-0624

www.brookespublishing.com

"Paul H. Brookes Publishing Co." is a registered trademark of
Paul H. Brookes Publishing Co., Inc.

Typeset by Integrated Publishing Solutions, Grand Rapids, Michigan.
Manufactured in the United States of America by
Versa Press, East Peoria, Illinois.

All case studies in this book are based on the authors' actual experiences. In
all instances, names have been changed; in some instances, identifying
details have been altered to further protect confidentiality.

The work for this volume by Kerri L. Briggs was completed in her private
capacity. No official support or endorsement by the U.S. Department of
Education is intended or should be inferred.

Library of Congress Cataloging-in-Publication Data

Reading in the classroom: systems for the observation of teaching and learning
    / edited by Sharon Vaughn and Kerri L. Briggs.
        p.   cm.
    Includes bibliographic references and index.
        ISBN 1-55766-651-2
    1. Reading (Elementary).   2. Observation (Educational method).
LB1573 .R2794   2003
372.41—dc22   2003060005

British Library Cataloguing in Publication data are available from the British
Library.

Reading
in the
Classroom

Contents

About the Editors

Sharon Vaughn, Ph.D., Texas Center for Reading and Language Arts, College of Education, The University of Texas, Austin, Texas 78712

Dr. Vaughn is the H.E. Hartfelder/Southland Corporation Regent's Chair at The University of Texas. She is Director of the Texas Center for Reading and Language Arts and Editor-in-Chief of the *Journal of Learning Disabilities*. She has written numerous book and research essays about issues related to students with learning disabilities and their difficulties, with particular focus on interventions that improve reading and social outcomes.

Kerri L. Briggs, Ph.D., 400 Avenue SW, Washington, D.C. 20202

Dr. Briggs is Special Assistant to the Assistant Secretary for Elementary and Secondary Education at the U.S. Department of Education. In this capacity, Dr. Briggs contributes to the implementation of efforts associated with the No Child Left Behind Act of 2001 (PL 107-110). Prior to that, she was Director of Evaluation at the Texas Center for Reading and Language Arts at The University of Texas. She has co-authored several journal articles and book chapters about reading, school-based management, leadership, and charter schools.

About the Contributors

Mary Abbott, Ph.D., Juniper Gardens Children's Project, University of Kansas, Kansas City, Kansas 66101

Dr. Abbott is Assistant Research Professor at the Juniper Gardens Children's Project at the University of Kansas. Her areas of expertise include literacy instruction for students with severe reading challenges and the translation of research to practice.

Scott Baker, Ph.D., Eugene Research Institute, 132 East Broadway, Suite 747, Eugene, Oregon 97401

Dr. Baker received his doctorate in school psychology in 1993. Since then, he has pursued a full-time research career at the Eugene Research Institute and the University of Oregon. His research interests include the prevention of reading difficulties and the education of English-language learners. Dr. Baker is currently Principal Investigator on three research projects funded by the Office of Special Education Programs.

Meaghan Edmonds, M.A., Texas Center for Reading and Language Arts, College of Education, The University of Texas, Austin, Texas 78712

Ms. Edmonds is Research Associate at the Texas Center for Reading and Language Arts at The University of Texas. Ms. Edmonds holds a master's degree in curriculum and instruction, and she is pursuing a doctorate in quantitative research methods. While working at the Center, she has been a part of the Teacher Reading Academy's core development team and has worked on several program evaluation projects. Her academic interests include observational studies of instructional practices and policy evaluation.

Barbara R. Foorman, Ph.D., University of Texas–Houston Medical School, 7000 Fannin Street, Suite 2443, Houston, Texas 77030

Dr. Foorman is Professor of Pediatrics and Director of the Center for Academic and Reading Skills at The University of Texas–Houston Medical School. Dr. Foorman directs research projects funded by federal grants, and she is on the editorial board of many journals. She is actively involved in outreach to public schools and to the general public.

Russell Gersten, Ph.D., Instructional Research Group, 2525 Cherry Avenue, Suite 300, Signal Hill, California 90755

Dr. Gersten is Director of the Instructional Research Group, a nonprofit educational research institute in Long Beach, California. His research interests are reading instruction for English learners and effective means for translating research into practice.

Roland H. Good III, Ph.D., School Psychology Program, College of Education, University of Oregon, Eugene, Oregon 97403

Dr. Good is Associate Professor in the School Psychology Program at the University of Oregon. He teaches measurement, statistics, and research design courses at the graduate level and conducts research on the Dynamic Indicators of Basic Early Literacy Skills (DIBELS). He received his undergraduate degree in elementary and special education and has taught in elementary general education and special education. He earned his doctorate in school psychology from The Pennsylvania State University and has worked as a school psychologist. Dr. Good is Co-principal Investigator for the Early Childhood Research Institute on Measuring Growth and Development and a member of the Reading Leadership Academy Assessment Committee.

Anne W. Graves, Ph.D., Department of Special Education, San Diego State University, 5200 Campanada Drive, San Diego, California 92037

Dr. Graves teaches credential candidates and conducts research in reading and writing instruction in the Department of Special Education at San Diego State University.

Charles R. Greenwood, Ph.D., Juniper Gardens Children's Project, University of Kansas, Kansas City, Kansas 66101

Dr. Greenwood is Director of the Juniper Gardens Children's Project at the University of Kansas. He is also Senior Scientist in the Schiefelbusch Institute for Life Span Studies and Courtesy Professor in the Department of Human Development and Family Life and the Department of Special Education at the University of Kansas. A former special education teacher and school psychologist, he is best known for his work on instructional and behavioral intervention strategies.

Noel Gregg, Ph.D., Department of Special Education, University of Georgia, 324 Milledge Hall, Athens, Georgia 30602

Dr. Gregg is Distinguished Research Professor in the Department of Special Education at the University of Georgia. Her research and writing focus on assessment, young adults with learning disabilities, and written language disorders.

Marcia L. Grek, Ph.D., Florida Center for Reading Research, Florida State University, 227 North Bronough Street, Suite 7250, Tallahassee, Florida 32301

Dr. Grek is Director of Curriculum and Instructional Projects at the Florida Center for Reading Research at Florida State University. She is a former classroom teacher and a reading educator with extensive experience in professional development. Her research interests include preventing reading difficulties and professional development in early literacy for teachers.

Diane Haager, Ph.D., Division of Special Education, California State University, Los Angeles, California 90032

Dr. Haager is a researcher and teacher educator in reading and learning disabilities. She is Professor in the Division of Special Education at California State University, Los Angeles, where she instructs teachers in methods for teaching students with high-incidence disabilities. Her research interests include reading instruction for English-language learners and students at risk for reading failure, accommodations and instructional methods for students with learning disabilities, and social competence.

Beth Harry, Ph.D., Department of Teaching and Learning, School of Education, University of Miami, Coral Gables, Florida 33124

Dr. Harry is Professor in the Department of Teaching and Learning at the University of Miami. Her research and teaching focus on the intersections among special education, family, and multicultural issues, including the disproportionate representation of culturally and linguistically diverse students in special education. Dr. Harry completed her primary and secondary education in her native Jamaica, earned her bachelor's and master's degrees in Canada, and earned her doctorate at Syracuse University.

Ed Kaméenui, Ph.D., Institute for the Development of Educational Achievement, University of Oregon, Eugene, Oregon 97403

Dr. Kaméenui is Professor in the College of Education and directs the Institute for the Development of Educational Achievement at the University of Oregon. His areas of specialization are early literacy research, schoolwide reading improvement, design of high-quality educational tools, and design of instruction.

Ruth A. Kaminski, Ph.D., Area of Special Education, College of Education, University of Oregon, Eugene, Oregon 97403

Dr. Kaminski is Research Assistant of School Psychology in the College of Education at the University of Oregon. Dr. Kaminski conducts research related to assessment and intervention for promoting school success with children in preschool and early elementary school. She is a co-author with Roland H. Good III of *The Dynamic Indicators of Basic Early Literacy Skills (DIBELS) Assessment System* (Sopris West, 2003).

Ae-Hwa Kim, Ph.D., Texas Center for Reading and Language Arts, College of Education, The University of Texas, Austin, Texas 78712

Dr. Kim is Research Assistant of the Texas Center for Reading and Language Arts at The University of Texas. Her interests include technology applications to reading and reading comprehension intervention for students with disabilities.

Janette Klingner, Ph.D., Department of Educational Equity and Cultural Diversity, University of Colorado, Boulder, Colorado 80309

Dr. Klingner is Associate Professor in the Department of Educational Equity and Cultural Diversity at the University of Colorado at Boulder. She was a bilingual special education teacher for 10 years before earning a doctorate in reading and learning disabilities from the University of Miami. Her research focuses on outcomes for students with learning disabilities in general education classrooms, reading comprehension instruction, and the disproportionate representation of culturally and linguistically diverse students in special education.

Nancy Mather, Ph.D., Department of Education, University of Arizona, Tucson, Arizona 85750

Dr. Mather is Associate Professor of Special Education at the University of Arizona in Tucson. Her current interests are early literacy assessment and instructional interventions. She is co-author with Richard Woodcock and Kevin McGrew of the *Woodcock-Johnson III* (Riverside, 2001).

Patricia G. Mathes, Ph.D., Texas Institute for Reading Research, Southern Methodist University, 3108 Fondern, Room 210, Dallas, Texas 75275

Dr. Mathes is Professor of Reading and Director of the Texas Institute for Reading Research at Southern Methodist University. Her research focuses on the prevention and intervention of reading disabilities.

Christopher Schatschneider, Ph.D., Florida Center for Reading Research, 227 North Bronough Street, Suite 7250, Florida State University, Tallahassee, Florida 32309

Dr. Schatschneider is an active researcher investigating individual differences in early reading development. He is also trained in research methodology and applied statistics.

Deborah C. Simmons, Ph.D., Institute for the Development of Educational Achievement, University of Oregon, Eugene, Oregon 97403

Dr. Simmons is Associate Professor of Education and Associate Director of the Institute for the Development of Educational Achievement at the University of Oregon. Her areas of expertise include schoolwide reading improvement;

primary-grade intervention for reading difficulties; curriculum design, including principles of effective teaching; and curriculum evaluation and adaptation.

Sylvia B. Smith, Ph.D., Eugene Research Institute, 132 East Broadway, Suite 747, Eugene, Oregon 97401

Dr. Smith is Research Associate at the Eugene Research Institute. Her interests include instructional design analyses of beginning reading core and supplemental programs; development of early literacy programs and indicators of early literacy, language, and social growth and development; training and implementation of the Dynamic Indicators of Basic Early Literacy Skills (DIBELS) data system; and implementation of early literacy and language professional development systems.

Keith M. Sturges, M.A., AEL Regional Education Laboratory, Post Office Box 1348, Charleston, West Virginia 25325

Mr. Sturges is an applied anthropologist whose interests include service access and use, community change, and directed school change. He currently conducts applied research for AEL, a regional education laboratory in Charleston, West Virginia, to determine strategies to improve the academic success of students attending schools that do not meet state requirements.

Yolanda Tapia, Juniper Gardens Children's Project, University of Kansas, Kansas City, Kansas 66101

Ms. Tapia is Field Research and Training Coordinator with the Juniper Gardens Children's Project at the University of Kansas. Her background in applied linguistics has prepared her for the challenges of developing evaluation instruments, improving instruction, and researching communication behaviors and language acquisition for first- and second-language learners.

Joseph K. Torgesen, Ph.D., Florida Center for Reading Research, 227 North Bronough Street, Suite 7250, Florida State University, Tallahassee, Florida 32309

Dr. Torgesen is Professor of Psychology and Education in the Department of Psychology at Florida State University and Director of the Florida Center for Reading Research. His research interests include instructional methods for the prevention and remediation of reading disabilities and assessment practices for the early identification of children who are at risk for reading difficulties.

Joshua Wallin, Institute for the Development of Educational Achievement, University of Oregon, Eugene, Oregon 97403

Mr. Wallin is Research Assistant for the Institute for the Development of Educational Achievement at the University of Oregon. He is System Administrator and Head Programmer for the Dynamic Indicators of Basic Early Literacy Skills (DIBELS) data system.

Foreword

Since the 1970s, an enormous amount of progress has been made in understanding how children learn to read, why many have trouble learning to read, and what components of instruction are necessary to help almost all children become good readers. In spite of a solid research foundation on which to base practice, general and special education classrooms have yet to achieve the rates of success that are possible. Education's chronic challenge is how to teach those students who depend on schooling to learn: students from poorer and low-performing schools, students of racial and ethnic minorities, students whose first language is not English, and students with learning disabilities and other challenges.

If effective reading instruction could be accomplished with the dissemination of scientifically based, comprehensive reading instruction programs, the sophisticated science represented in this book would be unnecessary. Several researchers of this volume document the limitations of even the best-designed instructional programs and methods. The tools an educator teaches with are only one factor that accounts for student achievement. Many other variables must be accounted for, and many of those are difficult to identify, describe, and quantify. Bringing those variables into focus, however, is necessary in order to make progress in teacher selection, preparation and licensing, coaching and mentoring, and evaluation. Unless we can be better informed and able to address teachers' knowledge, intentions, behavior, and ability to engender reading skill and motivation in children, we may continue to prescribe overly simplistic (and expensive) solutions for a public health problem that undermines the lifelong prospects of large segments of our society.

This collection is much more than a description and validation of innovative means for observation of reading instruction. The contributors probe the internal workings of functioning classrooms using an array of theory-driven tools and methodologies. They approach questions that must be answered with an appreciation not only for the complexity of teaching but also for the intangible nature of teacher–student communication: If time spent teaching a skill such as writing does not necessarily create better writers, what does account for student achievement? How can an educator teach a program with fidelity but still obtain poor results? How much can a good program help novice teachers obtain better results? What are the limitations of highly scripted instruction, and why and for whom do the limitations exist? If teachers are differentiating instruction and responding to student variability effectively, what are they actually doing? If a teacher is effective with students learning English as a second (or third) language, how is that teacher adjusting his or her verbal and nonverbal interactions with those students? Can we show that teachers' content knowledge or language proficiency is related to student outcomes?

This book contains some surprising findings and some valuable observation tools. Its ground-breaking content will help educators and researchers with varied purposes, including evaluation of curriculum; organization of professional development for teachers of regular and special education and for teachers of English-language learners (ELLs); evaluation of fidelity of standards-based instruction; and design of preservice teacher education. This volume is a noteworthy contribution to our field.

Louisa C. Moats, Ed.D.

Preface

In this era of standards, assessments, accountability, and expectations for improved student achievement, policy makers at all levels are paying particular attention to reading achievement. The latest findings from the National Assessment of Educational Progress are that nearly 60% of low-income fourth-grade students cannot read at a basic level. Determined to improve this situation, President George W. Bush and the U.S. Congress passed legislation—Reading First, the reading component of the No Child Left Behind Act of 2001 (PL 107-110)—that not only provides significant funds but also emphasizes the importance of reading instruction that is grounded in science-based research. As states begin to implement newly funded reading initiatives, the implementation of this research in the classroom is crucial. Policy makers and educators are focused on the essential features of the classroom environment that are necessary for success. Although the outcome of this focus is certainly improved reading achievement, policy makers and educators may be left unable to explain differences in outcomes without serious consideration of what is happening in the classroom. One methodology for gathering information that provides those explanations and answers questions about recommended practices in reading instruction and policy effectiveness is classroom observation.

With increased focus on classroom practice and science-based research, high-quality research methodologies that can answer policy implementation questions are crucial. However, while working on national and state reading initiatives and multiple research projects, we realized that this important body of work was typically mentioned only briefly in reports, journal articles, and chapters. This work includes the systems for observation of classrooms, which forms the basis for important findings and research discussions about reading instruction. Colleagues across the United States were publishing significant work that would shape our understanding of reading instruction, but their methodologies for making these findings had yet to be fully explored or discussed. Often, length of published articles allowed inadequate space to provide all of the necessary information about definitions, training, development, reliability, validity, and limitations for a classroom observation system. This book is devoted to providing that space and thus to enabling other researchers, scholars, and educators to gain access to high-quality classroom observation systems.

Kennedy (1999) described classroom observations as *first-level approxima-tions,* indicators that estimate or approximate student learning. (As a point of contrast, the highest-level approximation would be testimony from teachers or principals about the effects of policies on their teaching or on learning.) As first-level approximations, these observation systems have certain clear advantages and disadvantages. Classroom observations are direct means of examining the content and complexity of student learning, and they have high face validity. Conversely, as Kennedy noted, classroom observation systems lack standardization and agreement about definitions of events. This book addresses both concerns. First, by outlining each system, this volume encourages further studies that can use these systems and refine the instruments so that they become accurate approximations of classroom events and student learning. Standardization in classroom observation will begin to improve as the procedures for training observers and collecting data with these instruments are made public. Second, each chapter, while discussing unique systems, answers similar questions of development, use, data analysis, and application. This uniform process is a step toward defining key events in the classroom.

This book includes detailed discussion of the most current and representative classroom observation systems used by prominent reading and writing researchers. Each chapter describes these systems within the context of reading instruction and other instructional settings. Furthermore, the chapters in this book address measurement and observational procedures for recording classroom behavior and reading instructional strategies. In a broad sense, this book describes and provides examples of the many useful ways teachers, researchers, and other educational stakeholders can capitalize on the already designed instruments and observational scales for recording teacher–student behavior in classrooms.

These observation systems, each designed by different teams of researchers and other educators, are responses to a particular problem or research question, some of which educators and decision-makers address on a daily basis. In addressing a problem or question, these researchers attempted to devise systematic procedures influenced by a range of methodologies (e.g., ethnographic, behavioral) to collect information about interactions and activities in the classroom. Thus, each system has a particular focus—some quite narrow, others broader—and collects a specific type of information (see Table 1).

Each chapter addresses several characteristics of the classroom observation system. Each system

- Represents a procedure for better understanding particular questions and issues related to teaching and learning
- Links research on scientifically based reading and writing practices to systems for recording teacher or student behavior
- Relates to a particular issue (e.g., classroom climate) and/or addresses reading

- Reflects high standards of research methodology. (Each system has been used in the field and tested for its reliability and provides descriptions of use and misuse.)
- Transfers useful information to other researchers who wish to address similar issues

By compiling descriptions of these systems in one book and by reporting on the validity and reliability of each system, this text provides an important resource that allows educators to gain access to valuable tools to standardize their classroom observations. Furthermore, the chapters in this book serve as a resource to researchers who are interested in identifying and using observational procedures for their work.

In Chapter 1, Barbara R. Foorman and Christopher Schatschneider explain the development and use of instruments for observing classrooms in two urban school districts. The first instrument analyzes how teachers used classroom time to provide reading instruction in 20 categories, including specific reading concepts (e.g., oral language, comprehension), classroom management, instructional directions, and feedback. Using multiple data sources for their work, the authors explain the use of other instruments for measuring teaching effectiveness (i.e., Texas Teacher Appraisal System and a checklist for teacher competencies), implementation fidelity of specific reading programs,

Table 1. Characteristics of chapters and observation instruments

Lead author	Population described	Type of data collected	Focus of instrument
Foorman	Urban elementary classrooms	Quantitative	Time and teacher
Edmonds	Elementary classrooms	Quantitative and qualitative	Instructional events and teacher
Greenwood	Urban, inner city students	Quantitative	Students, teacher, and classroom
Kim	Various: general education, special education, and bilingual	Quantitative and qualitative	Teacher, students, and classroom
Haager	English-language learners in elementary schools	Quantitative	Teacher
Klingner	Elementary schools, primarily minority	Qualitative	Teacher and students
Mather	Students developing writing skills	Quantitative	Students
Good	Beginning reading programs	Quantitative and qualitative	Classrooms
Grek	First grade students most at-risk for reading problems	Quantitative and qualitative	Teachers and paraprofessionals

teacher knowledge of reading instruction, and teacher opinions about program curricula.

Chapter 2 by Meaghan Edmonds and Kerri L. Briggs describes the Instructional Content Emphasis (ICE) instrument, which is multidimensional and grounded in the findings of the National Reading Panel and other seminal research. The ICE instrument documents the use of effective reading instruction (i.e., phonological awareness, phonics, fluency, comprehension, and vocabulary instruction) by focusing on instructional events within the classroom. It was designed to help observers understand to what extent teachers implemented effective instructional practices learned through a statewide professional development initiative. The authors also discuss various grouping techniques and instructional materials used by teachers during reading instruction.

In Chapter 3, Charles R. Greenwood, Mary Abbott, and Yolanda Tapia concentrate on the behavior of individual students, with a particular interest in the needs of disadvantaged students. Capitalizing on advances in technology, the authors describe a combination of instruments that guide observers to record ecobehavioral events about the student, teacher, and classroom through the use of a software system, Ecobehavioral Assessment Software System (EBASS), and coding scheme, Mainstream Version of the Code for Instructional Structure and Student Academic Response (MS-CISSAR). The authors provide detailed information about the use of these instruments and how they could be applied in other reading instructional settings.

Chapter 4 by Ae-Hwa Kim, Kerri L. Briggs, and Sharon Vaughn details the development over time of the Classroom Climate Scale (CCS). Used in a variety of settings, the CCS is designed to determine to what extent students with disabilities are provided with effective, research-based instruction tailored to their needs in classrooms. The scale focuses on classroom elements, including grouping practices, overall classroom climate, teacher-initiated behaviors, student-initiated behaviors, student participation and interaction, and reading instruction. The authors explain how the CCS was developed and then adapted for use in research about bilingual reading classrooms, resource room settings for students with learning disabilities, and resource room settings for students with emotional and behavior disorders.

In Chapter 5, Diane Haager, Russell Gersten, Scott Baker, and Anne W. Graves focus on identifying reading instruction that is most effective for English-language learners (ELLs), a growing population in the United States. By developing an observation scale, the authors investigated the literacy-related instructional practices of primary-grade teachers for ELL students. The scale includes three parts: items related to general instructional practices that are likely to be effective for literacy instruction, items related to English language development, and items specific to reading/language arts instruction. Using data collected with their instrument, Haager and her colleagues document teachers' use of effective instructional practices and also observe a positive relationship between the use of these strategies and students correctly reading more words per minute.

In Chapter 6, Janette Klingner, Keith M. Sturges, and Beth Harry explain how to conduct ethnographic observations, from the initial step of gaining access to the final steps of data analysis. The authors draw from their studies of the Success for All (SFA) curriculum and the student referral process for special education in several elementary schools. They end the chapter with a summary of findings drawn from their ethnographic observations about the uses of the SFA curriculum in the schools. This analysis highlights the usefulness of ethnographic research by explaining how the implementation of SFA is shaped and changed by the school context.

Chapter 7 by Nancy Mather and Noel Gregg approaches the issue of classroom observations from the perspective of the teacher instead of the researcher. The authors explain two instruments teachers may use for informally assessing students' writing abilities: the Written Language Profile, a detailed assessment for an individual student that measures the proficiency of a student on 25 distinct writing skills, and the Class Written Language Profile, a summarization tool organized around 13 global writing elements. The authors discuss each skill and element and highlight the problems that students with writing difficulties may face.

Chapter 8 by Roland H. Good III, Ruth A. Kaminski, Sylvia B. Smith, Deborah C. Simmons, Ed Kaméenui, and Joshua Wallin describes how to use the Dynamic Indicators of Basic Early Literacy Skills (DIBELS) data system, an outcomes-driven model used to analyze school-based data on basic early literacy skills, in order to determine effective beginning reading programs. The authors outline five essential components of successful reading programs and include guidelines for using the DIBELS data to make decisions about adjusting the core reading curriculum in order to improve students' reading outcomes.

Chapter 9 by Marcia L. Grek, Patricia G. Mathes, and Joseph K. Torgesen utilizes quantitative and qualitative observational methods to provide evidence and understanding about similarities and differences in the supplemental instruction of certified teachers compared with paraprofessionals. Teachers and paraprofessionals taught small groups of first graders who were most at risk for reading problems. The observation measure recorded critical components that corresponded with their supplemental intervention reading program, including instructional pacing, adherence to the lesson plan, providing independent practice, correcting errors using appropriate scaffolds, teaching to mastery, maintaining student attentiveness, and eliciting student responses. Similarities and differences between certified teachers and paraprofessionals are also described.

REFERENCE

Kennedy, M.M. (1999). Approximations to indicators of student outcomes. *Educational Evaluation and Policy Analysis, 21*, 345–363.

This book is dedicated to the outstanding professionals with whom we have worked at the Texas Center for Reading and Language Arts. Though it is difficult to list all of them because they are so many, we would like to recognize in particular Diane P. Bryant, Shari Levy Sharbaneau, Mark Luetzelschwab, Pam Bell Morris, Martha Smith, Sylvia Linan Thompson, Kim Twiddy Rodriguez, and all of the outstanding teachers and educators who have guided us along the way.

We would also like to dedicate this book in remembrance of Sandy McCracken Briggs. Throughout her life, she enjoyed teaching children through music, was an avid reader, and encouraged people to face new challenges. She would be proud to know that this devotion continues with her daughter and through this work.

Measurement of Teaching Practices During Reading/ Language Arts Instruction and Its Relationship to Student Achievement

BARBARA R. FOORMAN AND CHRISTOPHER SCHATSCHNEIDER

Reading initiatives at local, state, and national levels in the United States call for scientifically based reading instruction. Several consensus documents agree about what the content of this instruction should be—the National Research Council's *Preventing Reading Difficulties in Young Children* (Snow, Burns, & Griffin, 1998), the *Primary Literacy Standards* (New Standards, 1999), and the report of the National Reading Panel (2000). All of these documents agree on the importance of explicit instruction in the alphabet principle, integrated with reading for meaning and opportunities to learn. Specifically, this includes all support instruction that builds phonemic awareness and phonemic decoding skills, fluency in word recognition and text processing, construction of meaning, vocabulary, spelling, and writing skills (Foorman & Torgesen, 2001). But beyond agreement on the *content* of scientifically based reading instruction, little agreement exists regarding the *implementation*

This work is supported by Grant #R01 HD30995 from the National Institute of Child Health and Human Development, "Early interventions for children with reading problems."

of this instruction. We cannot answer such basic questions as, "What does good reading instruction look like? How much time should teachers spend in different reading/language arts activities in order to maximize student outcomes? How much of good teaching is a matter of teacher knowledge, classroom management, or student engagement?"

To answer these questions, we reviewed the literature on classroom observation instruments and began to pilot our own instruments in a longitudinal investigation of the conditions under which children learn to read. The investigation followed approximately 1,400 children (98% of whom were African American) in kindergarten through fourth grade; these children were in 112 classrooms in 17 high-poverty schools in Houston and Washington, D.C. The literature review and longitudinal investigation reveal much. In this chapter, we review the literature on existing instruments for observing reading/language arts instruction, describe the classroom observational instruments we developed, and provide preliminary descriptions of how these measures of classroom behaviors relate to student outcomes.

OBSERVATIONAL SYSTEMS FOR CLASSROOM READING INSTRUCTION

Classroom observational systems range widely from descriptive frameworks and narrative descriptions to coding of teacher–student communication and time-sampling of discrete behaviors. An example of a descriptive framework is the Reading Lesson Observation Framework (RLOF; Henk, Moore, Marinak, & Tomasetti, 2000). The RLOF consists of a set of expectations for teaching behaviors during reading/language arts instruction time. Thus, the RLOF serves as a tool that district supervisors can use to align teaching behaviors with district philosophy. The instrument consists of seven domains with 5–11 indicators in each. The seven domains are classroom climate, prereading phase, guided reading phase, postreading phase, skill and strategy instruction, materials and tasks of the lesson, and teacher practices. Responses are recorded in one of four ways: observed and of satisfactory quality, observed and of very high quality, either not observed or of unsatisfactory quality, and not applicable. No inter-rater reliability for the RLOF was provided by Henk and colleagues (2000).

There are many qualitative approaches to conducting classroom observations (Wolcott, 1988). One method, adopted by Pressley, Wharton-McDonald, Mistretta-Hampston, and Echevarria (1998), uses a grounded-theory approach to identify common elements of literacy instruction in six fourth-grade and sixth-grade classrooms. Consistent with this approach, data collection and analysis in Pressley and colleagues' study occurred simultaneously. Data consisted of field notes from classroom observations, interviews with the teachers, and classroom artifacts. During classroom observations, student engagement was calculated every 10–15 minutes as the proportion of students who appeared to be engaged productively in academic work. Validity and reliability were ensured by "triangulation of data, methods, and investigators" by collecting data across classrooms, by observing and interviewing, and by comparing inter-rater reliability across two investigators (Pressley et al., 1998, p. 169). Validity, or credibility, of data was further triangulated by negative-case analysis (i.e., looking for disconfirming data), prolonged engagement (i.e., having observers spend the majority of the school year in the classroom), and member checking (i.e., presenting data summaries to the teachers for verification). In this study, classrooms were found to be similar in the combination of authentic reading and writing experiences and explicit skills instruction. Classrooms differed with respect to methods and materials and whether important instructional elements were omitted, such as instruction in comprehension strategies or self-regulation.

Time-sampling approaches gained recognition as classroom observational techniques with Stallings, Robbins, and Presbrey's (1986) finding that time-on-task predicted achievement. Allington and McGill-Franzen (1989) took the utility of the time-on-task variable a step further by showing that disadvantaged, low-achieving students were better served through general education (via what was then called Chapter 1 and is now called Title I funding) than through special education. Specifically, students served through Chapter 1 received significantly more time per day (i.e., 35 minutes) in reading/language arts instruction than their peers in resource rooms, and the quality of instruction was better. No student outcome data, however, were provided. Allington and McGill-Franzen's (1989) student observation instrument required observers to code a number of instructional setting variables and note the clock time for transitions to new settings. Overall reliability during the 3-day training period was 86%.

An observational system that goes beyond reading/language arts instruction is the Ecobehavioral Assessment Systems Software (EBASS; Greenwood, Carta, Kamps, & Delquadri, 1995). The EBASS consists of three instruments: 1) CISSAR (Code for Instructional Structure and Student Academic Response), which is for observing general education kindergarten through twelfth-grade classrooms; 2) MS-CISSAR (the mainstream version of CISSAR), which is for observing children with special needs in any school setting; and 3) ESCAPE (Ecobehavioral System for Complex Assessments of Preschool Environments), which is for observing preschool- and kindergarten-age children with or without special needs. Each instrument has been validated and used in published research (e.g., Greenwood & Delquadri, 1988). EBASS runs on a laptop computer and prompts the observer to record events every 10 seconds. Each instrument contains student, teacher, and ecology categories. Student behavior is further categorized into academic responses or competing, nonacademic responses and task management behaviors. Academic responses consist of writing, playing an academic game, reading aloud, reading silently, academic talking, answering an academic question, and asking an academic question. Task management behaviors that support academic responding are attending to a task, raising a hand or signaling for help, looking for materials, moving to a new academic station, and playing appropriately. Teacher behaviors are subcategorized as teacher position (e.g., in front, at the teacher's desk, among students, at the side or the back of the classroom, out of the room) and teacher behavior (e.g., no response, teaching, other talk, approval, disapproval). Ecology events are categorized according to activity (e.g., reading, math, science), task (e.g., reading books, using workbooks, listening to the teacher's lecture, discussing with teacher), and structure (entire group, small group, or individual). The EBASS system provides data on 1) percent occurrence of each variable to compute inter-rater reliability or to compare across settings or occasions; 2) minute-by-minute variability in academic engagement; and 3) probability of student behavior, given particular concurrent teacher or ecology variables. EBASS has been used most widely to evaluate instruction in special education (Greenwood et al., 1995).

The observational system that most influenced our work was designed by Scanlon and Vellutino (1996). Their study of kindergarten activities and skills predicted first-graders' reading success. They developed a computer-driven, time-sampling procedure whereby an observer was prompted to observe the classroom for 10 seconds and then to answer six prompts: 1) instructional group (e.g., whole class, small group); 2) general focus (direct or indirect reading, writing, language development, other academic areas, art and physical education, general management, informal interaction); 3) teacher purpose (e.g., modeling, telling information, instructing through question and answer, giving feedback, listening and watching); 4) materials (e.g., trade book; textbook; student composition; words, letters, or sentences written; oral text or presentation); 5) specific focus (text, word identification, letter names or sounds, phoneme awareness, graphic features, word meaning, text meaning, recitation, general information); and 6) expected response (read silently, read orally, respond orally, listen and look, write, other). Inter-rater reliability of 85% was obtained and maintained throughout data collection. Results revealed considerable variability in time allotment across teachers of these primarily half-day programs, and nearly a majority of time was typically devoted to management or other non-instructional activities. They found that the proportion of time devoted to phonemic awareness activities was related to reading outcomes in first grade for children who are at risk but not for children who were not identified as being at risk.

DESCRIPTION OF NEW CLASSROOM OBSERVATION MEASURES

Through our experience describing classroom instruction for the 112 teachers participating in our early reading interventions grant, we have refined and created new measures of reading/language arts teaching behaviors and student engagement; typical instructional strategies; treatment fidelity; teaching effectiveness; and teachers' knowledge, experience, and attitudes. High inter-rater reliabilities (> .80) have been obtained on the observational measures, and our group has trained other research teams to use several of these measures in their reading research. Ten-second prompts are cued by an audiotape player; all observational forms are scannable and are entered immediately into the database.

Although focused on literacy development, we are also interested in instruction outside of the reading/language arts block, especially social studies and science instruction, during which literacy instruction increasingly takes place as students progress through the primary grades. Therefore, observers attend at least one class of social studies and one of science during the year to complete the minute-by-minute observational form used during reading/language arts instruction. Observers also record a narrative account regarding the extent to which literacy instruction is incorporated into social studies and science.

Time by Activity

The quantity and quality of time allotment during the reading/language arts block is critically important to understanding teaching effectiveness (Allington, 1991). Accordingly, we modified a procedure used by Scanlon and Vellutino (1996) to quantify time spent on various reading/language arts behaviors. Using the audiotape-recorded designation of minutes, observers code the instructional format and content of teaching within each minute. At the end of each timed observation, observers use a 1–5 scale to note the overall quality of instruction exhibited during the reading/language arts block, as well as assign separate quality ratings for reading, spelling, oral language, and writing instruction. Table 1.1 shows the four categories for instructional format, which range from whole class to small groups to all students working on their

Table 1.1.   Categories for instructional format and instructional content used in the time-by-activity instrument

Category	Item	Description
Instructional format	Whole class or very large group	Activity or instruction involves or is directed toward the whole class or a very large group.
	Teacher with small group or cooperative group (three to six students)	The teacher works with a small or cooperative group while other students are working.
	All students working on their own, individually or in groups, with teacher monitoring	*All* students are engaged in individualized activities. The teacher is moving around the room, observing, commenting, and so forth.
	All students work on their own, individually or in groups, *without* teacher monitoring	*All* students are engaged in individual activities. The teacher is *not* observing but is engaged in another activity, such as working at his or her desk.
Instructional content	Oral language/ discussion (not related to written stimulus)	The teacher is leading an activity that is intended to develop students' verbal skills. This includes a variety of activities that help to develop vocabulary, grammar, and syntax. Here are some examples: asking children to identify things (e.g., body parts, colors, days); working on directional terms; discussing the items and activities associated with a special place such as the beach; discussing days of the week, names of months, seasons, and so forth. This can also take the form of sharing in which the teacher elicits or allows children to talk about their personal experience, tell a story, and so forth. Other examples include the teacher talking; asking students for responses or asking questions; listening to student responses; and listening games, activities, or songs (e.g., calendar and morning message).
	Book and print awareness/ conventions	Some examples include conventions of print use and the format of a book, including title page, author, reading left to right, and genre of book.
	Phonemic awareness	This refers to all instruction that is targeted at directing the children's attention to the sounds in language and/or manipulating those sounds. These activities do *not* include explicit reference to the text. In some cases, text may be present, but the teacher may not be providing explicit instruction about the link between the sounds and the text. Other examples include rhyming; blending; syllable or phoneme segmentation; working with initial, middle, or ending phoneme; and phoneme deletion or substitution.

Category	Item	Description
	Alphabet letter recognition and reproduction	Examples include reciting or singing the alphabet, identifying letter names and sounds, and practicing letter formation and alphabetical order.
	Alphabetic instruction	This refers to any instruction that is intended to help students understand that written letters of the alphabet are used to represent the sounds in words. It includes instruction regarding which letters make which sounds. Other examples include rules for letter–sound correspondence, identification of vowels and consonants, and work with blends and digraphs.
	Structural analysis	This refers to instruction about meaningful parts of words (i.e., morphemic units). Examples include instruction regarding plurals, possessive words, prefixes, suffixes, verb tenses, root words, derivations, and etymology.
	Word work (with text)	This refers to any instruction with text at the word level, including words on the board, on word walls, or in books or other print mediums. Kinds of word work include blending or sounding out words, teaching of "sight words," segmenting words into syllables or phonemes, rhyming words (with text), and writing words.
	Vocabulary	The teacher focuses on developing the children's knowledge of the meaning of words through definitions, antonyms, or synonyms or through application to sentences.
	Previewing to prepare for reading	This refers to all discussions of topics and issues related to something the teacher and students will read or have read before that was related to the upcoming reading. For example, if they read a book about going to the beach, the teacher might ask who has gone to the beach. It differs from the discussions for oral language development because the emphasis is on knowledge that is linked to what is going to be read or has been read.
	Spelling in the context of reading	This usually occurs in passing. A teacher might ask students to spell a word that was just read. This is not an extended spelling lesson.
	Reading text/books	This describes activities that go beyond the word level (all types of text). *Students must be able to see the text.* Examples include the teacher reading aloud (alone, without students), student(s) reading aloud (with or without the teacher), and students reading silently.

(continued)

Table 1.1.   *(continued)*

Category	Item	Description
	Students read their own writing	This describes activities in which students are peer- or self-editing or reading their writing to the class, a group, or an individual.
	Reading comprehension	This describes activities that occur during or after reading. The teacher focuses on the children's understanding of the text they are reading or hearing. This includes using semantic or syntactic cues to make sense of decoding; asking students to identify facts, characters, setting, plot, main idea, or story details; asking students to predict, summarize, draw conclusions, compare and contrast, or evaluate; and modeling strategies that students can use to help with comprehension such as outlining, story mapping, and so forth.
	Spelling (spelling is specific focus)	This usually involves an extended spelling lesson and some sort of spelling workbook. Examples include the teacher focusing on letter–sound correspondence as the instructional unit (e.g., short vowels, long vowels, consonant blends, digraphs, vowel teams), and the teacher illustrating words that do not follow phonetic spelling rules and are not easily sounded out (e.g., *the, who, sight*).
	Writing composition (more than single words)	These are activities in which children are asked to create stories, journal entries, recipes, or essays, for example, and to express these ideas by writing them on paper. This includes students writing creative compositions or essays, the teacher dictating words or sentences, students copying and constructing words or sentences with teacher guidance, journal writing, and instruction in the writing process (e.g., editing, drafting, outlining).
	Grammar, capitalization, and punctuation	This describes instruction in the rules of grammar, capitalization, or punctuation.
	Giving directions/ passing out materials (relevant to reading instruction)	
	Nonreading instruction	This describes instruction that is discipline-oriented or other (e.g., teacher out of classroom, general announcement).
	Feedback	This describes feedback that is corrective, praising, or punitive.
	Predictable text	This describes explicit discussion and reading of predictable text, (i.e., text that repeats a particular phrase over and over)
	Uncodable	This is used only for those behaviors that are completely uncodable in any content area.

own, in which the teacher is or is not monitoring student behavior. Table 1.1 also summarizes and explains the 20 categories for content. Content includes reading/language arts activities (e.g., oral language, alphabetic instruction, reading comprehension, spelling, writing), giving directions or passing out materials, nonreading instruction, feedback (e.g., corrective, praising, punitive), and uncodable activities. We have subdivided nonreading instruction into discipline-related and other. Intraclass correlations of the 20 time-by-activity categories are given in Table 1.2. These correlations were computed from an ANOVA model comparing simultaneous ratings of a teacher by two observers. The majority of these correlations is above .90, well above acceptable standards. Four of the correlations range from .78 to .89, which is excellent. The three that fall below this range—.50 (uncodable), .59 (book and print awareness), .67 (phonemic awareness)—are relatively low-incidence activities for first and second grades.

A comparison of time-by-activity data for first and second grades is provided in Figure 1.1 for the Houston and Washington, D.C., classrooms. Time spent on each content category has been summed across the school year for the three to six observations of each of the 112 participating teachers and represented as a percentage of total time. In both sites the reading/language arts period was scheduled for a mini-

Table 1.2.   Intraclass correlations among time-by-activity indicators

Indicator	Correlation
Oral language/discussion	0.97
Book and print awareness/conventions	0.59
Phonemic awareness	0.67
Alphabet letter recognition and reproduction	0.81
Alphabetic instruction	0.89
Structural analysis	0.98
Word work (with text)	0.98
Vocabulary	0.98
Previewing to prepare for reading	0.92
Spelling in the context of reading	0.93
Reading text/books	0.98
Reading their own writing	0.95
Reading comprehension	0.78
Spelling	0.91
Writing composition (more than single words)	0.94
Grammar, capitalization, and punctuation	0.98
Giving directions/passing out materials (relevant to reading instructions)	0.96
Nonreading instruction	0.91
Feedback	0.79
Uncodable	0.50

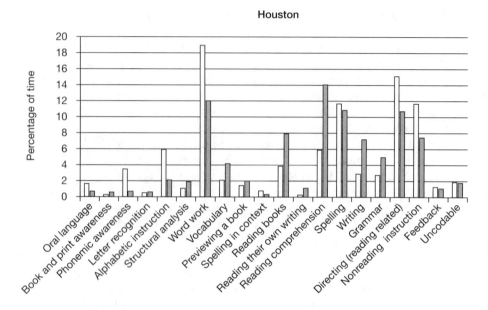

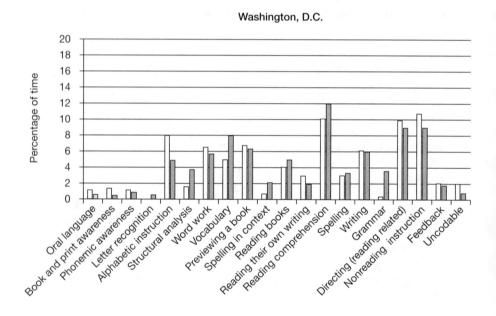

Figure 1.1. Time spent in reading/language arts activities in first and second grades. The top graph describes Houston. The bottom graph describes Washington, D.C. (*Key:* ☐ = first grade, ■ = second grade)

mum of 90 minutes, but the actual time ranged from 79 to 180 minutes in individual classrooms.

In first-grade classrooms in Houston, the two most frequent activities were word work (17%) and directing (15%). Spelling (12%) and nonreading activities (11%) are also notable. Other activities that are more frequent in first-grade Houston classrooms, relative to second-grade Houston classrooms, are alphabetic instruction (6%), phonemic awareness (3%), and oral language (2%). The low percentages for these prereading and early-reading activities are not surprising, given that they are more central to kindergarten and beginning-of-first-grade curricula. Activities that appear more frequently in second grade, relative to first grade, are reading comprehension (13%), reading books (8%), writing (7%), grammar (6%), and vocabulary (4%). In second-grade Houston classrooms, a relatively high percentage of time is still devoted to word work (12%), spelling (11%), directions (10%), and nonreading activities (7%).

Grade-level differences in time allotment in Washington, D.C., classrooms are not nearly so apparent. First-grade classrooms devote more time to nonreading-related activities (12%), directions (10%), and alphabetic instruction (8%); however, differences in second grade are small. Second-grade percentages that exceed first-grade percentages are reading comprehension (12%), vocabulary (8%), reading books (5%), grammar (4%), and structural analysis (4%).

Time allotment for various literacy activities can vary by curriculum. A major reason for the relative similarity in grade-level profiles in Washington, D.C., is that six of nine participating schools used Houghton Mifflin's *Invitations to Literacy* (1996) reading program, which emphasizes reading comprehension from the beginning of first grade. The other three Washington, D.C., schools used the same Open Court program as the Houston schools used. In our research site in Houston, three of the schools used Success for All (Slavin, Madden, Dolan & Wasik, 1996), two used Open Court Reading's Collection for Young Scholars (1995), and three used Reading Mastery I (Englemann & Bruner, 1995). To examine differences in time allotment by curriculum, we grouped the 20 time-by-activity content codes into the following four domains of reading/language arts instruction:

- Word work: Phonemic awareness, alphabetic instruction, letter recognition, word work

- Reading comprehension: Reading comprehension, previewing a book, reading books

- Language: Oral language, vocabulary, reading own writing, writing, grammar

- Nonreading instruction: Nonreading behaviors such as discipline, time when the teacher is out of classroom, or announcements over the intercom

Time allotments for each domain tell us the percentage of time a teacher focuses on work-level instruction, text-level instruction, and oral language instruction. The activities reading own writing and writing deserve their own domains; however, in the first- and second-grade classrooms in the Houston and Washington, D.C., schools, these activities accounted for a relatively small percentage of total time (less than 8%) and, therefore, are collapsed with oral language activities. We have omitted the spelling domain (using a speller or spelling in the context of the reading basal) because the reading curricula were equally inattentive to spelling and the percentage of time allocated to spelling accounted for relatively little time in these classrooms (less than 10% overall).

Time-by-activity data are presented by curricula for the Houston teachers in Figure 1.2 and the Washington, D.C., teachers in Figure 1.3. Open Court Reading (1995) was used in both sites. In first-grade Houston classrooms, teachers using Open Court and Reading Mastery (Englemann & Bruner, 1995) devoted greater percentages of time (about 32%) to word work than to reading comprehension or language arts. In contrast, teachers using Success for All allocated time more evenly between these three domains. In second-grade Houston classrooms, teachers using Success for All and Open Court allocated about 27% of time to reading comprehension, about 24% to language, and about 15% to word work. This stands in contrast to Reading Mastery, with 36% allocated to word work and 16% to reading comprehension and language arts.

In first-grade Washington, D.C., classrooms, teachers using Open Court allocated 43% of their instructional time to word work, 9% to reading comprehension, and 11% to language arts. This is comparable to the pattern for the first-grade teachers in Houston. For teachers in Washington, D.C., using Houghton Mifflin (1996), the corresponding percentages were 20%, 25%, and 24%. This is similar to the pattern for first-grade teachers using Success for All in Houston. In Washington, D.C., second-grade teachers' allocation of time looked more similar across curricula, except for a greater emphasis on reading comprehension and less on word work in Houghton Mifflin's program. Interestingly, the percentages of nonreading behaviors ranged from 10% to 16% across curricula, grades, and sites except for in second-grade Houston classrooms in which Reading Mastery was used, where nonreading behaviors made up 5% of time allocation. These data reflect the tradeoffs

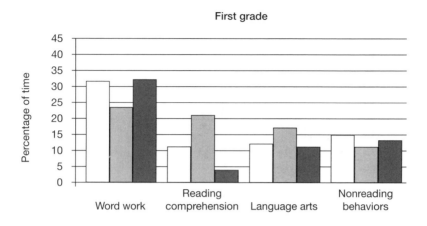

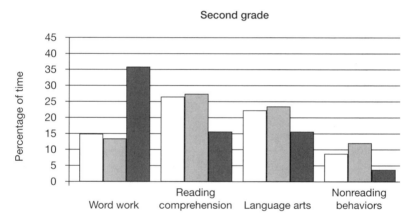

Figure 1.2. Time-by-activity ratings by curriculum in Houston. The top graph describes the first grade. The bottom graph describes the second grade. (*Key:* □ = Open Court, ▦ = Success for All, ■ = Reading Mastery)

inherent in allocation of fixed amounts of time in reading/language instruction, as well as the different instructional emphases in reading curricula.

Student Engagement

In addition to coding the instructional format and the content within the first 15 seconds of each minute of the reading/language arts block, observers note in 10-second intervals whether each of four students randomly selected off the class roster are engaged in on-task or off-task

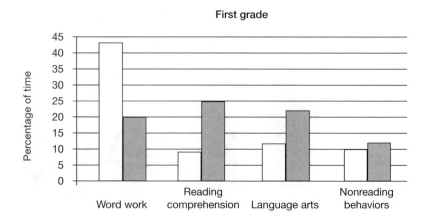

First grade

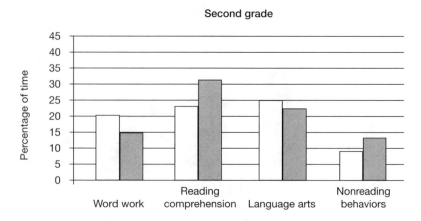

Second grade

Figure 1.3. Time-by-activity ratings by curriculum in Washington, D.C. The top graph describes the first grade. The bottom graph describes the second grade. (*Key:* ☐ = Open Court, ■ = Houghton Mifflin)

behaviors. Because language arts blocks typically vary from 90 to 120 minutes, data are analyzed as percentage of time. Thus, we are able to report the percentage of student on-task and off-task behaviors across the year. If classrooms are observed three times per year, student engagement data are available for 12 randomly selected students, or approximately half the students in the classroom. It is also possible to target the engagement of particular students or those representing certain achievement levels (see Pellegrini, 2001, for the advantages and disadvantages of sampling and recording rules for direct observations of children).

Typical Strategies Used by
Teachers During Reading/Language Arts

The time-by-activity and student engagement data indicate how time is spent during reading/language arts and the overall quality of that time, but they do not indicate the instructional strategies teachers typically employed. Therefore, at the end of each timed observation period, observers complete a form regarding the instructional strategies exhibited during the reading/language arts block. This form is partly inspired by the coding of word recognition strategies developed by Juel and Minden-Cupp (2000) and the narrative records of how teachers typically deliver content used by Pressley and colleagues (1998). The Juel and Minden-Cupp (2000) study included four teachers, and Pressley and colleagues' (1998) study included ten teachers. To accommodate larger number of teachers and observers, we developed a scannable, true/false form with 3–5 items in 10 domains (oral language, listening comprehension, phonemic awareness, letter–sound instruction, word identification, vocabulary, reading comprehension, writing, spelling, and management/motivation). For example, under reading comprehension, observers record a true/false response, depending on whether the teacher did the following:

- Predominantly asked literal, "right there in the text" questions
- Predominantly asked inferential questions (e.g., predicting based on prior knowledge, summarizing/drawing conclusions, comparing and contrasting, evaluating the author's intent)
- Offered instruction on how to use comprehension strategies while students read (e.g., skimming, note taking, highlighting, using visual imagery and/or think-alouds)
- Taught reading comprehension

These metacognitive strategies become increasing important as students shift from learning to read to reading to learn. The items on this typical strategies form are listed in Table 1.3. The true/false format allowed us to achieve high inter-rater reliability ($>.80$). We plan to examine relationships among teaching effectiveness, typical strategies, and student learning.

Teaching Effectiveness

We used two forms to measure teaching effectiveness. Both emerged out of the effective schools literature (e.g., Stallings et al., 1986; Ysseldyke & Christenson, 1993). The first is a checklist of teacher compe-

Table 1.3. Typical strategies used by a teacher during reading/language arts (with true/false responses)

Strategy	Items
Oral language	Encouraged students to express their ideas verbally
	Oral language taught
Listening comprehension	Asked literal questions, (i.e., answer was in the oral presentation)
	Asked inferential questions (e.g., predicting based on prior knowledge, summarizing/drawing conclusions, comparison and contrasting, evaluating the author's intent)
	Prompted and guided students to accurately retell a story
	Listening comprehension taught
Phonemic awareness (manipulation of sounds in speech)	Explicit phonemic awareness instruction taught without printed letters or text
	Explicit phonemic awareness instruction taught focused on individual phonemes
	Explicit phonemic awareness instruction taught focused on syllables
	Phonemic awareness taught
Letter–sound instruction	Letter–sound associations taught without printed words or text
	Letter–sound associations taught in isolation (with written letters or manipulation) rather than in the context of trying to sound out a word
	Letter–sound associations taught in context of sounding out words
Vocabulary (instruction of word meanings)	Taught from a predetermined list in the program manual
	Taught from personal or class-generated list
	Vocabulary taught
Word identification (decoding unfamiliar words)	Focused on sounding words out
	Focused on whole word/visual memory/contextual strategies
	Word identification taught
Reading comprehension	Predominantly asked literal, "right there in the text" questions
	Predominantly asked inferential questions (e.g., predicting based on prior knowledge, summarizing/drawing conclusions, comparison and contrasting, evaluating the author's intent)
	Offered instruction in how to use comprehension strategies while students read (e.g., skimming, note taking, highlighting, evidence of use of visual imagery, think-alouds)
	Reading comprehension taught
Writing	Primarily used word- and sentence-level writing rather than multi-sentence writing
	Used a plan-write-revise model for writing
	Had one-to-one miniconferences with students
	Provided instruction in punctuation, capitalization, grammar, or handwriting
	Writing taught

Strategy	Items
Spelling	Provided direct instruction in how to spell the words on the list (e.g., letter–sound patterns, word structure, spelling rules)
	Used spelling program primarily as seatwork
	Spelling instruction was solely in the context of reading/writing instruction
	Spelling taught
Management/motivation	Taught students strategies for organizing their time and assignments and for working independently in the absence of direct teacher supervision
	Created a stimulating and motivating classroom environment

tencies in five categories: 1) planning (e.g., the lesson sequence is followed appropriately), 2) management (e.g., the teacher maintains a classroom environment that minimizes distractions and is appropriate for learning), 3) instruction (e.g., the teacher presents and delivers the lesson effectively), 4) monitoring of students' learning (e.g., the teacher records student progress efficiently), and 5) personal characteristics (e.g., the teacher is knowledgeable about how children learn to read). Each category has four to eight items that are rated on a 6-point scale from "all the time" to "never" or "no opportunity to observe," except for the personal characteristics category, in which the anchors go from "very true" to "not at all true." Observers complete this checklist twice in the middle of the year to obtain test–retest reliability. Again, inter-rater reliability has been high (>.80). The items on this checklist are listed in Table 1.4.

The second measure of teaching effectiveness is completed toward the end of the school year by supervisory research staff members. This second measure is called the Texas Teacher Appraisal System (TTAS; Texas Education Agency, 1984) and is available from the Texas Education Agency. The TTAS rates student–teacher interaction during a 45-minute lesson according to a supervisor, in contrast to the teacher competency checklist, which is a more global instrument completed by observers who have been in the teacher's classroom several times. The TTAS was used for administrative performance appraisals by Texas school districts from 1986 to 1990, at which point it was replaced by an appraisal instrument that required administrators to observe teacher performance throughout the year rather than in a single lesson. To validate the content of the TTAS, the Texas Education Agency asked 30,000 teachers to rate TTAS items on observability, importance, and frequency of use.

Table 1.4.   Components of teacher competency rating form

Planning	The lesson sequence is followed appropriately.
	The teacher plans effectively for instruction.
	The teacher seems to be organized and has all of the materials necessary for instruction easily accessible.
	The teacher maintains lesson plans.
Management	The teacher maintains a classroom environment that minimizes distractions and is appropriate for learning.
	The teacher has well-established instructional routines.
	The teacher maximizes the amount of time available for instruction (e.g., brief transitions, appropriate timing and pacing of teaching).
	The teacher has clearly stated classroom rules and procedures and communicates expectations about classroom behavior.
	The teacher manages student behavior effectively in order to avoid disruptions and to provide productive learning opportunities.
Instruction	The teacher presents and delivers the lesson effectively (using eye contact, variation of tone, animation).
	The teacher provides many and equal opportunities for students to participate.
	The teacher emphasizes appropriate content.
	The teacher provides sufficient practice.
	The teacher models thinking and learning.
	The teacher is aware of lesson objectives.
Monitoring of students' learning	The teacher records student progress effectively.
	The teacher uses the data in order to make judgments and decisions about student performance.
	The teacher monitors student responses effectively.
	The teacher provides clear, direct, and frequent feedback to the students.
	The feedback provided by the teacher is appropriate to lesson objectives.
	The teacher provides feedback in a positive manner.
	The teacher assigns tasks that are relevant to instructional goals and objectives.
	The teacher corrects students' errors to extend instruction.
Personal characteristics	The teacher is knowledgeable about how children learn.
	The teacher is interested in the program being used.
	The teacher is aware of the students' level of ability and skill development and plans the instruction appropriately.
	The teacher has high but realistic expectations regarding students' learning and their progress.
	The teacher is generally motivated and keeps students actively involved by maintaining an effective learning environment.

Scoring procedures were delineated by a group of 45 subject-matter experts in 1986. A 1986 reliability study by Stallings and colleagues involving 28 teachers in five school districts indicated inter-rater reliability of .85 for the instrument.

The version of the TTAS we used consists of 49 indicators of the "quality or effectiveness of teaching behavior judged by their observed impact upon student behavior and the apparent success of students engaged in learning activities" that can be rated during a 45-minute snapshot of teaching (Texas Education Agency, 1984, p. 5). Another 16 indicators relate to professional growth and responsibilities and were not included in our measure of teaching effectiveness because of the difficulty of directly observing these activities. The 49 indicators fall into four domains (with nine dimensions): instructional strategies, classroom management and organization, presentation of subject matter, and learning environment.

A complete listing of the four domains, nine dimensions, and 49 indicators is given in Table 1.5. For each observed indicator, one point is assigned. The total number of points can be interpreted according to a scale of teaching effectiveness provided by the Texas Educational Agency. Preliminary analyses of 112 second- and third-grade teachers from the Houston and Washington, D.C., samples of teachers show that Kuder-Richardson (KR-20) reliabilities for all dimensions and domains were high, ranging from .72 to .93 (Phillips, 2001). The sample size of 112 was insufficient to perform factor analyses of tetrachoric correlations among the dichotomously scored items on the TTAS. Instead, correlational means among items within and between dimensions and within and between domains were qualitatively examined for evidence of factorial structure. These examinations lend support for the dimensional structure intended and warrant the use of item sums for the four domains as indices of teaching effectiveness (Phillips, 2001).

Prior to the TTAS, we used a simple 1–7 global rating of teaching effectiveness and again achieved high inter-rater reliability (>.80). Also, the correlations between teaching effectiveness and teacher competency are very good, which is not surprising, given the overlap in domains of classroom management, instructional planning and presentation, and learning environment. The correlations between global ratings of effectiveness and components of teacher competency in the Houston and Washington, D.C., schools are presented in Table 1.6. There were strong positive correlations between global ratings obtained by master teachers and teaching competency ratings obtained by classroom observers. Moreover, Houston ratings of the quality of reading instruction completed at the end of the time-by-activity form correlates .59 with the global ratings of teaching effectiveness. Quality ratings were not available on the forms in Washington, D.C., until the following year be-

Table 1.5. Teaching effectiveness

Domain	Action	Examples
Instructional strategies	Provides opportunities for students to participate actively and successfully	Varies activities appropriately
		Interacts with groups appropriately
		Solicits student participation
		Extends responses/contributions
		Provides time for response/consideration
		Implements at appropriate level
	Evaluates and provides feedback on student progress during instruction	Communicates learning expectations
		Monitors student performance
		Solicits responses/demonstrations for assessment
		Reinforces correct response/performance
		Provides corrective feedback/clarifies/none needed
		Reteaches/none needed
Classroom management and organization	Organizes materials and students	Secures student attention
		Uses procedures/routines
		Gives clear administrative directions/none needed
		Maintains appropriate seating/grouping
		Has materials/aids/facilities ready
	Maximizes amount of time available for instruction	Begins promptly/avoids waste at the end of class
		Implements appropriate sequence of activities
		Maintains appropriate pace
		Maintains focus
		Keeps students engaged
	Manages student behavior	Specifies expectations for behavior/none needed
		Prevents off-task behaviors/none needed
		Redirects/stops inappropriate/disruptive behavior
		Applies rules consistently and fairly/none needed
		Reinforces desired behavior when appropriate

Domain	Action	Examples
Presentation of subject matter	Teaches for cognitive, affective, and/or psychomotor learning and transfer	Begins with appropriate introduction
		Presents information in appropriate sequence
		Relates content to prior/future learning
		Defines/describes concepts (e.g., skills, attitudes, interests)
		Elaborates critical attributes
		Stress generalization/principle rule
		Provides for application
		Closes instruction appropriately
	Uses effective communication skills	Makes no significant errors
		Explains content/tasks clearly
		Stresses important points/ dimensions
		Uses correct grammar
		Uses accurate language
		Demonstrates written skills
Learning environment	Uses strategies to motivate students for learning	Relates content to interests and experiences
		Emphasizes the value and importance of activity or content
		Reinforces and praises efforts
		Challenges students
	Maintains supportive and negative criticism	Avoids sarcasm and negative criticism
		Establishes a climate of courtesy
		Encourages slow and reluctant students
		Establishes and maintains positive rapport

Note: Adapted from the Texas Teacher Appraisal System.

cause they were developed initially in Houston and then used in Washington, D.C. Furthermore, preliminary data analyses with the 658 first- and second-graders in the Houston schools show that, on average, the percentage of time that students are engaged during reading/language arts instruction correlates .73 with ratings of teaching effectiveness.

Fidelity of Reading Instruction

If teachers are using a particular reading program and it is desirable to know how well they are implementing the program, then a fidelity

Table 1.6.   Correlations of global effectiveness with components of teaching competency

Components of competency	First grade		Second grade	
	Houston (n = 20)	Washington, D.C. (n = 21)	Houston (n = 22)	Washington, D.C. (n = 20)
Planning	.72[a]	.75[a]	.66[b]	.59[b]
Management	.76[a]	.46[c]	.84[a]	.61[b]
Instruction	.44	.49[c]	.59[b]	.42
Monitoring of students' learning	.52[c]	.53[c]	.61[b]	.51[c]
Personal characteristics	.63[b]	.78[b]	.74[a]	.59[b]
Overall competency	.72[a]	.62[b]	.77[a]	.57[b]

[a]$p < .001$
[b]$p < .01$
[c]$p < .05$

checklist should be completed by an observer who knows the program well. For example, the reading reform model Success for All (Slavin et al., 1996) asks the facilitator to complete an implementation checklist. Weak implementation, as indexed on the fidelity form, triggers modeling and coaching by the facilitator.

For research purposes, we report fidelity as the percentage of expected components correctly implemented. The less scripted the program, the more difficult it is to determine fidelity and the less likely fidelity will be linked to student outcomes. For example, our fidelity form for the Houghton Mifflin (1996) program was similar to the RLOF (Henk et al., 2000). Fidelity was very high across the teachers in the six schools in Washington, D.C., using this curriculum. However, variability in student achievement across these classrooms was high and unrelated to fidelity. We find that the ratings of time-by-activity and teaching effectiveness and the proportion of the curriculum actually covered were more relevant to explaining achievement outcomes.

Teacher Surveys Related to Reading Instruction

We used two teacher surveys to discover what teachers know about teaching reading and what teachers think about the reading curricula they use. The following sections describe each of these surveys.

Teacher Knowledge Survey   It is important to understand what teachers know about teaching reading. One way to measure this knowledge is to give teachers a pretest prior to providing professional development and a posttest after professional development. Accordingly, we have developed a survey (based on Moats, 1994, 2000) for teachers in kindergarten through second grade that assesses their knowledge regarding speech sounds (e.g., how many speech sounds are in the word *edge*), morphology (identifying prefixes and suffixes), phonological patterns (e.g., why the second *m* in *moment* is not doubled), and orthographic rules (e.g., change *y* to *i* when adding endings, as in *easier*). In an attempt to base the survey more on performance, we have added questions pertaining to a running record of oral reading errors and a writing protocol. Thus, we look to see if high teacher knowledge relates to high teaching effectiveness.

In preliminary data from 83 third- and fourth-grade teachers in Houston and Washington, D.C., schools, the correlations between TTAS and the teacher knowledge survey administered at the beginning and end of year were moderate ($r = .39$ and $r = .30$, $p < .001$, respectively). The cautionary tale here is that paper-and-pencil tests of teacher knowledge do not necessarily translate into teaching effectiveness. Professional development needs to follow the teacher into the classroom in a coaching model that translates knowledge into practice (Foorman & Moats, 2003).

Teacher knowledge surveys typically include questions about demographics (e.g., gender, ethnicity), educational background (degrees and certifications), years of teaching experience, and specialized training experiences. In order to link perceptions of preparedness with teacher knowledge and student learning (Mather, Bos, & Babur, 2001; McCutchen et al., 2002), we also include questions such as, "How well do you think you are prepared to teach children to read?" and "How well do you think you are prepared to teach struggling readers how to read?" Often background and experience questionnaires are combined with teacher knowledge and attitude surveys. One such example is the 55-item teacher survey from the National Reading Research Center (Baumann, Hoffman, Duffy-Hester, & Ro, 2000).

Survey of Teacher's Opinions About Program Curricula The Survey of Teacher's Opinions About Program Curricula has four parts (Foorman, Francis, Fletcher, Schatschneider, & Mehta, 1998). The first part asks the teacher to rate his or her response on a scale of 1 (definitely no) to 5 (definitely yes) to four questions about the literacy program they are currently using:

1. If you were responsible for curriculum decisions in your district, would you recommend that resources (e.g., materials, staff development) be provided for this reading program in the future?

2.   Would you recommend the reading program you are using to a colleague?

3.   Would you recommend the reading program for use with all children of the appropriate age?

4.   Would you recommend the reading program for children with special needs?

The second part of the survey consists of 10 statements about reading instruction to be rated "strongly disagree" to "strongly agree" (e.g., children should have daily opportunities to practice matching letters and sounds; children should have daily opportunities to write and read their own stories; most children learn to read through exposure to good literature and do not need explicit instruction in letters and letter sounds). The third part of the survey consists of four questions about how often teachers participate in school-related activities (e.g., meeting with other teachers to discuss instruction, curriculum development, instructional objectives for language-minority children, children with disabilities). The final part of the survey lists the components of the reading curriculum used by the teacher (e.g., phonemic awareness, big book reading). The teacher rates how valuable each of these components is for teaching children to read.

We found that 53 first-grade teachers in eight Title I schools who were delivering instruction that varied with respect to the explicitness of alphabetic code instruction differed significantly in their responses to the first two questions of the first part of this attitudes survey. Teachers with the most explicit approach (called *direct code*) were more likely than teachers with a moderately explicit approach (called *embedded code*) to recommend their instruction to the district. Teachers using the direct-code approach were more likely than teachers using either an embedded-code or an implicit-code (which is the least explicit) approach to recommend their instruction to a colleague. The other parts of the survey do not tend to show differences across teacher groups because of the social desirability of the response. For this reason, we strongly recommend triangulating teacher survey data with observations of classroom instruction and with student achievement.

RELATIONSHIP OF NEW
CLASSROOM MEASURES TO STUDENT OUTCOMES

We are in the midst of analyzing the relationships between teacher data and student outcomes in our Houston–Washington, D.C., longitudinal data set. In Table 1.7, we present correlations between teaching effectiveness and scores on the Letter-Word Identification, Word Attack,

Table 1.7. Correlations of teacher effectiveness with student outcomes for first and second grades

	First grade		Second grade	
Measure	Houston (n = 20)	Washington, D.C. (n = 21)	Houston (n = 22)	Washington, D.C. (n = 20)
Letter-Word Identification	.64[a]	.68[a]	.28	.56[b]
Word Attack	.56[b]	.55[b]	.19	.49[c]
Passage Comprehension	.62[b]	.70[a]	.18	.41
Phonemic awareness	.57[b]	.58[b]	.22	.47[c]
Spelling dictation	.52[c]	.58[b]	.22	.47[c]

Note: Letter-Word Identification, Word Attack, and Passage Comprehension are from the Woodcock-Johnson Psychoeducational Battery–Revised (Woodcock & Johnson, 1989). Spelling dictation is from the Kaufman Test of Educational Achievement (Kaufman & Kaufman, 1985). Phonemic awareness is from a prepublication version of the Comprehensive Test of Phonological Processing (Wagner, Torgesen, & Rashotte, 1999).

[a] $p < .001$
[b] $p < .01$
[c] $p < .05$

and Passage Comprehension subtests of the Woodcock-Johnson Psychoeducational Battery–Revised (Woodcock & Johnson, 1989), phonemic awareness scores from a prepublication version of the Comprehensive Test of Phonological Processing (CTOPP; Wagner, Torgesen, & Rashotte, 1999), and spelling scores from the Kaufman Test of Educational Achievement (Kaufman & Kaufman, 1985). All achievement measures were obtained at the end of the school year. These correlations are positive and generally strong, except in the second grade in Houston.

Scanlon and Vellutino (1996) found that allocation of instructional time differentially influenced outcomes for children at different proficiency levels. In a similar fashion, we grouped our Houston and Washington, D.C., classrooms into high-performing and low-performing categories, based on a median split of average word reading performance at the beginning of the year (see Foorman et al., 1998, for a description of the measure). Classrooms in which fewer than 50% of the students performed below grade-level average on word reading were described as high initial status. Classrooms in which more than 50% of the students performed below grade-level average on word reading were described as low initial status. We are analyzing how initial classroom status, teacher effectiveness, and percentage of time spent on reading/language activities affect literacy outcomes of 852 first- and second-graders in Houston and Washington, D.C. (Foorman, Schatschneider, Fletcher, Francis, & Moats, 2003).

Figure 1.4 graphically displays time-by-activity ratings by initial classroom status and teacher effectiveness ratings in Houston, and Figure 1.5 displays the same information for Washington, D.C. Teacher effectiveness ratings are dichotomized around the median into groups of high ratings and low ratings. In Houston, highly rated teachers spent a greater percentage of time doing word work than teachers with lower ratings. Word work accounted for nearly 40% of instructional time for highly rated teachers in first-grade classrooms with high initial status. Surprisingly, this difference was more apparent in classrooms with high initial status than with low initial status, with the latter classrooms presumably being the ones to benefit the most from additional word work. The other striking difference was in the percentage of time spent on

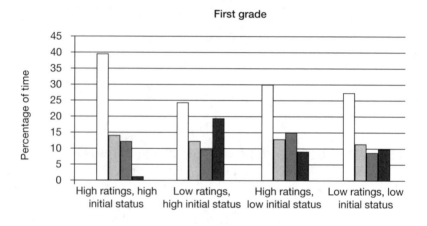

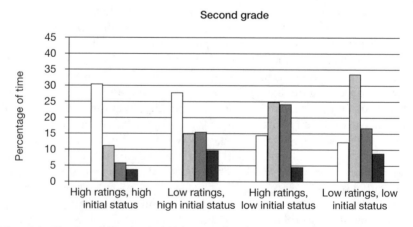

Figure 1.4. Time-by-activity ratings by initial status and teacher ratings in Houston. The top graph describes the first grade. The bottom graph describes the second grade. (*Key:* ☐ = Word work, ▣ = Reading comprehension, ▤ = Language arts, ■ = Nonreading behaviors)

reading comprehension in second grade. Houston classrooms with low initial status spent the majority of literacy instruction on reading comprehension, with the percentage being nearly 35% in second-grade classrooms with low initial status and low-rated teaching. Finally, in first and second grades in Houston, highly rated teachers more often tended to have less instructional time devoted to nonreading activities.

In the Washington, D.C., first-grade classrooms depicted in Figure 1.5, time-by-activity ratings are remarkably similar, except for the tendency for highly rated teachers in classrooms with low initial status to

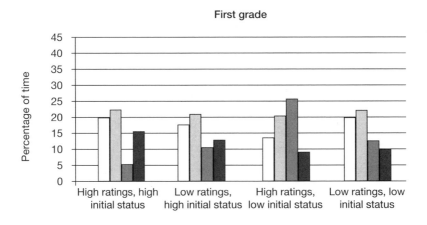

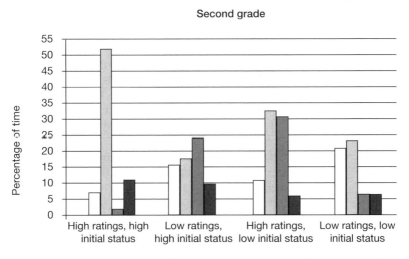

Figure 1.5. Time-by-activity ratings by initial status and teacher ratings in Washington, D.C. The top graph describes the first grade. The bottom graph describes the second grade. (*Key:* ☐ = Word work, ▨ = Reading comprehension, ▨ = Language arts, ■ = Nonreading behaviors)

spend 27% of instructional time in language activities. In second grade, the most striking finding is that highly rated teachers in classrooms with high initial status spent 52% of instructional time in reading comprehension activities. In low initial status classrooms, highly rated second-grade teachers increased time spent on language to nearly equal the percentage of time spent on reading comprehension (30%). Thus, across sites, teachers allocated instructional time differently depending on their teaching skill and the proficiency of their students. The resulting profiles of time-by-activity ratings were clearly influenced by the curricular materials at hand, as shown in Figures 1.2 and 1.3.

Finally, quality judgments must be considered along with quantity of instructional time. When examining writing performance in second and third grades in the Houston and Washington, D.C., schools (Foorman, Francis, Chen, & Schatschneider, 2001), we found that time spent on writing instruction did not predict writing outcomes, whereas quality judgments of writing instruction did. Specifically, teachers who were rated high on writing instruction had students with significantly better grammar and language scores, a greater number of words in their compositions, and a greater percentage of words sequenced correctly.

CONCLUSION

In this chapter, we have 1) described existing instruments that exemplify methods for observing reading/language arts instruction; 2) presented the measures we have developed out of our longitudinal study of reading development in kindergarten through fourth grades in Houston and in Washington, D.C., schools; and 3) provided preliminary data linking observations of classroom teaching to student outcomes. There are many conclusions. First, we can obtain reliable judgments of how teachers allocate instructional time and the quality of that time. Second, the curriculum that a teacher uses influences the allotment of instructional time. Third, students' performance affects teachers' decisions about allocation of instructional time, and these decisions vary by ratings of teaching effectiveness. Fourth, sheer quantity of instructional time does not necessarily affect outcomes; quality of instruction also needs to be considered. Fifth, teacher knowledge, as measured by paper-and-pencil tests, may not directly affect student achievement. It is the translation of knowledge into practice through coaching and mentoring that makes the difference. Thus, as we examine the conditions under which children learn to read, it is critically important to reliably measure classroom teaching in order to study its role in moderating students' skill development. We are currently analyzing our Houston–Washington, D.C., data to examine the impact of teaching in kindergarten through fourth grade on students' development and attainment of reading-related skills. In addition, we are adapting these observational measures to bilingual classrooms as we begin a longitudinal study of language and literacy development in Spanish-speaking children.

REFERENCES

Allington, R.L. (1991). Children who find learning to read difficult: School responses to diversity. In E.H. Hiebert (Ed.), *Literacy for a diverse society* (pp. 237–252). New York: Teachers College Press.

Allington, R.L., & McGill-Franzen, A. (1989). School response to reading failure: Instruction for Chapter 1 and special education students in grades two, four, and eight. *The Elementary School Journal, 89,* 529–542.

Baumann, J.F., Hoffman, J.V., Duffy-Hester, A.M, & Ro, J.M. (2000). The first R yesterday and today: U.S. elementary reading instruction practices reported by teachers and administrators. *Reading Research Quarterly, 35,* 338–377.

Englemann, S., & Bruner, E. (1995). *Reading mastery I.* Chicago: SRA/McGraw-Hill.

Foorman, B.R., Francis, D.J., Chen, D., & Schatschneider, C. (2001, June 1–3). *Does writing instruction improve reading?* Paper presentation at the annual meeting of the Society for the Scientific Study of Reading. Boulder, CO.

Foorman, B.R., Francis, D.J., Fletcher, J.M., Schatschneider, C., & Mehta, P. (1998). The role of instruction in learning to read: Preventing reading failure in at-risk children. *Journal of Educational Psychology, 90,* 37–55.

Foorman, B.R., & Moats, L.C. (2003). Conditions for sustaining research-based practices in early reading instruction. *Remedial and Special Education.*

Foorman, B.R., Schatschneider, C., Fletcher, J.M., Francis, D.J., & Moats, L.C. (2003). *The impact of instructional practices in Grades 1 and 2 on reading and spelling achievement in high poverty schools.* Manuscript submitted.

Foorman, B.R., & Torgesen, J.K. (2001). Critical elements of classroom and small-group instruction promote reading success in all children. *Learning Disabilities Research and Practice, 16,* 202–211.

Greenwood, C.R., Carta, J.J., Kamps, D., & Delquadri, J. (1995). *Ecobehavioral Assessment Systems Software (EBASS).* Lawrence: University of Kansas.

Greenwood, C.R., & Delquadri, J. (1988). Code for instructional structure and student academic response: CISSAR. In M. Hersen & A.S. Bellack (Eds.), *Dictionary of behavioral assessment techniques* (pp. 120–122). New York: Pergamon.

Henk, W.A., Moore, J.C., Marinak, B.A., & Tomasetti, B.W. (2000). A reading lesson observation framework for elementary teachers, principals, and literacy supervisors. *The Reading Teacher, 53,* 358–369.

Invitations to literacy. (1996). Boston: Houghton Mifflin.

Juel, C., & Minden-Cupp, C. (2000). Learning to read words: Linguistic units and instructional strategies. *Reading Research Quarterly, 35,* 458–492.

Kaufman, A.S. & Kaufman, N.L. (1985). *Kaufman Test of Educational Achievement.* Circle Pines, MN: American Guidance Service.

Mather, N., Bos, C., & Babur, N. (2001). Perceptions and knowledge of preservice and inservice teachers about early literacy instruction. *Journal of Learning Disabilities, 34,* 472–482.

McCutchen, D., Abbott, R.D., Green, L.B., Beretvas, N., Cox, S., Potter, N.S., Quiroga, T., & Gray, A.L. (2002). Beginning literacy: Links among teacher knowledge, teacher practice, and student learning. *Journal of Learning Disabilities, 35,* 69–86.

Moats, L.C. (1994). The missing foundation in teacher education: Knowledge of the structure of spoken and written language. *Annals of Dyslexia, 44,* 81–102.

Moats, L.C. (2000). *Speech to print: Language essentials for teachers.* Baltimore: Paul H. Brookes Publishing Co.

National Reading Panel. (2000). *Teaching children to read: An evidence-based assessment of the scientific research literature on reading and its implications for reading instruction.* Washington, D.C.: National Institute of Child Health and Human Development (NICHD).

New Standards. (1999). *Primary literacy standards.* Washington, D.C.: Center for Education and the Economy.

Open Court Reading. (1995). *Collections for young scholars.* Chicago: SRA/McGraw-Hill.

Pellegrini, A.D. (2001). Some theoretical and methodological considerations in studying literacy in social context. In S.B. Neuman & D.K. Dickinson (Eds.), *Handbook of early literacy research* (pp. 54–65). New York: The Guilford Press.

Phillips, H.L. (2001). *Multilevel investigation of the relationships of beliefs with behaviors, and of task and contextual performance with effectiveness.* Unpublished doctoral dissertation, University of Houston, Texas.

Pressley, M., Wharton-McDonald, R., Mistretta-Hampston, J., & Echevarria, M. (1998). Literacy instruction in 10 fourth- and fifth-grade classrooms in upstate New York. *Scientific Studies of Reading, 2,* 159–194.

Scanlon, D.M., & Vellutino, F.R. (1996). Prerequisite skills, early instruction, and success in first-grade reading: Selected results from a longitudinal study. *Mental Retardation and Developmental Research Reviews, 2,* 54–63.

Slavin, R.E., Madden, N.A., Dolan, L.J., & Wasik, B.A. (1996). *Every child, every school: Success for All.* Thousand Oaks, CA: Corwin Press.

Snow, C.E., Burns, M.S., & Griffin, P. (Eds.). (1998). *Preventing reading difficulties in young children.* Washington, DC: National Academy Press.

Stallings, J., Robbins, P., & Presbrey, L. (1986). Effects of instruction based on the Madeline Hunter model on students' achievement: Findings from a follow-through project. *The Elementary School Journal, 86,* 117–138.

Texas Education Agency. (1984). *Texas Teacher Appraisal System.* Austin: Author.

Wagner, R.K., Torgesen, J.K., & Rashotte, C.A. (1999). *Comprehensive Test of Phonological Processing.* Austin, TX: PRO-ED.

Wolcott, H.F. (1988). Ethnographic research in education. In R.M. Jaeger (Ed.), *Complementary methods for research in education* (pp. 187–249). Washington, DC: American Educational Research Association.

Woodcock, R.W., & Johnson, M.B. (1989). *Woodcock-Johnson Psychoeducational Battery–Revised.* Allen, TX: DLM Teaching Resources.

Ysseldyke, J.E., & Christenson, S.L. (1993). *The Instructional Environment System–II (TIES–II).* Colorado Springs, CO: Sopris West.

2

The Instructional Content Emphasis Instrument

Observations of Reading Instruction

MEAGHAN EDMONDS AND KERRI L. BRIGGS

Within the context of a national reading initiative, Texas (2000) crafted a statewide reading initiative that was far-reaching and multifaceted. The reading initiative was, in one sense, a tool to help students meet the expectations outlined in the state's curriculum standards in reading and ensure that every child could read on grade level by third grade. In conjunction with the reading initiative, the state also adopted new accountability measures that tied success in reading to promotion and retention decisions.

With such high stakes, policy makers were not satisfied to merely establish policy. Policy makers and educators alike needed to ensure that classroom instruction was aligned with state expectations and that students were given opportunities to learn the knowledge and skills outlined by the standards and measured by the state assessment. Because the statewide assessment served as a more global measure intended to determine school success, it did not provide detailed information about classroom instruction. To obtain information about what was happening in the classroom and whether quality instruction was being implemented in initiative-funded programs, state leaders called for an evaluation of several initiative programs.

EVALUATING STATE READING INITIATIVE PROGRAMS

A team of evaluators was asked to determine whether two reading initiative programs—state-funded, locally designed interventions for struggling readers and statewide professional development in reading for primary grade teachers—were having an effect on classrooms and students. More specific evaluation questions were within the overarching issue of program quality and effects: Are teachers delivering interventions that reflect both state content standards and current research about reading? Are teachers implementing the content presented in the professional development? Is the message about the importance of research-based instruction being heard and used? These questions had a common concern: What, how, and how well were students being taught during reading and language arts instruction?

The evaluations utilized a number of methods to make these determinations, including surveys of teacher practices, interviews with teachers and principals who were implementing the interventions and professional development, and results of student assessments other than the statewide reading assessment. Yet, providing answers to these questions required following the programs into the classroom, seeing them in action, and attaining an in-depth and accurate portrayal of classroom practice. Furthermore, state leaders were accustomed to using quantitative data to make decisions and understand the educational landscape. Although they wanted to know what was happening in the classroom, it was not sufficient to provide qualitative analyses; quantitative explanations of implementation were required. In response to the challenge of quantifying the content of reading and language arts instruction, the evaluation team developed the Instructional Content Emphasis (ICE) observation instrument to systematically categorize and code the content of reading and language arts instruction—including what components of reading instruction were emphasized, how students were grouped, and what materials were being used. In addition to the descriptive variables, the instrument captured student engagement and overall instructional quality. The following section outlines the specific purpose for which ICE was developed; the theoretical basis for the instrument's format and categories; examples of data produced by ICE; and practical uses of the instrument.

DEVELOPMENT AND DESCRIPTION OF THE INSTRUCTIONAL CONTENT EMPHASIS (ICE) INSTRUMENT

ICE was developed and refined over the course of two separate evaluations of policies related to the statewide reading initiative. The first project evaluated program-funded reading interventions for struggling readers in upper-elementary and middle schools. The second program, evaluated in the succeeding year, funded professional development on beginning reading instruction and primary-grade interventions for students at risk for reading difficulties.

Observations were included in the evaluation plan because observing reading and language arts instruction has been shown to be useful not only for determining instructional content but also for approximating student learning in reading. Specifically, observations of instructional content capture *opportunities to learn,* a key predictor of student achievement (Porter, 1993, 1994). It follows that the kind of work teachers ask their students to do—the instructional *content* of the class—offers a valid indication of the knowledge and skills students are developing (Kennedy, 1999).

Before creating ICE, the team conducted a thorough search of existing observation systems. The search uncovered multiple studies that used instruments for recording and coding universal classroom elements such as student–teacher interaction (e.g., Kerr, Kent, & Lam, 1985; Vogt, 1991), classroom environment (e.g., McIntosh, Vaughn, Schumm, Haager, & Lee, 1994), and pedagogical practices (e.g., Henk, Moore, & Marinak, 2000; Newman, Marks, & Gamoran, 1996). Few, however, would have enabled observers to capture the actual content or topics being covered during reading and language arts instruction. The disappointing search for a fitting instrument prompted the development of a unique observation instrument. ICE is essentially a quantitative system for coding the qualitative nature of classroom reading instruction. Using the ICE coding system, the evaluator can capture multiple aspects of the classroom including components of reading instruction, grouping patterns, materials used for instruction, student engagement, and the emphasis on content during instruction.

To measure instructional content, ICE captures the skills that students learned and used during reading instruction. This instrument places importance on what students learn during reading instruction, as opposed to the topic of instruction. For example, if students were reading a rhyme about weather, the ICE system would capture the fact that students were learning to rhyme or studying vocabulary words as opposed to the fact that they were learning about snow or rain. Certainly, these concepts—rhyming, vocabulary, and weather—are all important, but ICE was intended to estimate the extent to which instruction addressed the components of effective reading instruction, such as phonological awareness, phonics, fluency, comprehension, and vocabulary instruction.

When using the ICE instrument during observations of reading instruction, researchers focus on describing each *instructional activity,* defined as a distinct or unique activity in which the grouping and materials are coordinated around a certain domain or component of reading instruction. For example, an observation of a kindergarten reading lesson during which students participated in a rhyming activity, listened to a story read by the teacher, and practiced making the letter *h* in sand trays would include descriptions of three instructional activities.

These detailed descriptions are then coded with the ICE instrument, resulting in a numeric description for each instructional activity. ICE has four prescribed dimensions, each with several subcategories, for classifying reading instruction. The first two dimensions describe what is being taught. The third dimension describes how it is being taught. The final dimension describes the materials being used to teach. The four dimensions are

- *Main instructional category—Dimension A:* Main categories identify the broad domain of instructional content.

- *Instructional subcategory—Dimension B:* Subcategories classify the specific activities that occur, allowing for a more detailed description of content. The subcategories are broad enough so that activities that have common objectives but are known by several different names can be readily classified.

- *Grouping—Dimension C:* Instructional activities are categorized into one of five grouping patterns: whole class, small groups, pairs, independent, and individual.

- *Materials—Dimension D:* Coding options for materials used during instruction include multiple types of text (e.g., basal readers, patterns books) and a wide range of ancillary materials.

In addition to the four dimensions, the instrument contains categories for coding how long the activity lasts (i.e., content emphasis), how well students attend to what is being presented (i.e., student engagement), and a separate set of indicators for rating the overall instructional quality of the entire observation. The content emphasis code represents the amount of time spent on an instructional activity, not the amount of time a grouping pattern or material was used, and it is calculated based on the entire observation. The relative amount of time given to the activity is rated on an incremental scale ranging from 1 (incidental, an unplanned activity that took very little time) to 6 (maximum emphasis, occupying 91%–100% of observed instructional time). For example, a 15-minute activity in a 60-minute observation would be rated a 3, the code for low-moderate emphasis. By definition, a low-moderate activity occupies between 10% and 40% of the total observation time.

ICE also provides space for tallying and recording the amount of time spent on noninstructional activities that are both academic in nature (e.g., handing out materials, grading a test) and nonacademic (e.g., roll call, making announcements, talking about the upcoming field trip). Accounting for noninstructional time creates a context for judging the relative duration of instructional opportunities provided and allows the observer to examine how well teachers use classroom time.

Student engagement for each activity is rated on a Likert-type scale (1 = low engagement, 2 = medium engagement, 3 = high engagement). Indicators used for rating engagement stipulate that *low engagement* is assigned to activities during which fewer than half the students are actively listening or participating. Under the ICE system, students following along but not necessarily vocally participating are considered to be engaged. Figure 2.1 provides an example of a numeric description with codes for all six categories (see the appendix for coding categories).

For coding the overall quality of observed instruction (versus individual activities), seven quality indicators are rated on a scale from 1 (unacceptable) to 4 (outstanding). Specific quality indicators include 1) classroom management, 2) classroom environment, 3) instructional balance, 4) level of instructional scaffolding, 5) level of student self-regulation, 6) academic expectations, and 7) teaching in context. ICE users consider the observed instruction in its entirety when rating the seven quality items.

Validity and Reliability

The multidimensional, taxonomical design of the instrument was derived from the Reform Up Close study of instructional content in high school mathematics and science classes (Porter, 1994; Smithson & Porter, 1994). Previous studies that have used content area standards as the basis for categorizing instructional content (Porter, 1994; Saxe, Gearhart, & Seltzer, 1999) served as a model for creating the instrument's taxonomy.

To be valid, the instrument had to provide coding options that accurately portrayed what was occurring in the classroom, particularly the content of reading instruction. Content validity was established by a thorough literature review and through consultation with experts in the field. Instructional categories and subcategories in ICE were culled from a variety of sources documenting instructional practices found in beginning reading instruction, upper-elementary and middle school reading and language arts classes, and reading intervention programs (Bond & Dykstra, 1997; Graves & Dykstra, 1997; Morrow, Tracey, Woo, & Pressley, 1999; Pressley, 1998; Pressley, Rankin, & Yokoi, 1996; Pressley, Wharton-McDonald, Mistretta-Hampston, & Echevarria, 1998; Pressley, Wharton-McDonald, Mistretta-Hampston, & Yokoi, 1997; Searfoss, 1997; Stahl, 1992; Wharton-McDonald, Pressley, & Mistretta-Hampston, 1998). Instrument developers also reviewed national and state reading standards (Center for the Improvement of Early Reading Achievement, 1998; National Center on Education and the Economy, 1999; Texas Education Agency, 2000) and research on best practice in literacy instruction (Educational Research Service, 1999; Gambrell & Mazzoni, 1999; Juel, 1994; National Reading Panel, 2000; Osborn & Lehr, 1998; Snow, Burns, & Griffin, 1998).

Because policy makers were interested in determining what students were being taught and the extent to which classroom instruction was aligned with the research, seminal research on the components of effective reading instruction served as the basis for developing ICE's categories. The seminal work (Adams, 1990; National Reading Panel, 2000; Snow et al., 1998) has led to an increased consensus about the definition of effective reading programs and a solid research base on what constitutes good teaching in beginning reading. This body of research provides converging and convincing evidence that proficiency in certain foundational skills influences later reading achievement. ICE coding categories were built around these reading components—the same components that were the basis for the initiative's professional development and the state content standards in reading for the primary grades. A critical aspect of the reading initiative was educating the teaching workforce about this research and infusing this research into reading instruction, making research-based instruction a key variable in the evaluation projects for which ICE was developed.

Information for the other dimensions were drawn from a number of sources. The grouping categories for Dimension C were drawn from the Classroom Climate Scale (see Chapter 4). The materials identified in Dimension D were based on the evaluators' knowledge of classrooms and refined during the pilot tests. Quality indicators were selected from the work reviewed for Dimensions A and B and from research on effective teaching (e.g., Brophy, 1979; Porter & Brophy, 1988).

Although the included categories for coding instruction are certainly not exhaustive, they represent the most common types of reading activities implemented in elementary and middle school classrooms. Including *common* instructional activities, not just the most effective, protected against the possibility of observing instruction that defied classification. However, because ICE includes categories of instruction that the research has shown to be effective, one can argue that students who have the opportunity to learn the content represented on the instrument are likely to develop skills needed for success in reading. This premise makes ICE a theoretically valid measure of instructional quality.

To increase reliability, indicators for each subcategory were developed (see the Appendix). Drawn from descriptions of reading activities found in the best practices literature, the indicators define the parameters of the subcategories by providing specific examples of instruction associated with a given coding category. For example, within the comprehension subcategory (in Dimension A), the corresponding indicators for the subcategory "Prior knowledge/predicting" (in Dimension B) are 1) students preview the material before reading, 2) students predict outcomes based on prior knowledge, and 3) students participate in activities designed to measure their level of knowledge before reading.

Using ICE requires some familiarity with reading instruction. Observers, for example, must be able to differentiate between phonological awareness instruction and phonics-based activities. Although training observers on the ICE system takes a good deal of time and effort, raters are highly reliable once trained. For the two evaluations during which ICE was further developed, an inter-rater reliability rate of 91% was achieved.

Decisions regarding the scope and specificity of ICE's main dimensions, and subcategories within the dimensions, were informed by the literature and restricted by practicality. The initial list of instructional topics was reduced to include only those instructional topics that appeared in either the state content standards, more than one major research source, or both. Instrument refinement followed a pilot in primary-grade classrooms. A panel of educators, university professors, and researchers also reviewed the instrument's format and categories

Instructional content observed: *Four students in a small group place plastic letters on an alphabet arc. All students are focused. (5 minutes out of a 30-minute observation)*		
Dimension	Category title	Numeric code
Dimension A	*Alphabetics*	*1*
Dimension B	*Alphabetic knowledge*	*3*
Dimension C	*Small group*	*2*
Dimension D	*Manipulatives*	*2*
Content emphasis	*Low to moderate*	*3*
Student engagement	*High*	*3*

Figure 2.1. Example of a coded instructional activity.

and provided valuable feedback. Input from these authorities in the field established that the instrument measured what it purported to—instructional content of reading and language arts instruction.

The Original ICE

Because the two projects evaluated different grade levels, two versions of ICE resulted. The original version of ICE, used in the first evaluation, reflected instructional content appropriate for upper-elementary and middle school reading and language arts instruction. This original version contains five Dimension A topics, each with a number of subcategories (Dimension B). In total, there are 32 items in Dimension B:

- *Word Level* includes seven subcategories: decoding instruction, vocabulary instruction in context, vocabulary instruction out of context, vocabulary root words, spelling instruction, fluency, and independent reading.

- *Comprehension* includes seven subcategories: predicting/previewing, background knowledge, identifying purpose of story, monitoring comprehension during reading, identifying main idea and summarizing, application/analysis/evaluation, and teaching of comprehension skills.

- *Thinking Skills* includes six subcategories: brainstorming, separating fact from fiction, examining multiple options/answers, developing research questions, interpreting information, and teacher modeling of critical thinking skills.

- *Writing Skills* includes six subcategories: writing on passages read in class, writing involving library resources, creative writing, expository writing, teaching writing processes, and sharing writing.

- *Assessment* includes six subcategories: written comprehension questions, formula/format writing, vocabulary/spelling tests, writing tests, standardized tests, and book reports.

Primary Grade ICE

The second version, referred to as the primary grade ICE, maintained the original structure but was adapted to capture the nuances of primary-grade reading instruction. Revisions included adding categories for critical components of beginning reading. The primary grade version also benefited from a year of use and analysis of data from the original version and from a research base that was more definitive for younger readers (e.g., Snow et al., 1998). For example, Dimension B subcategories from the original version included reading and language arts topics not typically seen in primary grades (e.g., writing involving library or other research resources) and excluded important instructional topics associated with beginning reading (e.g., phonological awareness).

The primary grade version of ICE contains five Dimension A topics, each with a number of Dimension B subcategories. In total, there are 22 items in Dimension B.

- *Alphabetics* includes seven subcategories: concepts of print, phonological awareness, alphabetic knowledge, word study/phonics, spelling, oral language development, and multiple-cueing systems.
- *Fluency* includes three subcategories: partner reading, repeated reading, and modeling fluency.
- *Reading* includes four subcategories: guided oral reading, choral reading, independent reading, and listening to text read aloud.
- *Comprehension* includes four subcategories: vocabulary, prior knowledge/predicting, comprehension monitoring, and story structure and analysis.
- *Writing and Language Arts* includes four subcategories: dictation, independent writing and publishing, grammar and punctuation, and handwriting instruction.

Two additional categories—student engagement and overall instructional quality—make the primary grade version of ICE unique. Whereas the first version captured instructional content almost exclusively, the revised version introduced more process variables.

FINDINGS

Although complex analysis of ICE data is possible, the findings presented in this chapter resulted from relatively basic analyses conducted to answer policy makers' questions about the instructional content of initiative-funded programs. The following presents an example of data for each of ICE's four primary dimensions. Instructional content descriptions were culled from evaluation reports that summarized observation data gathered using the ICE system.

During the second evaluation project, two components of one larger policy were evaluated: 1) professional development on strategies for primary-grade reading instruction and 2) interventions designed for primary-grade students at risk for reading difficulties. The purpose in evaluating the first component was to determine the extent to which teachers were implementing evidence-based reading strategies presented during professional development sessions delivered throughout the state. Regarding the second component, policy makers were interested in the content and focus of program-funded interventions for struggling readers in kindergarten and first grade. Specifically, the evaluators were charged with examining whether students had the opportunity to learn the foundational skills that predicate reading success.

For the evaluation, 13 schools from 10 districts were selected. Districts were selected on the basis of the following criteria: participation in the state reading initiative, a sufficient number of students participating in the intervention, and a willingness to participate in the evaluation. Districts were also selected from around the state and included urban and rural areas. The following conclusions from the evaluation reports characterize reading instruction from a variety of angles: which topics were most emphasized (Dimensions A and B); the relationship between grouping patterns and student engagement (Dimension C and student engagement), and materials commonly used during primary-grade reading instruction (Dimension D).

Dimensions A and B: Topics
Emphasized in Primary-Grade Reading Instruction

Evaluation data gathered from more than 100 observations in 36 classrooms revealed that students were indeed participating in balanced reading instruction, as espoused by the professional development sessions the teachers had attended and as supported by the research on effective reading instruction (Briggs, Edmonds, & Twiddy, 2000a, 2000b). Figure 2.2 depicts the instructional content of observed kindergarten classrooms, and Figure 2.3 represents instructional content in first-grade classrooms. As illustrated, kindergarten instruction emphasized phonics and prereading skills, which includes instruction in oral language development, book and print concepts, and phonological awareness. Instruction observed in first-grade classrooms focused less on prereading skills and provided students with more opportunities to practice reading text, instruction that is consistent with grade-level expectations (Snow et al., 1998).

One critical component of effective reading instruction rarely observed was the opportunity for students to become more rapid and more accurate readers. This could be explained by the fact that developing fluency among students is often part of other activities (e.g., reading text) and not an activity that most teachers conduct during a scheduled observation. Taken together, ICE data provided evidence

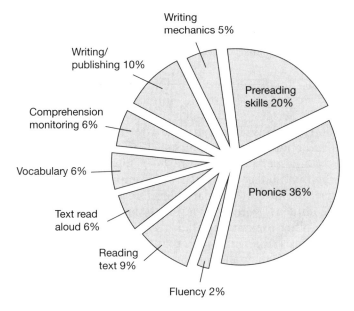

Figure 2.2. Instructional content in kindergarten classrooms. To more easily display observation data, some ICE categories were collapsed. For example, "prereading skills" includes instruction in oral language development, book and print concepts, and phonological awareness.

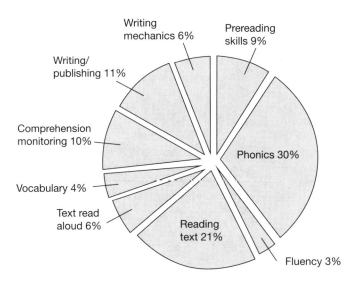

Figure 2.3. Instructional content in first-grade classrooms. To more easily display observation data, some ICE categories were collapsed. For example, "prereading skills" includes instruction in oral language development, book and print concepts, and phonological awareness.

that students had opportunities to develop early literacy skills, practice reading, and enhance their understanding of text through comprehension and vocabulary instruction—all components of an effective reading program.

Observations of interventions for struggling readers in kindergarten and first grade showed an intensive concentration on foundational skills (Briggs et al., 2000a, 2000b). ICE data illustrated that intervention programs offered struggling readers instruction in prereading skills and phonics-related topics such as alphabetic understanding, word study, and spelling (see Figure 2.4). Opportunities for students to develop their vocabulary, grammar, and comprehension skills were less emphasized. Because the primary objective of observed programs was to provide students with a strong basis in prereading and decoding skills, these other topics most often received the lowest rating on the content emphasis scale, indicating that they occurred during teachable moments rather than as a planned activity.

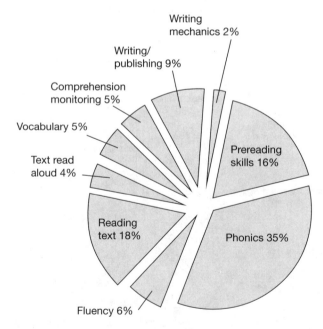

Figure 2.4.   Instructional content during intervention sessions. To more easily display observation data, some ICE categories were collapsed. For example, "prereading skills" includes instruction in oral language development, book and print concepts, and phonological awareness.

In sum, the data gathered through the primary grade version of ICE revealed that teachers were delivering instruction that reflected the statewide professional development. Students were receiving many opportunities to learn fundamental skills in decoding and comprehension. It was less evident that students received many opportunities to increase fluency, although it was suspected that this instruction occurred outside of the observations. Although teachers still relied on whole-class instruction, they were working with small groups of students and tailoring those opportunities to their needs. The interventions reflected even more concentrated efforts at improving the reading skills of students; a key focus was improving their ability to hear sounds in words and decode written text.

Dimension C and Student Engagement: The Relationship Between Grouping Patterns and Student Engagement

One revealing finding gleaned from ICE data was the significant relationship between certain grouping patterns used for reading instruction and student engagement. Observed teachers worked with the entire class most frequently, followed by small-group instruction (Briggs et al., 2000a). All but three observed teachers used a variety of grouping patterns during general reading instruction. First-grade students were more engaged and on task while in small groups for reading instruction than when working with the entire class, in pairs, or alone (Briggs et al., 2000a, 2000b)—an encouraging finding considering the relative emphasis given to this grouping pattern. This finding should also provide encouragement to teachers who may believe that small-group instruction opens up the door to too many behavior problems.

Instruction delivered in observed intervention programs occurred most often in a small-group setting. Among the observed intervention activities, 70% were conducted within a small-group setting (Briggs et al., 2000b). Furthermore, Briggs and colleagues (2000b) showed that student engagement was significantly higher when instruction was delivered as part of an intervention that occurred in small groups or pairs than when students worked independently.

Dimension D: Common Materials Used in Reading Instruction

ICE data allowed the evaluation team to determine the most common types of text used for reading instruction in the grade levels observed. Observed kindergarten teachers used trade books and big books most often. Decodable text proved to be the most popular text type in first-grade reading instruction. These findings provided evidence that the observed teachers were indeed using a variety of text types with their students.

IMPLICATIONS AND DISCUSSION

ICE was developed for the express objectives of two specific evaluation projects. Yet, the instrument's design lends itself to multiple uses and has the ability to produce data that describe a range of instructional practices during reading. ICE is at once generic enough to use when observing a variety of reading and language arts programs but specific enough in the coding system to yield detailed, descriptive information on exactly what is being taught during reading and language arts instruction. The data yielded by this system of quantifying instructional content can inform the decisions and actions of teachers, program coordinators, curriculum evaluators, campus administrators, and policy makers. Among the instruments many uses, both researchers and practitioners can

- Systematically evaluate the content of an existing or newly adopted curriculum
- Compare the instructional content of intervention, general, and advanced language arts programs
- Determine the use and frequency of student grouping patterns
- Monitor the implementation of curriculum or instructional materials
- Determine levels of implementation for newly introduced programs
- Check the instructional content data from other sources (e.g., teacher interviews, curriculum manuals, self-reported practices)

Perhaps the most practical instrument application is using the system to gather empirical evidence of the reading instructional opportunities provided to students. Instruction provided, opportunities to learn, and achievement are inextricably linked, especially when the measure of achievement assesses specific performance standards, as was the case with the reading initiative under which ICE was developed. Because implementation of content standards is nested within teachers' instruction, classroom observation becomes a necessary method for determining whether instruction that is provided is aligned with what is *expected*. If students are to be held accountable through assessments of reading performance, then determining students' opportunities to learn the content assessed becomes a critical and ethically imperative concern. The ICE instrument offers a means for systematically making those determinations on the basis of more than self-reports or non-structured observation notes. The resulting empirical data offer answers to the questions about the many dimensions of reading instructional content—including topics emphasized, grouping patterns implemented, and materials used. Use of the instrument in more rigorous, large-scale studies offers the hope of being able to assert with confidence that teachers are indeed providing students with effective reading instruction.

REFERENCES

Adams, M.J. (1990). *Beginning to read: Thinking and learning about print.* Cambridge, MA: MIT Press.

Briggs, K.L., Edmonds, M., & Twiddy, K. (2000a). *Evaluation report of the Student Success Initiative, 1999–2000: A report to the 77th Texas Legislature* (Report No. AD01 105 06). Austin: Texas Education Agency.

Briggs, K.L., Edmonds M.S., & Twiddy, K. (2000b). *Evaluation report of the Student Success Initiative, 2000–2001: A report to the Texas Education Agency* (Unpublished report). Austin: Texas Center for Reading and Language Arts.

Bond, G.L., & Dykstra, R. (1997). The cooperative research program in first-grade reading instruction. *Reading Research Quarterly, 32*(4), 348–427.

Brophy, J.E. (1979). Teacher behavior and its effects. *Journal of Educational Psychology, 71*(6), 733–750.

Center for the Improvement of Early Reading Achievement. (1998). *Standards for primary-grade reading: An analysis of state frameworks.* Retrieved October 1, 1998, from http://www.ciera.org/ciera/publications/report-series/inquiry-3/report31.html

Educational Research Service. (1999). *Reading at the middle and high school levels: Building active readers across the curriculum.* Arlington, VA: Author.

Gambrell, L.B., & Mazzoni, S.A. (1999). Principles of best practice: Finding the common ground in best practices in literacy instruction. In L.B. Gambrell, L.M. Morrow, S.B. Neuman, & M. Pressley (Eds.), *Best practices in literacy instruction* (pp. 11–21). New York: The Guilford Press.

Graves, M.F., & Dykstra, R. (1997). Contextualizing the first-grade studies: What is the best way to teach children to read? *Reading Research Quarterly, 32*(4), 342–344.

Henk, W.A., Moore, J.C., & Marinak, B.A. (2000). A reading lesson observation framework for teachers, principals, and literacy supervisors. *The Reading Teacher, 53*(5), 358–369.

Juel, C. (1994). *Learning to read and write in one elementary school.* New York: Springer-Verlag.

Kennedy, M.M. (1999). Approximations to indicators of student outcomes. *Educational Evaluation and Policy Analysis, 21*(4), 345–363.

Kerr, D.M., Kent, L., & Lam, T.C. (1985). Measuring program implementation with a classroom observation instrument: The interactive teaching map. *Evaluation Review, 9*(4), 461–482.

McIntosh, R., Vaughn, S., Schumm, J., Haager, D., & Lee, O. (1994). Observations of students with learning disabilities in general education classrooms. *Exceptional Children, 60,* 249–261.

Morrow, L.M., Tracey, D.H., Woo, D.G., & Pressley, M. (1999). Characteristics of exemplary first-grade literacy instruction. *The Reading Teacher, 52*(5), 462–476.

National Center on Education and the Economy. (1999). *Reading and writing grade by grade.* Pittsburgh, PA: Author.

National Reading Panel. (2000). *Report of the National Reading Panel: Teaching children to read* (NIH Pub. No. 00-4754). Washington, DC: U.S. Department of Health and Human Services.

Newman, F.M., Marks, H.M., & Gamoran, A. (1996). Authentic pedagogy and student performance. *American Journal of Education, 104,* 280–312.

Osborn, J., & Lehr, F. (Eds.). (1998). *Literacy for all: Issues in teaching and learning.* New York: The Guilford Press.

Porter, A.C. (1993). *Opportunity to learn* (Brief No. 7). Madison, WI: Center for Organization and Restructuring of Schools.

Porter, A.C. (1994). *Reform of high school mathematics and science and opportunity to learn* (Report No. RB-13). Madison: University of Wisconsin, Consortium for Policy Research in Education.

Porter, A.C., & Brophy, J. (1988). Synthesis of research on good teaching: Insights from the work of the Institute for Research on Teaching. *Educational Leadership, 45*(8), 74–85.

Pressley, M. (1998). *Reading instruction that works: The case for balanced teaching.* New York: The Guilford Press.

Pressley, M., Rankin, J., & Yokoi, L. (1996). A survey of instructional practices of primary grade teachers nominated as effective in promoting literacy. *The Elementary School Journal, 96*(4), 363–384.

Pressley, M., Wharton-McDonald, R., Allington, R., Block, C.C., Morrow, L., Tracey, D., Baker, K., et al. (1998). *The nature of effective first-grade literacy instruction* (Research Report No. 11007). Albany, NY: National Research Center on English Learning and Achievement.

Pressley, M., Wharton-McDonald, R., Mistretta-Hampston, J., & Echevarria, M. (1998). Literacy and instruction in 10 fourth- and fifth-grade classrooms in upstate New York. *Scientific Studies of Reading, 2,* 159–164.

Pressley, M., Wharton-McDonald, R., Mistretta-Hampson, J., & Yokoi, L. (1997). *A survey of the instructional practices of grade-5 teachers nominated as effective in promoting literacy* (Research Report No. 85). Athens: University of Georgia, National Reading Research Center.

Saxe, G.B., Gearhart, M., & Seltzer, M. (1999). Relations between classroom practices and student learning in the domain of fractions. *Cognition and Instruction, 17*(1), 1–24.

Searfoss, L.W. (1997). Connecting the past with the present: The legacy and the spirit of the First-Grade Studies. *Reading Research Quarterly, 32*(4), 433–438.

Smithson, J., & Porter, A. (1994). *Measuring classroom practice: Lessons learned from efforts to describe the enacted curriculum—the Reform Up Close Study* (Research Report No. 31). Madison: University of Wisconsin, Consortium for Policy Research in Education.

Snow, C., Burns, M.S., & Griffin, P. (Eds.). (1998). *Preventing reading difficulties in young children.* Washington, DC: National Academy Press.

Stahl, S.A. (1992). Saying the "p" word: Nine guidelines for exemplary phonics instruction. *The Reading Teacher, 46*(8), 618–625.

Texas Education Agency. (2000). *Texas Essential Knowledge and Skills: Reading/language arts.* Austin: Author.

Vogt, M.E. (1991). An observation guide for supervisors and administrators: Moving toward integrated reading/language arts instruction. *The Reading Teacher, 45*(3), 206–211.

Wharton-McDonald, R., Pressley, M., & Mistretta-Hampston, J. (1998). Literacy instruction in nine first-grade classrooms: Teacher characteristics and student achievement. *Elementary School Journal, 99*(2), 101–128.

Indicators for Instructional Content Emphasis Instrument

DIMENSION A: 1. ALPHABETICS
Dimension B. Subcategories of Alphabetics

1.1. *Concepts of print.* Students are learning how books and print work.

- Learning that print moves from left to right
- Learning the parts of a book, how to handle books
- Identifying the author, illustrator, and title
- Identifying the difference between letters, words, and sentences
- Learning concepts of print during read alouds

1.2. *Phonological awareness.* The focus is on the ability to recognize the sounds in spoken language and how they can be segmented, blended, and manipulated. (Activities are characterized by the absence of print.)

- Identifying sounds
- Using alliteration or rhyming
- Segmenting sentences into spoken words
- Segmenting words into syllables or blending syllables into words
- Blending and segmenting onset and rime
- Dividing spoken words into individual sounds

1.3. *Alphabetic knowledge.* Students are learning to recognize, name, and write letters.

- Distinguishing upper- and lower-case letters
- Learning to print letters; focusing on identifying letters. (Students may be using different types of materials to master this skill, not just pencil and paper.)

Item wording has been slightly revised for inclusion in this volume.

1.4. *Word study and phonics.* The alphabetic principle is the idea that letters represent sounds and sounds can be represented by letters.

- Acquiring letter–sound correspondence
- Decoding (using letter–sound correspondence knowledge in reading)
- Blending activities involving print
- Making and/or sorting words with common characteristics
- Studying words with common letter combinations
- Learning irregular words
- Learning common spelling patterns for purposes of reading/decoding
- Learning to connect sound to print through spelling activities
- Studying syllable patterns or other structural clues for decoding
- Learning words in context
- Receiving phonics/word study instruction, including implicit instruction (e.g., the teacher states a rule as the child reads but does not provide direct instruction)

1.5. *Spelling.* Students are learning to remember and reproduce conventional spelling.

- Writing words in response to a word study lesson. (Differs from phonics in that the task focuses on recall and response to a particular set of words.)
- Studying and/or practicing a particular spelling pattern. (More likely among older primary-grade students.)

1.6. *Oral language development/discussion.* Focus is on listening and speaking to communicate meaning.

- Discussing academic content (not logistic or disciplinary matters)
- Engaging in discussion about words, books, songs, or relevant topics
- Developing understanding of words or concepts
- Listening to the teacher talking to extend understanding of the word, and not necessarily learning a specific definition for a word

1.7. *Multiple-cueing system.* Focus is on using other cueing systems to read.

- Using the pictures to identify words
- Using prior knowledge or understanding to read
- Using word order to read

DIMENSION A: 2. FLUENCY
Dimension B.   Subcategories of Fluency

2.1. *Partner reading.* Students read aloud with a partner to develop speed, accuracy, or intonation.

2.2. *Repeated reading.* Students engage in repeated reading either with the class, small group, or one-to-one for the purpose of developing speed, accuracy, and/or intonation.

2.3. *Modeling fluency.* The teacher reads aloud to the student(s) with the intent of modeling speed, accuracy, and/or intonation.

DIMENSION A: 3. READING
Dimension B.   Subcategories of Reading

3.1. *Guided oral reading.* Students engage in reading either with the class, in small groups, or one-to-one. (Students may need the teacher's help to read aloud.)

- Receiving guidance from a teacher, peer, or parent
- Sharing the reading task with a teacher or peer(s)
- Receiving guidance about how to use semantic and syntactic clues to read

3.2. *Chorale reading.* Class reads aloud as a group simultaneously.

3.3. *Independent reading.* The student reads text independently, either silently or orally.

3.4. *Listening to text read aloud.* Students listen to books read aloud (by the teacher or books on tape).

DIMENSION A: 4. COMPREHENSION
Dimension B.   Subcategories of Comprehension

4.1. *Vocabulary*

- Developing print or oral vocabulary in the context of reading or discussion
- Learning vocabulary words through direct instruction
- Learning vocabulary through other instructional events (implicit instruction)
- Using context knowledge to confirm meaning
- Using word lists and story words to learn vocabulary

4.2. *Prior knowledge/predicting*

- Previewing the material before reading
- Predicting outcomes based on prior knowledge

- Participating in activities designed to measure level of knowledge before reading a book

4.3. *Comprehension monitoring.* Monitoring may occur during or after reading. Conversation tends to be discussion-oriented with little focus put on a product or goal. The teacher and students summarize the story, as the intent of discussion or activities.

- Learning to be aware of one's own understanding of text
- Learning specific comprehension strategies
- Answering questions during or after reading
- Using comprehension strategies, such as searching for clues, asking for help, rereading passages
- Discussing or responding to reading with the teacher and/or other students
- Students discuss elements not explicitly found in the text
- Retelling a story
- Summarizing a story's main events
- Identifying the main idea
- Putting story events into a sequence

4.4. *Story structure and analysis.* The teacher and students analyze the story with a specific goal in mind. This is not likely to be an incidental activity, and students may have a product or shared understanding once activity is completed. These activities occur after reading the text.

- Learning through instruction using graphic or semantic organizers that represent material and assist in comprehension
- Learning to use story structure to facilitate comprehension and recall
- Categorizing text
- Identifying and understanding story elements, such as plot, character, and setting
- Learning through instruction in text features, such as cause and effect
- Learning to integrate ideas and make generalizations from text

DIMENSION A: 5. WRITING AND LANGUAGE ARTS
Dimension B.   Subcategories of Writing and Language Arts
5.1. *Dictation*

- Sharing the writing tasks with the teacher and/or other students
- Dictating to the teacher what is to be written (or vice versa)

- Receiving help with constructing written versions of thoughts or responses to reading

5.2. Independent writing/publishing

- Producing writing products independently, which can be drawings, scribbles, words, or sentences
- Sharing writing with the class or a partner
- Learning to group words into coherent sentences or phrases when writing

5.3. Grammar and punctuation

- Learning through instruction in grammatical elements, such as nouns, verbs, proper names, and pronouns
- Learning to form and use punctuation marks

5.4. Handwriting instruction

- Practicing the proper formation of letters. (Focus is on correctness of formation and not on identification.)
- Learning about and practicing the proper size, spacing, posture, and strokes of letters

3

Ecobehavioral Strategies

Observing, Measuring, and
Analyzing Behavior and Reading Interventions

CHARLES R. GREENWOOD, MARY ABBOTT, AND YOLANDA TAPIA

The observational instruments described in this chapter evolved from a 20-year line of research seeking to improve the academic and social success of urban children. Of particular interest in the early 1980s, when we began this work, was how to explain and prevent the achievement gap between low-income and other children. Because disproportionate numbers of children in racial minorities are poor, both poverty and minority-group status were intertwined with the issue of academic success then and today (see Greenwood, 1996b; Greenwood, Carta, Kamps, & Arreaga-Mayer, 1990, for reviews). In preceding years, some have believed that the gap, including reading achievement, was explained by one's race and genes (i.e., nature) and not by poverty, opportunity to learn, or schooling experience (i.e., nurture) (Jensen, 1980). Our own research sought an explanation in terms of alterable variables under the control of classroom teachers (Greenwood, 1996a, 1996b).

Following up on the observations of others in elementary schools (e.g., Hops & Cobb, 1973), our observations in urban Title I elementary schools (i.e., schools serving majority populations of low-income African American students) suggested that these students were not overly burdened by behavior and conduct problems, compared with students of similar grade levels in non–Title I schools. What was striking, however, was the fact that the students were simply not highly engaged in reading, writing, or discussing academic subject matter during instruction (see Greenwood, Delquadri, & Hall, 1984). Compared with teachers in non–Title I schools, teachers in Title I schools were more likely to lecture while using the chalkboard or the overhead projector. Their students were expected to simply observe and listen. We observed that, during reading instruction, students in Title I classrooms actually spent little time reading prepared materials or text. We also observed that students in the lowest reading group actually met less for supervised reading instruction than did students in higher functioning groups because they were always scheduled last, before recess or lunch breaks. If the other groups' reading time ran long that day, the lowest group's time was cut short.

We sought to capture these informal observations using a formal observational assessment instrument in research on the issue of how well reading instruction actually promoted students' reading behavior and other academic responses. However, the existing instruments were neither technically adequate (e.g., reliability, validity) nor sensitive to what we wanted to study; that is, they were unable to explain individual students' academic behavior in the context of instruction. An observational approach was selected for this purpose rather than the teacher report approach because of the latter's low validity with respect to what actually transpires in the classroom (Hartmann & Woods, 1990).

The direct observational measures we reviewed had a number of insensitivities, including 1) only recording global behaviors (e.g., attention or on-task behaviors) instead of specific academic behaviors (e.g., reading silently, reading aloud, writing), 2) the inability to disaggregate individual academic behaviors for analysis (e.g., reading versus writing), and 3) the inability to explore the teacher's behaviors and classroom ecological situations of which observed reading behaviors were a function. Earlier methods were not sensitive to the momentary interactions—the temporal relationships among ecology, teacher, and student behavior events.

Achieving these abilities in a single observational instrument required a conceptual framework that linked separate streams of changing classroom situations, teacher behaviors, and student behaviors (Greenwood, 1996a; Greenwood, Peterson, & Sideridis, 1995; Morris & Midgley, 1990). We made this link using a taxonomy of behavioral and ecological event definitions combined with a time sampling method of recording that allowed detailed analyses of the instructional experiences and performance of individual students. The detailed analyses included 1) reports of the percentage occurrence of specific student behaviors, teacher behaviors, and classroom ecological situations during instruction and 2) reports of the teacher behavior and ecological situations during instruction that either accelerated or decelerated students' reading behaviors above or below base levels of occurrence. The first set of analyses were helpful in describing the range of events and their base levels of occurrence, and the second set of analyses revealed what promoted the classroom behaviors (e.g., reading aloud) for individuals and groups of students.

This chapter describes the conceptual framework, measurement taxonomy, observational instrument, and findings that emerged from the use of this instrument as strategies of ecobehavioral assessment and analysis, with a focus on reading and reading instructional intervention issues. After describing these strategies, we focus on examples that help explain why a student is or is not learning to read, what reading strategies work best for some students, and how teachers organize reading instruction for students (e.g., materials, grouping) in general education classrooms to include students with disabilities for instruction. We conclude by considering the role of these strategies in reading research and practice.

In our experience, answering these questions has required answers to additional questions:

1. What are the actual reading experiences of individual students in a classroom?
2. What classroom instructional acts and conditions are provided?
3. How and when do reading behaviors change and grow over time in instruction, from kindergarten to fourth grade?
4. Of what classroom instructional acts and conditions are reading behaviors a function?
5. What are the effects of instructional interventions on reading behavior and formative measures of reading achievement?

THE ECOBEHAVIORAL CONCEPTUAL/ANALYTIC FRAMEWORK

In order to address these questions, we chose several beliefs and principles to guide the development of our instruments, setting them apart from other observational instruments. First, on the basis of several well-established theories of instruction (e.g., ecological, behavioral, developmental, educational), we inferred that classroom ecology and teacher behavior are alterable variables under the control of classroom teachers as components of their instructional interactions with students. As such, we concluded that these instruction variables influence and are influenced by student behavior and learning. Second, answering questions and generating hypotheses about the effects of instruction require measurement of a representative sample of instruction received by individual students. The instructional conditions of which individual reading behaviors are a function cannot be addressed without substantial information about the classroom ecology and the teacher's behavior, along with student behavior over time and sessions. Previously, observational instruments had been exclusively ecological or exclusively behavioral (e.g., Greenwood, Carta, & Dawson, 2000); the ecobehavioral framework, however, integrated streams of classroom ecology, teacher behaviors, and student behaviors recorded by an observer one moment to the next, as they changed over time.

Third, as may already be obvious, we made the behavior of individual students the primary unit of analysis in these ecobehavioral strategies, not the behavior of the class of students or the teacher. Making the student the primary unit of analysis requires data collected on one student for a sustained period of time. Thus, in our strategies, momentary observations are conducted for a single student for the total observation time. This student-focused feature in ecobehavioral strategies is critical to revealing the unique instructional conditions of which reading behaviors are a function. Other observation instruments are often designed to describe the average occurrences of student behaviors by rotating momentary observations of one student, then another, and another, possibly including all students in the class. This type of observational sampling is typically designed to represent average class behavior levels and does not lend itself nearly as well to addressing questions of behavioral function, as does the ecobehavioral focus on one student at a time in a single observation.

Fourth, like all instruments, these strategies needed to be technically sound, that is, reliable and valid. Fifth, the strategies needed to be as friendly and economical as possible in order to be used in schools beyond the sole purpose of instructional intervention research. For example, only one observer should be required to conduct primary observations and produce useful data in a time frame short enough that teachers could act on the results in terms of monitoring progress, instructional decision making, and changing instruction.

The major advance represented by the ecobehavioral strategy was the ability to analyze the temporal associations and joint occurrences of ecological, teacher, and student events. This feature resulted in answers to questions such as, How often is Ramón reading aloud during reading instruction (the base level of occurrence)? What ecological and teacher behavior events are typically occurring concurrently as Ramón is reading aloud? Furthermore, before and after implementing an instructional intervention for Ramón, has the occurrence of reading aloud increased, or is it changing or decreasing? Have the ecological and teacher behavior events logically linked to a planned change in instruction actually changed as expected when compared with Ramón's reading behaviors before and after intervention? Thus, for individual students and for groups of students (by pooling separate observations of individual students), answers to these and similar questions (e.g., has the change in Ramón's oral reading during instruction influenced his rate of progress on reading curriculum-based measurement [CBM] probes?) can be addressed.

Observational Instruments (Mainstream Version of the Code for Instructional Structure and Student Academic Response)

A number of ecobehavioral observation instruments exist for use in schools (i.e., general and special education classrooms, English as a second language [ESL] programs, preschools), child care, and home settings (Greenwood et al., 2000) that are based on this model. For the purposes of this discussion, however, we focus on the Mainstream Version of the Code for Instructional Structure and Student Academic Response (MS-CISSAR) because of its relevance to reading for students with and without disabilities in elementary and secondary classrooms. The MS-CISSAR is a multiple-event classroom observation system (Kamps, Greenwood, & Leonard, 1991). It is an update of an earlier version, the Code for Instructional Structure and Student Academic Response (CISSAR; Greenwood & Delquadri, 1988; Stanley & Greenwood, 1981). The update was made to represent the ecological events of special education in combination with those of the general education classroom. As children with disabilities were increasingly included in the general education classroom in the 1980s and 1990s, this update improved the MS-CISSAR's sensitivity to the instruction of children with and without disabilities in similar settings.

As can be seen in Table 3.1, the individual events were organized under the three categories of ecology, teacher, and student, and each category was separated into subcategories. For example, student events were organized under three subcategories: academic responses, task management responses, and inappropriate responses. *Academic responses* were defined as active responses to academic situations, commands, and instructions. *Task management responses* were defined as enabling behaviors, that is, behaviors that positioned a student to make an academic response, given an opportunity to do so. *Inappropriate responses* were defined as undesirable behaviors, those behaviors that interfere or compete with the occurrence of academic and task management responses (see Greenwood, Carta, Kamps, & Delquadri, 1993). This particular breakdown was guided by our own research indicating that individual and composite academic responses were positive correlates of academic achievement (Greenwood et al., 1984) and also by the exist-

Table 3.1. Taxonomy for the Mainstream Version of the Code for Instructional Structure and Student Academic Response

Category	Subcategory	Number of events	Example
Student	Academic responses	6	Reading aloud, silent reading
	Task management	7	Getting attention, raising a hand
	Inappropriate responses	8	Disrupting, looking around
Ecology	Setting	11	Regular classroom, resource room
	Activity	19	Reading, spelling, math
	Task	9	Reader, worksheet
	Physical arrangement	3	Entire group, divided group
	Instructional structure	5	Independent, one-to-one
Teacher	Teacher definition	9	Regular education, peer tutor
	Teacher behavior	15	Reading aloud, academic talk
	Approval	3	Approval, disapproval
	Teacher focus	4	Target student, other
Total		99	

ing observational research literature at that time with respect to enabling and undesired classroom behaviors. Using this taxonomy as the basis for classroom observation, we were able to empirically describe not only the occurrence of a student's active academic responses but also levels of key enabling and problem behaviors.

Similarly, subcategories were used to group into classes classroom ecological and teacher behavior events. The subcategories of ecology were the *setting, activity, task, physical arrangement, and instructional structure.* These events described the physical location (setting), the subject matter (activity), the type of materials or media (tasks), the seating arrangement (physical arrangement), and the instructional arrangement (instructional structure). The teacher subcategories were teacher definition, teacher behavior, approval, and teacher focus. These events described who the teacher was (teacher definition), what the teacher was doing (teacher behavior), the teacher's use of approval and/or disapproval (approval), and to whom the teacher's behavior was directed (teacher focus; e.g., focus directed toward the student being observed, toward others, toward all).

Each of these individual events has a precise definition, and observers learned these from studying a training manual, using a computer-assisted tutorial (Greenwood, Carta, Kamps, Terry, & Delquadri, 1994), and practicing in a classroom. Interobserver agreement checks qualified observer trainees as certified MS-CISSAR observers (Greenwood, Carta, et al., 1993). For example, some of the reading-related MS-CISSAR event definitions include the following:

1. *Reading aloud* is defined by "those instances in which the student being observed is looking at a book, passage, chart, computer screen, or blackboard, and reading aloud what is written."

2. *Silent reading* is defined by "those instances in which the student is observed looking at print materials and eye movements indicate scanning of letters, words, sentences, or numbers."

3. *Activity-reading instruction* is defined "as an activity whose primary goal is the translation of written letters into words and the comprehension of words, phrases, sentences, and paragraphs."

4. *Teacher behavior—reading aloud* is defined "by those instances where the teacher is reading aloud to or in concert with one or more student(s)."

In summary, the MS-CISSAR taxonomy of ecobehavioral events provides a rich description of classroom ecology, teacher, and student events that can be analyzed at the single-event level, as a profile of events within a subcategory, or in the case of student behavior, as composite subcategory scores. The latter are formed by simply adding the percentages of the individual events within the subcategory.

Observational Procedure

The typical procedure for conducting MS-CISSAR observations is through use of a portable notebook computer and a custom-developed software system, the Ecobehavioral Assessment Software System (EBASS; Greenwood, Carta, et al., 1993; Greenwood & Hou, 1995). The software was written for Microsoft's disk operating system (MS-DOS) and runs in the Microsoft Windows environment. Momentary time sampling is used to pace and prompt the observers to record the events in the three major categories. The observer is asked to record one of the event categories (ecological, teacher, or student) every 20 seconds over the total time of the observation. At the first time sample, the observer is asked to record *ecological* events by selecting those that have occurred from the list of ecology choices in the MS-CISSAR taxonomy. Twenty seconds later, the observer is asked to enter the *teacher* events that have occurred by again selecting from those in the relevant sections of the teacher event taxonomy. Twenty seconds later, the observer is prompted to enter the occurrence of *student* events from those in the student section of the taxonomy. This cycle of ecology, teacher, and student event recording is repeated every 1 minute of the observation at 20-second intervals. These 1-minute records are used in the analysis of data.

The behavior of the observer is prompted by a change in the computer screen and a volume-controlled, audible signal. At this signal, the observer is taught to look, record, and wait, followed by another cycle of look, record, and wait in the next 20 second-interval, and all following intervals. In the momentary time sampling procedure used, the observer is required to identify only those events occurring at the "look" time point and then record that event. Using this method, the observer is not responsible for tracking the duration or the onset/offset of all possible events, and thus, the complexity inherent in handling so many events accurately is kept at a manageable level. It has been shown that observers using momentary time sampling can reliably record a large number of events and that momentary time sampling, as compared with whole-interval or partial-interval recording procedures, provides estimates most like those of real-time event and duration recording (Ary, 1984; Powell, 1984; Powell, Martindale, & Kulp, 1975).

Observer Training

The EBASS system provides a range of materials and media in support of individual or group learning of the MS-CISSAR instrument. These supports include a step-by-step description in the EBASS Practitioner's Manual, videotapes that illustrate the MS-CISSAR taxonomy of events, and a computer-assisted tutorial. The tutorial provides practice recording of classroom event scenarios and feedback on one's mastery of definition usage. Also provided is a calibration videotape for testing one's interobserver agreement against a standard set of events. The actual sequence of training includes reading from the manual, working on the tutorial to achieve high levels of definition mastery, making practice observations in the classroom, and doing interobserver agreement checks with a trainer and/or the video calibration tape to qualify as a trained and reliable MS-CISSAR observer (Greenwood, Carta, et al., 1993).

Additional Considerations

Other features of the EBASS software provide a user-friendly environment for conducting observations, managing a caseload of observations, and analyzing observation data that extends its use to school-based studies of instructional intervention, as well as research-based studies.

Conducting Observations The observer may adapt the MS-CIS-SAR taxonomy to be used in a particular observation. Options include using the full taxonomy of events or leaving out one or several event categories in order to make the observation more specific. For example, if one only wants to record student behavior, ecological and teacher events can be eliminated using the software. Similarly, one may leave out ecological events and just record teacher and student events. Although one may eliminate some categories, the system precludes changing the events used or their definitions in the taxonomy in order to maintain MS-CISSAR as a standardized taxonomy. Standardization allows comparisons of observational data across students, classrooms, schools, and observers because the same events and definitions are applied. This is unlike some observational software that allows one to provide an idiosyncratic set of events and definitions (Tapp & Wehby, 1993).

Before and after an observation, the observer may write text notes or impressions regarding that particular observation. The software also allows the user to select where the data will be stored, to the computer's hard drive or to an auxiliary drive. An advantage of storing the data to an auxiliary drive is that one's caseload of observations can be taken off the computer. Because the EBASS program is typically loaded on the hard drive, others can share the computer without the danger of confidential information being unintentionally left on the computer.

Considerations for Planning Observations

Invariably, contemplating the use of the MS-CISSAR evokes a range of questions concerning exactly who, how long, and how many observations are needed to achieve intended purposes. Answering these questions is largely related to the purpose and the design. There is no simple answer to these questions, but planning can usually address them within the resources available.

Who? Who will be observed is largely related to the initiating purpose and context for using MS-CISSAR in the first place. If the observations are to be conducted by school psychologists in a local district, students who are referred for behavioral problems or reading delays may be observed. If observations are to be conducted for teacher consultation, program evaluation, or research purposes, they may focus on students with and without some set of concerns (e.g., students with and without disabilities, low versus high achievers) with the potential of informing decisions. For cases in which normative information is concerned, a sampling frame may be used to schedule observations of students in a range of programs, classrooms, grade levels, and so forth to provide information that is representative of the larger universe of factors.

How Long? In general, the length of any observation need only be long enough to represent the situations and student behavior of interest. The length of individual MS-CISSAR observations is always a critical issue because observation length includes and excludes some of the possible range of ecological and teacher events that are allowed to influence the student behavior observed. For example, observations during formally scheduled reading instruction provide a distinctly different ecological and teacher event context for student behavior than observations during arithmetic or science. Similarly, observations in reading for less than the entire session (60 or more minutes) may not represent the entire reading session unless a sampling pattern of multiple observations is constructed so that an individual student is observed in similar situations at the beginning, middle, and end of the reading period. By constructing sampling frames using multiple short observations, one can construct a plan that represents the desired contexts of interest in the data collected.

How Many? In general, more observations are better because repeated observations also help represent session-by-session variations in the contexts to be assessed, as well as variations in student behavior. Multiple observations across days allow estimates of variance that might be of importance in understanding the stability or instability of student behavior. At minimum, three sessions are needed to establish trends over time. Observations across days also allow representation of school and classroom schedule effects in the data. For example, representing schedule variation may be important when it is known that reading instruction on Monday, Wednesday, and Friday is different from reading instruction on Tuesday and Thursday. In this case, it may be helpful to collect enough data (Monday–Thursday observations) to represent this weekly variation. The question of how many observations are needed may be answered by a sampling frame that allows adequate representation of the situations of interest in the observation.

Data Analysis

EBASS provides a range of analytical tools. In addition, the observation data may be exported in a format readable by the statistical software and thus used with other statistical/analytical software or database software. Analyses in EBASS can be applied to a single observation, to multiple observations of the same student, or to groups of observations of multiple students. Simply marking the observations to be included in an analysis is all that is required.

Percentage Occurrence   The percentage occurrence of each event (e.g., reading aloud) and subcategory composites (e.g., academic responding) is provided by the EBASS. These results are helpful in understanding the levels of particular events and the profiles of events within subcategories. Looking at occurrence profiles is often helpful in identifying stand-out events—those occurring most or least often—and the pattern of event occurrence. For example, by selecting the particular event and a range of observations for a student on different dates, graphs displaying percentage occurrence information and trends over time can be produced. These data are helpful in monitoring progress and growth over time and within intervention over time.

Conditional Probability   The conditional probability analyses in EBASS may be used to study the instructional events of which student behavior is a likely function. Tools in the software allow one to select single student behaviors (e.g., reading aloud) or consolidate several behaviors (e.g., reading aloud and reading silently) and identify the ecological and teacher events to be evaluated. Results are represented in terms of the base level of student behavior (i.e., the unconditional probability) and the probabilities of student behavior given the ecological and teacher behavior events of interest (i.e., conditional probabilities). These analyses are helpful in identifying the conditions that are promoting reading behavior during instruction and in tracking changes in the function of instruction over time and within interventions designed to promote the behavior interest.

Profile Analyses   Profile analyses allow one to compare a target student's performance with that of an index, or typical, peer in the same classroom or with normative peer observations. Tools in the EBASS software allow the user to identify the target and index students' observations to be used in the analysis, as well as which event categories are to be profiled and compared. For example, one may wish to compare the occurrence of reading behavior of a target student with a normative peer or a normative group. The analyses compare the two profiles and display indices of their similarity and dissimilarity. Profile analyses are useful in identifying children who are largely dissimilar from normative expectations of performance.

Profile analyses may also be applied to the problem of assessing how a student's performance compares with the performance of typical students in another classroom or with another teacher. Motivating these analyses may be the issues of future placement and finding a good match between the target student's behavior and environmental conditions, compared with those existing within several future placement setting alternatives (Agar & Shapiro, 1995).

Summary

To this point, we have introduced the rationale, goals, tools, and distinctive features of ecobehavioral observation strategies. This has included the ecobehavioral conceptual framework; the MS-CISSAR taxonomy; the EBASS software; issues related to learning, planning, and conducting observations; and specific types of analyses relevant to issues of research and practice in the teaching of reading. We now turn to a brief review of ecobehavioral observation findings in the literature based on these strategies and some example results from a longitudinal intervention study of reading interventions in kindergarten through fourth grade.

SOME FINDINGS FROM THE LITERATURE
BASED ON ECOBEHAVIORAL STRATEGIES

Greenwood and his colleagues developed their first ecobehavioral observation instrument in 1981 (Greenwood, Delquadri, Stanley, Terry, & Hall, 1985; Stanley & Greenwood, 1981, 1983). They reported that students in both Title I and other elementary classrooms were surprisingly unengaged in active academic responding during daily instruction. This was true for students who attended Title I schools and were at risk than it was for students at other schools. Replicating these findings, later studies (Greenwood, 1991; Greenwood, Delquadri, & Hall, 1989) reported that students in Title I schools were engaged 11 minutes per day fewer than students in other classrooms, based on the CISSAR instrument. They noted that at this daily rate of engagement over the elementary school period, without substantive early intervention to change this daily trend, students in Title I schools would require 365 additional hours of school time beyond their time in elementary grades to catch up to the amount of instruction received by students in other schools (Greenwood, Hart, Walker, & Risley, 1994).

Greenwood and Delquadri's (1995) longitudinal intervention study of the effects of ClassWide Peer Tutoring (CWPT) on the acceleration of

students' academic engagement and basic skills achievement demonstrated a range of positive effects (Greenwood, 1991; Greenwood et al.,
1989; Greenwood, Terry, Marquis, & Walker, 1994). They reported that
early and sustained use of CWPT implemented by classroom teachers
in reading, spelling, and arithmetic, beginning in first grade and progressing through fourth grade, increased students' engagement in academic responding during instruction, as measured by CISSAR and increased achievement on the Metropolitan Achievement Test (MAT). In
middle school, follow-up assessments indicated continued higher levels
of achievement in reading, language, and math on the Comprehensive
Test of Basic Skills (CTBS) and reduced the need for special education
services for students in the CWPT group (Greenwood, Terry, Utley,
Montagna, & Walker, 1993). In high school, follow-up assessments indicated a significant reduction in the number of students in the CWPT
group dropping out of high school, compared with control and comparison groups whose teachers did not use CWPT (Greenwood & Delquadri, 1995).

This longitudinal intervention study produced both correlational
and experimental evidence of a relationship between accelerated academic responding during instruction and accelerated achievement for
students who were at risk. Findings reported by Cooper and Speece
(1990a) extended Greenwood and Delquadri's (1995) findings to groups
who were at risk for being referred to special education services, as
compared with students who were at risk due to socioeconomic factors.
They reported significantly different mean levels of students' academic
responding for first-grade students referred for special education services (at risk) versus first-grade students who were not referred (Cooper
& Speece, 1990b). The difference favored higher performance of the non-
referred group over the referred group and replicated an association between students' level of academic responding and at-risk/delay status.

Using these relationships between academic responding and
achievement, Greenwood and colleagues (Greenwood, Arreaga-Mayer,
& Carta, 1994; Greenwood, Carta, Arreaga-Mayer, & Rager, 1991;
Kamps, Leonard, Dugan, Boland, & Greenwood, 1991) undertook an
effort to identify and promote those instructional practices that were
found to be naturally effective. Using the MS-CISSAR, they identified
students who were high achievers and who were highly engaged during academic instruction. For these students, their teachers were observed and interviewed in order to characterize and operationally define the instructional procedures that these teachers used to instruct
these highly engaged, high-achieving students. These procedures were
then taught to and implemented by other teachers in an attempt to
demonstrate that, compared with their baseline teaching procedures,

these newly identified procedures would produce more engagement in academic responding and accelerate achievement. Results from several studies of students with and without disabilities indicated that the identified practices were repeatable by other teachers who implemented them at high levels of fidelity and produced more engagement and improved academic outcomes (Greenwood et al., 1991; Kamps, Leonard, et al., 1991).

Ysseldyke, Thurlow, and their colleagues conducted a series of studies examining differences in instructional experiences received by students in regular and special education classrooms using the CISSAR beginning in the 1980s (e.g., Thurlow, Ysseldyke, Graden, & Algozzine, 1984; Ysseldyke, Christenson, Thurlow, & Bakewell, 1989; Ysseldyke, Thurlow, Christenson, & Weiss, 1987). This work produced a number of important findings supported by CISSAR data. Two of these were reports of 1) the relatively low levels of student engagement during instruction and 2) the lack of major differences in CISSAR indicators across general and special education classrooms. They reported mean levels of academic responding in the 40%–50% range for students in both general and special education. In one study, they reported that when the teacher directly instructed students, students typically spent 70% of their time passively watching and listening with no opportunity to actually read (O'Sullivan, Ysseldyke, Christensen, & Thurlow, 1990), replicating findings for the general education classroom report by Greenwood and colleagues (1984).

Marston, Deno, Kim, Diment, and Rogers (1995) compared six alternative instructional approaches in the teaching of reading in the Minneapolis public schools: computer-assisted instruction, Science Research Associate's Direct Instruction, direct instruction using Holt materials, effective teaching, peer tutoring, and reciprocal teaching. The MS-CISSAR was used to provide indicators of students' academic responding/engagement and teachers' instructional behavior. Of interest was comparison of the teacher and student behavioral characteristics of each instructional approach and how these processes related to students' growth in reading fluency as measured by a reading CBM. Of particular relevance to this chapter's focus, each instructional approach produced a distinctive pattern, or footprint, of teacher and student behaviors consistent with the approach being used. This suggests that implementation of the approach (i.e., teacher behavior) and students' behavior reflect important differences in response to instruction.

For example, *reciprocal teaching* is a teacher-led approach concentrated on teacher–student discussion, interaction, and talk focused on the subject matter. MS-CISSAR data reflected just this footprint. In comparisons with the other approaches, the teacher was most engaged (in rank order) in looking at the students, asking questions, and reading aloud to them. Students experiencing reciprocal teaching spent most of their time (in rank order) looking at the teacher and engaging in academic talk. In contrast with CWPT, based on the Jenkins and Jenkins (1982) model, students were most engaged (in rank order) in oral reading and looking at their tutor or tutee. Tutors (the teachers) were most engaged in academic talk with their tutee, talk about task management, and academic questions.

Logan, Bakeman, and Keefe (1997) used the MS-CISSAR to investigate the effects of instructional variables on the behavior of students with disabilities in the general education classroom. For students with moderate to severe disabilities, the key research question concerned which particular classroom situations and teacher behaviors best promoted the academic engagement of students included for instruction in the general education classroom. They reported that for these students, one-to-one, small-group, and independent-working arrangements were associated with higher levels of engaged behaviors than was whole-class instruction. They recommended that teachers use these arrangements more often with students with disabilities and reduce the time spent in whole-class instruction, along with a number of other similar recommendations based on MS-CISSAR analyses of the functional relationship between instruction and students' academic behavior.

Thus, published research using the CISSAR and MS-CISSAR has produced a range of important findings with implications for developing and validating instructional interventions. One of these findings is the positive relationship between the level of academic responding during instruction and growth in achievement. This relationship has been demonstrated by correlations and by experimental interventions in comparisons to control groups where CWPT was used to accelerate students' responding and practice. The relationship was also demonstrated by studies that first identified teaching practices related to high levels of academic responding and achievement and then tested their effects when implemented by other teachers. A second finding indicates generally low levels of academic responding and lack of differences in academic responding between students in general versus special education classrooms. Third, different reading instructional interventions produce different forms of teacher and student behaviors that often align with theoretically different procedures. Fourth, different instructional arrangements produce different profiles of student academic responding and other classroom behaviors. Each of these findings based on observational measurement of classroom instructional interactions contributes importantly to understanding the effects, potential effects, and lack of effects of instruction on student performance and instruction's relationships to different forms of academic progress.

FINDINGS FROM OBSERVATIONAL RESEARCH ON READING INTERVENTION

From a multiyear study of the effects of a schoolwide model designed to bridge the gap between research and practice in reading/literacy instruction (Abbott, Walton, Tapia, & Greenwood, 1999), we present some analyses illustrative of the type we used to monitor the effects of a range of reading interventions on the behavior of students learning to read. The purpose of the schoolwide model was to help a faculty member in one elementary school identify and implement research-based reading and literacy practices. The model was a multiyear partnership that set in place collaboration, consultation, and ongoing professional development activities in the school. This effort involved 10 teachers in kindergarten through fourth grade (Abbott et al., 1999). A list of research-based practices that we helped various teachers identify and implement over 3 years is displayed in Table 3.2.

This research investigated the extent to which implementation of the model changed teachers' practices and, in turn, accelerated student's growth in reading and reduced the number of early reading failures. Central to this goal was changing teachers' instructional practices and students' engagement in reading behavior and enabling behaviors beginning with students in kindergarten through second grade in the first year of the project. In subsequent years, teachers in first through third grades (in the second year of the project) and second through

Table 3.2.   Cumulative list of reading-related interventions implemented

Intervention	Grade level usage
Storybook	Kindergarten
Phonemic awareness	Kindergarten, 1
Repeated reading	Kindergarten, 1
Partner reading	1, 2, 3
Initial reading blending	1
Early intervention reading	1
Writer's workshop	1, 2, 3, 4
Phonics in story content	1
Word family books	1
Dolch words (nonwords)	1
Reading (classwide peer tutoring)	2, 3, 4
Spelling (classwide peer tutoring)	2, 3, 4
Partner reading/questions	3, 4
Reciprocal teaching	3, 4

fourth grades (in the third year of the project) were the focus of this collaboration in an effort to keep in place a high-intensity literacy intervention experience for the original kindergarten, first-, and second-grade cohorts as they progressed through their next 3 school years.

MS-CISSAR and reading CBM data were collected for 36 students beginning in the first year of the project. Because resources were not available to observe all students in a classroom in all 3 school years, target students for progress monitoring were selected so as to represent the class average as follows: readers with low ($n = 2$), average ($n = 2$), and high ($n = 2$) skill in each of two classrooms in one elementary school' s kindergarten, first grade, and second grade. This produced 12 students per grade cohort at the start of the study. The progress of these students was monitored over the next 3 years. Because nine students moved out of the study, they were replaced for progress monitoring purposes as needed, bringing the total number of students who were observed to 45. Students were observed a total of nine times (on three, four, and two occasions in the first, second, and third school years of the study beginning February, 1997, and ending November, 1998). Once started, observations were spaced at least 1 month apart and at most 2 months apart. Observations were repeated as frequently as schedule and resources allowed.

Reading/literacy interventions were implemented classwide with all students over the entire 3 years of the collaborative project. The overall mean number of interventions actually received per student was 6.6 (with a standard deviation of 1.5) over the entire project. Over the 3 years, the kindergarten cohort received a mean number of 8 interventions, and the first- and second-grade cohorts received a mean number of 6 interventions ($F[2,41] = 5.10$, $p = .011$). Tukey HSD post-hoc tests between means indicated that a significantly more intensive program was provided to the youngest cohort, as compared with either the first-grade cohort ($p < .04$) or the second-grade cohort ($p < .03$). Students in the kindergarten cohort received an additional two strategies over all 3 years.

What Were the Actual Reading Experiences of Students in a Classroom?

EBASS enables one to produce a summary of all MS-CISSAR individual observations or all observations pooled over all students. When pooled over all students, these results provided a summary description of the entire multiyear reading intervention effort. One salient finding from these results was that 99% of the observations were taken in the general classroom setting, as was planned. Perhaps more interesting was the fact that of the scheduled reading times reported by teachers that were observed, 50% of this time was recorded as reading, 26% was recorded as language arts, 11% was recorded as spelling, and various other smaller times (totaling 13%) were devoted to other subject matter in the list (or profile) of MS-CISSAR activities. Similarly of interest was the profile of tasks with reading texts (readers) used by students 29% of the time and paper and pencil, worksheets, and other media tasks used most, in order of occurrence. Instructional structure during these observations was primarily whole class (42%), small group (21%), independent (20%), and one-to-one (16%).

The teacher definition during this observed time was primarily the general classroom teacher (83%). Reflecting the intervention effort, however, was peer tutoring, occurring 7% of the time, with student teachers (4%), and aide/paraprofessionals (2%) accounting for smaller portions of observed time. The teacher was most often engaged in academic talk (25%), provided attention to students (25%), asked questions (10%), talked about management (9%), and read to students (8%). Teachers provided equally small amounts of approval and disapproval, in the 4% range.

Students spent 20% of their time reading (reading aloud at 10% and reading silently also at 10%). Writing occurred 14% of the time observed. In all, students were engaged in composite academic responding 47% of the time. Time spent in task management behaviors was highest for attention at 29%. Similarly, time spent in inappropriate behaviors was highest for looking around at 6%. Collectively, these summary data illustrated evidence of an effort by teachers to teach reading and of students engaged in reading behaviors, emitting appropriate enabling behaviors, with relatively low levels of problem behavior. In addition, one should be impressed with the diversity in quality and quantity of these experiences as reflected in these MS-CISSAR events.

Of Which Classroom Instructional Acts and Conditions Were Reading Behaviors a Function?

Questions and hypotheses about the best conditions for reading behavior during this reading instruction were addressed using conditional probability analyses in EBASS. These results are displayed in Figure 3.1 in table and graph formats, as produced by EBASS. On the left side of the figure, the observed ecological models (in this case, defined by activity, task, and teacher definition) are displayed, including their frequencies and percentages of occurrence. On the right side for each model, the conditional probabilities of reading aloud and reading silently are combined for each ecological model. Using the same complete project data set described in the last analysis, 20 ecological models

Ecological categories
A = Activity, B = Task, C = Teacher definition

Student category: Academic responding. Student behaviors: Reading aloud, reading silently

#	Ecological models (at least 1% of data)			Fre-quency	Per-centage	Fre-quency	Conditional probability	Z score	Signif-icance
1	A = Reading	B = Readers	C = Peer tutor	409	3.5	259	0.63	18.359	.001
2	A = Reading	B = Readers	C = Student	161	1.4	91	0.57	9.768	.001
3	A = Reading	B = Readers	C = Regular	3,154	27.2	1,112	0.35	15.494	.001
4	A = Reading	B = Workbooks	C = Regular	483	4.2	129	0.27	2.682	.010
5	A = Reading	B = Worksheet	C = Regular	835	7.2	161	0.19	-1.046	
6	A = Spelling	B = Worksheet	C = Regular	504	4.3	94	0.19	-1.126	
7	A = Spelling	B = Other media	C = Regular	146	1.3	25	0.17	-1.016	
8	A = Language	B = Workbooks	C = Regular	205	1.8	35	0.17	-1.216	
9	A = Reading	B = Other media	C = Regular	1,023	8.8	129	0.13	-5.613	.001
10	A = Language	B = Other media	C = Regular	564	4.9	67	0.12	-4.616	.001
11	A = Language	B = Paper/pencil	C = Regular	1,345	11.6	151	0.11	-7.404	.001
12	A = Language	B = Worksheet	C = Regular	448	3.9	50	0.11	-4.459	.001
13	A = Reading	B = Discussion	C = Regular	594	5.1	43	0.07	-7.138	.001
14	A = Language	B = Discussion	C = Regular	314	2.7	22	0.07	-5.339	.001
15	A = Spelling	B = Worksheet	C = Peer tutor	195	1.7	13	0.07	-4.331	.001
16	A = Language	B = Listen/lecture	C = Regular	192	1.7	12	0.06	-4.423	.001
17	A = Spelling	B = Paper/pencil	C = Peer tutor	182	1.6	9	0.05	-4.690	.001
18	A = Reading	B = Paper/pencil	C = Regular	426	3.7	19	0.04	-7.316	.001
19	A = Spelling	B = Paper/pencil	C = Regular	233	2.0	9	0.04	-5.652	.001
20	A = Reading	B = Listen/lecture	C = Regular	192	1.7	7	0.04	-5.204	.001
	Total sequences used:			11,605	83.4%	2,437			
	Total sequences recorded:			13,919					

Probability of student behaviors, given the ecological model

0.0 0.1 0.2 0.3 0.4 0.5 0.6 0.7 0.8 0.9 1.0

Unconditional probability (0.21) is the probability of student behaviors independent of model.

Figure 3.1. Results of conditional probability analyses using the Ecobehavioral Assessment Software System (EBASS), presented in table and graph formats.

of activity–task–teacher definition occurred, 10 of which were in reading. These reading models involved students' use of readers, workbooks, other media, paper and pencil, worksheet, discussion, and lecture occurring with peer tutors, student teachers, and the regular education teachers. Each model is listed in rank order by the size of its associated conditional probability of student reading behavior occurring.

The base-level probability of reading behavior (the unconditional probability) in the project was 21% occurrence. As can be seen, the instructional conditions most associated with the occurrence of reading behavior during reading instruction were use of reading texts in combination with a peer tutor, with a probability of .63. The next highest probabilities of reading behavior during reading instruction were use of reading texts with a student teacher (.57) and with a classroom teacher (.35). Also interesting were the instructional situations that did not promote reading behavior, those with probabilities of reading significantly lower than the unconditional probability of .21. As seen in Figure 3.1, 12 instructional arrangements significantly decreased reading behavior, including language and spelling activities, reading, and tasks that included other media, such as worksheets, workbooks, discussion, paper and pencil, and lecture. In these instructional situations, reading behavior was unlikely to occur. Given a goal of increasing students' active reading behavior during instruction, the implications of these findings, is to use more peer tutoring or partner reading or to change procedures used by the other teachers working with these students to enable more active reading of text materials.

Similar analyses could be conducted examining reading behavior probability as influenced by variations in student grouping, instructional structure, teacher behavior, and the focus of teacher behavior, depending on the purposes and interests of the investigators in these factors as represented in the MS-CISSAR taxonomy. Having described the collective reading experiences of these students and teachers and examined some of the accelerators and decelerators of reading behavior within this total dataset, we turn to an examination of one second-grade student with a reading delay. We also present the effects of interventions in first through third grades on his reading behavior during instruction and on his reading CBM over time.

How and When Do Reading
Behaviors Grow and Change Over Time?

We were particularly concerned about the first measured performance of one student, Dyshane, observed in November of second grade when researchers and teachers began monitoring his reading CBM progress.

At this assessment, after 2 years of schooling, he was reading only 18.0 correct words per minute (CWPM) in first- and second-grade reading material, compared with his second-grade peers (*n* = 12) who were reading at a mean rate of 60.6 CWPM. He was not learning to read, and he was at risk for reading failure (see Figure 3.2). Some 3 school years later at his last measurement, he was reading 75.0 CWPM in fourth-grade material, compared with his cohort's mean of 113.2 CWPM. His growth in reading fluency in instruction level material over this entire period was 1.7 CWPM per month in school, slightly higher than his grade cohort's mean rate of 1.4 CWPM per month in school. Although Dyshane had only closed the gap marginally, the good news was that he was reading sufficiently well in fourth-grade material that he was not referred for special educational services.

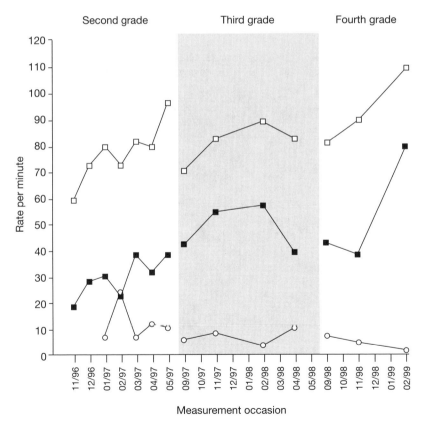

Figure 3.2. Dyshane's reading curriculum-based measurement (CBM) fluency over three grade levels. (*Key:* □ = Class's correct words per minute [CWPM], ■ = Dyshane's CWPM, ○ = Dyshane's errors per minute [EWPM])

Visual examination of the annual progress of both the cohort and Dyshane indicates a slowing of CBM progress in the second year with acceleration in the last year (see Figure 3.2). The mean rate of progress in second grade was 4.4 CWPM per month of school for the cohort, compared with the rate of progress for Dyshane, which was 2.8, double that of the overall rates for 3 years. These data suggest stronger intervention effects were achieved in the first year of the project. Dyshane received five strategies implemented by his teachers collectively in second through fourth grades. Each of his teachers implemented Writer's Workshop in each year. His second-grade teacher implemented CWPT in reading, and his third-grade teacher implemented partner reading. His fourth-grade teacher only implemented Writer's Workshop. Figure 3.3 further explains the behavioral effects of these instructional interventions as measured by MS-CISSAR.

In February, March, and April 1997, MS-CISSAR observations of Dyshane's experiences with reading CWPT in second grade indicated

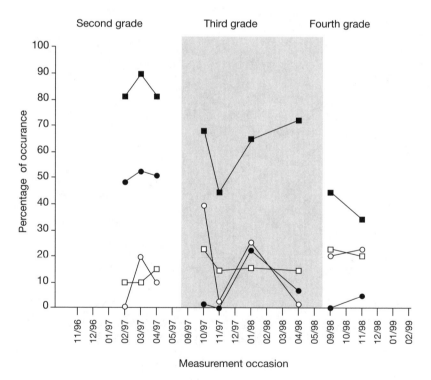

Figure 3.3.   Dyshane's reading and other behaviors during reading instruction sampled over three grade levels. (*Key:* ■ = Composite academic responding, ● = Reading aloud, ○ = Reading silently, □ = Attention)

very high levels of reading aloud (about 50% of intervals observed) and emerging levels of silent reading in the 10% range. Relatively low levels of attention were occurring during reading instruction. Highest, however, was the student's composite academic responding, the sum of his reading behaviors and writing, task participation, and talk about academics. As might be expected, these high levels of reading aloud produced during reading instruction varied with his monthly growth in CWPM in this year (see Figure 3.3).

With a new teacher in third grade and change to the partner reading strategy, the effects on student reading behavior during instruction became variable and less clear. Overall, reading aloud declined substantially, and silent reading increased in two of the four observations (October 1997 and January 1998). Partner reading was used to evoke silent reading. The level of attention remained about the same, in the 15% range. Also decreased from the prior year was composite academic responding. Dyshane's CBM progress continued and his rate of reading errors (EWPM) remained low and stable. However, in April 1998, his CWPM dropped substantially and his EWPM increased, perhaps due to this overall lower level of reading behavior during instruction in third grade.

In fourth grade, in the absence of any specific reading intervention, composite academic responding declined even further; however, silent reading was relatively high and stable at about 20% occurrence in the September and November 1998 observations, compared with third grade, when it was much more variable. An interesting development was his continued slower rate of growth in CWPM in the first half of fourth grade but with improving accuracy. This was followed by a large improvement in both CWPM and EWPM at the last measurement point, February 1999. In all, using these MS-CISSAR data, it was possible to associate reading behavior during instruction with reading CBM progress of this student over 3 years.

How Do Two Students Differ in Their Instructional Experiences in the Program?

Using the EBASS profile analysis tool, it was possible to compare students' classroom experiences and behaviors. Figure 3.4 compares a high-achieving student (Trey) with Dyshane during a single-observation occasion in the context of who was teaching them (i.e., teacher definition) during instruction based on the total number of observations of each of these students in the project at second grade. Like the conditional probability analysis, these data are presented in table and graph formats. The teacher definition types are listed in the upper left column

Teacher definition	Dyshane		Trey		Discrepancy profile			Dyshane's profile (n = 94)	Trey's profile (n = 63)	Discrepancy profile
	Frequency	Percentage	Frequency	Percentage	Difference	Difference squared	D Statistic			
Regular	35	37.23	21	33.33	3.90	15.21				
Special education	0	0.00	0	0.00	0.00	0.00				
Aide/Para	0	0.00	0	0.00	0.00	0.00				
Student	0	0.00	1	1.59	-1.59	2.52				
Volunteer	0	0.00	0	0.00	0.00	0.00				
Related service	0	0.00	0	0.00	0.00	0.00				
Substitute	45	47.87	0	0.00	47.87	2,291.76				
Peer tutor	13	13.83	41	65.08	-51.25	2,626.52				
No staff	0	0.00	0	0.00	0.00					
Missing	1	1.06	0	0.00	1.06	1.13				
Total	94		63		105.67	4,937.147	70.264835			

Figure 3.4. The performance of Trey, a high-achieving student, compared with the low performance of Dyshane during a single-observation occasion in the context of who was teaching them (i.e., teacher definition). (*Note:* If the D statistic is equal to zero, then the profiles are exactly the same. As the D statistic gets larger than about 20%, the profiles become more and more dissimilar.)

of the figure, along with their frequency and information about the percentage of occurrence for a selected target student (Dyshane's profile) and a selected comparison student (the profile of the index student, Trey). The data for the percentage of occurrence were differenced, forming a discrepancy profile and a profile-similarity statistic computed (the Euclidian Distance or D-Statistic; Nunnally, 1967).

As can be seen, the D-statistic was larger than 70.3, indicating a high degree of dissimilarity in the profiles of who taught them during reading and how long they were taught. The regular education teacher (35%), a substitute teacher (48%), and a peer tutor (14%) taught Dyshane. In contrast, a peer tutor (65%) and the regular education teacher (33%) taught Trey. In both cases, these data indicate a relative high exposure of these two students to peer tutors and reading partners and Dyshane's greater exposure to the substitute teacher. As in prior analyses, use of the MS-CISSAR observation data in reading resulted in a useful account and comparison of the instructional experiences of students in reading. Due to space limitations, however, it is not possible to explore the many other and potentially insightful analyses possible within the context of the MS-CISSAR taxonomy and the interests of the investigator.

CONCLUSION

This chapter describes ecobehavioral assessment and analysis strategies with implications for research on reading instruction and reading/literacy interventions. Issues related to conceptual framework, instruments, observer training, procedures of observation, and methods of analysis are addressed. Early work on these strategies reveals that students' behavior during their teachers' efforts to instruct them plays an important role in how fast they learn basic academic skills including reading. Particularly relevant has been the concern over low levels of academic responding produced in special and general education settings and the fact that the instruction provided is all too often not functionally related to high levels of academic responding, neither in oral or silent reading. To date, ecobehavioral observational assessment strategies have contributed to both current and new knowledge about the instruction of children at risk and with disabilities in special and general education settings. For students with disabilities in general education settings, academic responding is best promoted by small-group, independent, or one-to-one structures with the teacher's focus on the student and with peer tutors and paraprofessionals acting as teachers.

More time spent in these arrangements is likely to lead to greater performance, better learning, and accelerated growth rates.

It was possible to illustrate some typical analyses of ecobehavioral events relevant to research on reading using ecobehavioral observational strategies in a longitudinal study of the effects of a model designed to change teachers' practices in local classrooms in order to prevent early reading failure. These analyses included summative results for all students and all observations over multiple years and results for only one individual at risk for early reading failure. These analyses included

1. Percentage occurrence to describe the quality and quantity of ecological, teacher, and student events

2. Conditional probability analyses to reveal the conditions of which classroom reading behavior was a function

3. Trends over time to reveal the quantity and variation of key indicators of student behavior

4. Profile analyses of similarities between a student with low achievement and a student with high achievement

5. Display of the covariation of change in reading behavior with change in reading CBM progress as a function of intervention over three school years

Implications for Research and Practice

Observational studies have an important role to play in research on reading instruction and classroom-based reading intervention. Because observational measurement is designed to record what actually happens in classrooms, rather than record reports of what happened, they bring a degree of ecological validity and technical adequacy that cannot be obtained otherwise. Conversely, observation measures are not impervious to error and inaccuracies may be induced in observational data by insufficient observer training, lack of observer monitoring, intrusive introduction of observers into classroom settings, drift in reliability over time, and by biases held by observers (e.g., expectations, prejudices). However, procedures of training and monitoring exist for reducing these sources of error to low levels (e.g., Hartmann & Woods, 1990, pp. 117–121).

The ecobehavioral strategies in this chapter provide an important means of looking at the compounded effects that result from the momentary interactions among classroom ecology, teacher, and student during instruction. Because of the conceptual and practical focus on observing one student to map his or her experiences and behavior during instruction in these ecobehavioral strategies, it is possible to empirically study effects for individual students and groups of students. To date, the MS-CISSAR has been used widely in special education intervention research and evaluations of instruction, including reading with a range of students with and without disabilities. One study, which used MS-CISSAR to observe high school classrooms that included students with disabilities, indicated that on average, all students spent 8.2% of instruction time using reading texts and 8.8% of time engaged in silent reading (8.2% for students in general education students, compared with 9.4% for students in special education) (Wallace, Anderson, Bartholomay, & Hupp, 2002).

All too often, however, these interactions, which are theoretically and experimentally necessary to accurately characterize whether the intended effects of specific reading interventions are present, are missed because of lack of measurement or because they are simply assumed to occur and are never measured directly. The lack of observational information contributes to weak research designs, the inability to develop hypotheses that are testable, and findings that cannot be explained. Too often in reading intervention research and practice, student behavior during instruction is considered an insignificant factor even when research has shown otherwise. Because of the user-friendly computer software and training materials and procedures (i.e., EBASS), MS-CISSAR observations and results can be available to both research and school personnel given the will and resources necessary to develop the capacity to use them. Clearly, the MS-CISSAR is not a tool for direct use by classroom teachers; however, with training and observation results provided by trained others (e.g., school psychologists, special educators), teachers can use the information to guide instructional decision making and evaluate local instructional practices.

REFERENCES

Abbott, M., Walton, C., Tapia, Y., & Greenwood, C.R. (1999). Research to practice: A "blueprint" for closing the gap in local schools. *Exceptional Children, 65*(3), 339–352.

Agar, C.L., & Shapiro, E. (1995). Template matching as a strategy for assessment of and intervention for preschool children with disabilities. *Topics in Early Childhood Special Education, 15*(2), 187–218.

Ary, D. (1984). Mathematical explanation of error in duration recording using partial interval, whole interval, and momentary time sampling. *Behavioral Assessment, 6,* 221–228.

Cooper, D.H., & Speece, D.L. (1990a). Instructional correlates of student's academic responses: Comparisons between at-risk and control students. *Early Education and Development, 1,* 279–300.

Cooper, D.H., & Speece, D.L. (1990b). Maintaining at-risk children in regular education settings: Initial effects of individual differences and classroom environments. *Exceptional Children, 57,* 117–127.

Greenwood, C.R. (1991). Longitudinal analysis of time engagement and academic achievement in at-risk and non-risk students. *Exceptional Children, 57,* 521–535.

Greenwood, C.R. (1996a). The case for performance-based models of instruction. *School Psychology Quarterly, 11*(4), 283–296.

Greenwood, C.R. (1996b). Research on the practices and behavior of effective teachers at the Juniper Gardens Children's Project: Implications for the education of diverse learners. In D. Speece & B.K. Keogh (Eds.), *Research on classroom ecologies: Implications for inclusion of children with learning disabilities* (pp. 39–67). Mahwah, NJ: Lawrence Erlbaum Associates.

Greenwood, C.R., Arreaga-Mayer, C., & Carta, J.J. (1994). Identification and translation of effective teacher-developed instructional procedures for general practice. *Remedial and Special Education, 15,* 140–151.

Greenwood, C.R., Carta, J.J., Arreaga-Mayer, C., & Rager, A. (1991). The behavior analyst consulting model: Identifying and validating naturally effective instructional models. *Journal of Behavioral Education, 1,* 165–191.

Greenwood, C.R., Carta, J.J., & Dawson, H. (2000). Observational methods for educational settings. In T. Thompson, D. Felce, & F.J. Symons (Eds.), *Behavior observation: Technology and applications in developmental disabilities* (pp. 229–252). Baltimore: Paul H. Brookes Publishing Co.

Greenwood, C.R., Carta, J.J., Kamps, D., & Arreaga-Mayer, C. (1990). Ecobehavioral analysis of classroom instruction. In S.R. Schroeder (Ed.), *Ecobehavioral analysis and developmental disabilities: The twenty-first century* (pp. 33–63). New York: Springer-Verlag.

Greenwood, C.R., Carta, J.J., Kamps, D., & Delquadri, J. (1993). *Ecobehavioral assessment systems software (EBASS): Practitioner's manual.* Kansas City: Juniper Gardens Children's Project, University of Kansas.

Greenwood, C.R., Carta, J.J., Kamps, D., Terry, B., & Delquadri, J. (1994). Development and validation of standard classroom observation systems for school practitioners: Ecobehavioral assessment systems software EBASS. *Exceptional Children, 61,* 197–210.

Greenwood, C.R., & Delquadri, J. (1988). Code for instructional structure and student academic response: CISSAR. In M. Hersen & A.S. Bellack (Eds.), *Dictionary of behavioral assessment techniques* (pp. 120–122). New York: Pergamon.

Greenwood, C.R., & Delquadri, J. (1995). ClassWide Peer Tutoring and the prevention of school failure. *Preventing School Failure, 39*(4), 21–25.

Greenwood, C.R., Delquadri, J., & Hall, R.V. (1984). Opportunity to respond and student academic performance. In W. Heward, T. Heron, D. Hill, & J. Trap-Porter (Eds.), *Behavior analysis in education* (pp. 58–88). Columbus, OH: Merrill.

Greenwood, C.R., Delquadri, J., & Hall, R.V. (1989). Longitudinal effects of classwide peer tutoring. *Journal of Educational Psychology, 81,* 371–383.

Greenwood, C.R., Delquadri, J., Stanley, S.O., Terry, B., & Hall, R.V. (1985). Assessment of eco-behavioral interaction in school settings. *Behavioral Assessment, 7,* 331–347.

Greenwood, C.R., Hart, B., Walker, D., & Risley, T.R. (1994). The opportunity to respond revisited: A behavioral theory of developmental retardation and its prevention. In R. Gardner, III, D.M. Sainato, J.O. Cooper, T.E. Heron, W.L. Heward, J.W. Eshleman, & T.A. Grossi (Eds.), *Behavior analysis in education: Focus on measurably superior instruction* (pp. 213–223). Pacific Grove, CA: Brooks/Cole.

Greenwood, C.R., & Hou, L.S. (1995). *Ecobehavioral Assessment Systems Software (EBASS)–Version 3.0: Technical manual.* Kansas City: The Juniper Gardens Children's Project, University of Kansas.

Greenwood, C.R., Peterson, P., & Sideridis, G. (1995). Conceptual method-ological and technological advances in classroom observational assessment. *Diagnostique, 20,* 73–100.

Greenwood, C.R., Terry, B., Marquis, J., & Walker, D. (1994). Confirming a performance-based instructional model. *School Psychology Review, 23,* 625–668.

Greenwood, C.R., Terry, B., Utley, C.A., Montagna, D., & Walker, D. (1993). Achievement placement and services: Middle school benefits of ClassWide Peer Tutoring used at the elementary school. *School Psychology Review, 22,* 497–516.

Hartmann, D.P., & Woods, D.D. (1990). Observational methods. In A.S. Bel-lack, M. Hersen, & A.E. Kazdin (Eds.), *International handbook of behavior modi-fication and therapy* (Vol. 2, pp. 107–150). New York: Plenum.

Hops, H., & Cobb, J.A. (1973). Survival behaviors in the educational setting: Their implications for research and intervention. In L.A. Hamerlynck, L.C. Handy, & E.J. Mash (Eds.), *Behavior change: Methodology, concepts, and practice* (pp. 193–208). Champaign, IL: Research Press.

Jenkins, J.R., & Jenkins, L.M. (1982). *Peer and cross-age tutoring.* Seattle: Univer-sity of Washington (ERIC Document Reproduction Service No. ED 238 844).

Jensen, A.R. (1980). *Bias in mental testing.* New York: The Free Press.

Kamps, D., Greenwood, C.R., & Leonard, B. (1991). Ecobehavioral assessment in classrooms serving children with autism and developmental disabilities. In R.J. Prinz (Ed.), *Advances in behavioral assessment of children and families* (pp. 203–237). New York: Jessica Kingsley.

Kamps, D., Leonard, B.R., Dugan, E.P., Boland, B., & Greenwood, C.R. (1991). The use of ecobehavioral assessment to identify naturally occurring effective procedures in classrooms serving students with autism and developmental disabilities. *Journal of Behavioral Education, 41,* 367–397.

Logan, K.R., Bakeman, R., & Keefe, E.B. (1997). Effects of instructional vari-ables on engaged behavior of students with disabilities in general education classrooms. *Exceptional Children, 63*(4), 481–498.

Marston, D., Deno, S.L., Kim, D., Diment, K., & Rogers, D. (1995). Comparison of reading intervention approaches for students with mild disabilities. *Excep-tional Children, 62*(1), 20–37.

Morris, E.K., & Midgley, B.D. (1990). Some historical and conceptual founda-tions of ecobehavioral analysis. In S. Schroeder (Ed.), *Ecobehavioral analy-sis and developmental disabilities: The twenty-first century* (pp. 1–32). New York: Springer-Verlag.

O'Sullivan, P.J., Ysseldyke, J.E., Christensen, S.L., & Thurlow, A.L. (1990). Mildly handicapped elementary students' opportunity to learn during read-ing instruction in mainstream and special education settings. *Reading Research Quarterly, 25,* 131–146.

Powell, J. (1984). On the misrepresentation of realities by a widely practiced direct observation procedure: Partial interval one-zero sampling. *Behavioral Assessment, 6,* 209–219.

Powell, J., Martindale, A., & Kulp, S. (1975). An evaluation of time-sampling measures of behavior. *Journal of Applied Behavior Analysis, 8,* 463–470.

Stanley, S.O., & Greenwood, C.R. (1981). *Code for instructional structure and student academic response (CISSAR): Observers' manual.* Kansas City: Juniper Gardens Children's Project, Bureau of Child Research, University of Kansas.

Stanley, S.O., & Greenwood, C.R. (1983). Assessing opportunity to respond in classroom environments through direct observation: How much opportunity to respond does the minority disadvantaged student receive in school? *Exceptional Children, 49,* 370–373.

Tapp, J., & Wehby, J. (1993). *Multiple option observation system for experimental studies (MOOSES).* Nashville, TN: Vanderbilt University (ERIC Document Reproduction Service No. ED 361 372).

Thurlow, M.L., Ysseldyke, J.E., Graden, J., & Algozzine, B. (1984). Opportunity to learn for LD students receiving different levels of special education services. *Learning Disability Quarterly, 7,* 55–67.

Wallace, T., Anderson, R.A., Bartholomay, T., & Hupp, S. (2002). An ecobehavioral examination of high school classrooms that included students with disabilities. *Exceptional Children, 68*(3), 345–359.

Ysseldyke, J.E., Christenson, S.L., Thurlow, M.L., & Bakewell, D. (1989). Are different kinds of instructional tasks used by different categories of students in different settings? *School Psychology Review, 18,* 98–111.

Ysseldyke, J.E., Thurlow, M.L., Christenson, S.L., & Weiss, J. (1987). Time allocated to instruction of mentally retarded, learning disabled, emotionally disturbed, and nonhandicapped elementary students. *Journal of Special Education, 21,* 43–55.

4

The Classroom Climate Scale

Observing During Reading Instruction

AE-HWA KIM, KERRI L. BRIGGS, AND SHARON VAUGHN

One of the aims of the Individuals with Disabilities Education Act (IDEA) of 1990 (PL 101-476) and subsequent amendments was to educate students with disabilities in the least restrictive environment. To ensure the successful provision of the least restrictive environment mandate, general education teachers are required to provide appropriate adaptations and accommodations for students with disabilities. The evidence strongly suggests that students with disabilities do not fare well in general education classrooms *where appropriate adaptations are not provided* (Baker & Zigmond, 1990; Fox & Ysseldyke, 1997; McIntosh, Vaughn, Schumm, Haager, & Lee, 1993; Vaughn & Schumm, 1994). Successful inclusion relies on teachers' willingness and capability to provide adaptations and accommodations for students with disabilities (Gartner & Lipsky, 1987). Thus, it is necessary to equip general education teachers to meet the needs of students with disabilities.

The logical first step to help general education teachers become well equipped to meet the needs of students with disabilities is to examine general education teachers' perceptions about the feasibility of accommodating students with disabilities in their classrooms. Schumm and Vaughn (1991) conducted a study to address this question. Findings revealed that the types of adaptations that were perceived by general education teachers as most desirable and feasible were those related to the social and motivational adjustment of the students with disabilities but that did not require any curricular or environmental changes on the part of the teacher (e.g., provide reinforcement and encouragement, establish a personal relationship). At the same time, the types of adaptations that were perceived as least desirable and feasible were those that required changes in the planning, curriculum use, and evaluation procedures in the general education classrooms (e.g., adapt long-range plans, adapt materials, adapt scoring/grading criteria). Similar findings were revealed in a study by Bryant, Dean, Elrod, and Blackbourn (1999) that examined perceptions of 20 elementary and secondary general education teachers about accommodations for students with learning disabilities (LD) in their classrooms. The general education teachers demonstrated that they favored accommodations that did not require the alteration of the content and teaching procedures and demanded less time to implement.

Given this understanding of general education teachers' perceptions about the feasibility of adaptations and accommodations, the next step is to examine *the current status of instructional practices regarding adaptations and accommodations for students with disabilities in general education classes.* McIntosh and her colleagues (1993) were interested in determining the extent to which general education teachers actually provided adaptations and accommodations to meet the diverse academic and social needs of students with LD in their classes. Through careful review of existing classroom observational instruments, McIntosh and her colleagues sought appropriate instruments that could address this research question, but no instrument was identified. One of the highest concerns with existing instruments was the inability to explore both teacher and student behaviors and interactions relative to accommodating students with LD. The existing instruments fell into the following categories: evaluating teachers (e.g., Bailey, 1984), examining teacher behavior or instructional practice (e.g., Callaway, 1988), examining students' social and behavior problems (e.g., Schumaker, Hazel, Sherman, & Sheldon, 1982), examining either teacher or student interaction (e.g., Dorval, McKinney, & Feagans, 1982), or examining interaction among students (e.g., Bryan & Bryan, 1978). No instrument had the capability to document both teacher and student behaviors relative to accommodating students with LD, as well as interactions between teachers and students or among students.

In response to the existing instruments, the Classroom Climate Scale (CCS) was developed to provide systematic observation of teacher and student behaviors, as well as interactions between teachers and students or among students during academic instruction in general education classrooms (McIntosh et al., 1993). With successful use of the CCS in general education classrooms, since 1993 the CCS was successfully adapted for use during reading instruction 1) in resource reading classes for students with LD (Moody, Vaughn, Hughes, & Fisher, 2000; Vaughn, Moody, & Schumm, 1998), 2) in resource reading classes for students with emotional/behavioral disorders (EBD) (Levy & Vaughn, 2002), 3) in general education reading classes (Schumm, Moody, & Vaughn, 2000), and 4) in bilingual reading classes (Fletcher, Bos, & Johnson, 1999).

The purposes of this chapter are to describe the original CCS and its adapted versions, to describe its use in several studies and to synthesize findings from the studies, and to provide a discussion on how the CCS instrument can serve as a research tool and on findings from the studies using the CCS.

DESCRIPTION OF THE CLASSROOM CLIMATE SCALE

The following sections describe the CCS and its adaptations. Versions of the CCS include the adapted CCS for use in resource reading classes for students with LD, the adapted CCS for use in resource reading classes for students with EBD, and the adapted CCS for use in bilingual reading classrooms.

The Original Classroom Climate Scale

The CCS was developed to provide reliable and valid information regarding teacher and student behaviors or interactions in a general education classroom (see the Appendix). The CCS was developed through a three-step process: conducting an extensive review of the literature and evaluation of classroom observation instruments, refining the components and items through a series of field testing in classroom settings, and developing performance indicators (i.e., behavioral descriptors) for each item.

In the development of the CCS, substantial considerations were given to the validity and reliability of the instrument. First, to ensure the construct validity of the CCS, McIntosh and colleagues (1993) conducted an extensive review of literature and other relevant observation instruments in developing the drafts of the CCS. To further enhance the construct validity of the CCS, they requested experts to review the CCS. In addition, they generated performance indicators that supply behavioral descriptors for each item of the CCS. Subsequently, they conducted an extensive field testing of the items and the performance indicators in classroom settings to verify their effectiveness in recording the desired behaviors. Following classroom observations with the CCS, McIntosh and her colleagues discussed individual items and revised the ambiguous items.

Second, to ensure high inter-rater reliability, an extensive training of observers was provided prior to data collection. During the training, the observers practiced coding the CCS in an actual classroom setting, and they were required to obtain an inter-rater agreement of higher than .85. Only those observers who met this requirement were involved in data collection.

The CCS developed through this comprehensive and extensive development process was used in observing 60 general education classrooms across grade levels (elementary, middle, and high school) (McIntosh et al., 1993). McIntosh and colleagues (1993) examined the extent to which general education teachers provided differentiated instruction for students with LD. At this time, the scale was not specifically for reading. The CCS contained four components:

1. Teacher-initiated behaviors (nine items), including instructional grouping, types of monitoring and modifications, use of praise, and teacher fairness and impartiality (e.g., use whole-class activities, monitor ongoing student performance, appear fair and impartial)

2. Student-initiated behaviors (five items), including students' level of involvement in class activities, asking for help and volunteering, and levels of frustration and confusion (e.g., appear engaged in task-related behavior, ask the teacher for help, appear frustrated or confused)

3. Student participation and interaction (three items), including interactions between the student and the teacher, class activities, and other students (e.g., interact with other students, interfere with the work/activity of other students)

4. Overall classroom climate (four items), including the consistency or discrepancy in assignments, materials, and location and involvement in class activities between students without disabilities and students with disabilities (e.g., is the entire class working on the same activity/assignment, do all the students use the same materials)

The first three components were rated on a 5-point Likert-type scale (1 = rarely, 2 = seldom [less than 20% but more than rarely], 3 = occasionally [20%–69%], 4 = frequently [70%–94%], 5 = most of the time [more than 95%]). The last component, overall classroom climate, required an answer of yes or no.

The Adapted Classroom Climate Scale for Use in Reading Classes for Students with LD

Since the original CCS was developed by McIntosh and colleagues (1993), it has been used in several studies and adapted to address the specific research questions of those studies. Vaughn and her colleagues (1998) were interested in examining the extent to which intensive and individualized, research-based reading instruction was provided to students with LD in elementary resource reading classes. In order to address the research question, Vaughn and her colleagues added items on research-based reading practices for students with LD. Using the adapted version of the CCS, they conducted systematic observations of 14 elementary resource reading classes for LD, and 2 years later, they followed up with the six teachers who were teaching students with LD in resource reading classes (Moody et al., 2000).

The adapted CCS had two parts, a quantitative section and a qualitative section. In the quantitative section, the measure allowed the observer to rate items about the teacher behavior and instruction that included 1) grouping practices (the amount of time in which whole-class activities, small-group activities, student-pairing activities, independent activities, and individualized activities occur) and 2) teacher behaviors (the degree to which a teacher responds to needs of students, monitors ongoing student performance, appears fair and impartial, communicates expectations, redirects off-task behavior, and provides positive feedback or negative comments). In addition, the measure allowed the observer to rate items about student behaviors and interactions that included the amount of time a student engages in a task, the degree to which the student interferes with the work of other students, and the level to which the student is confused or frustrated. Items in the quantitative section of the adapted measure were rated on a 5-point Likert-type scale (Moody et al., 2000) or a 4-point Likert-type scale (Vaughn et al., 1998).

In the qualitative section, the adapted measure provided the observer with guided questions: whether students work on the same activity, follow the same sequence of activities, and use the same or different materials; the description of teachers' adaptations for students; the occurrence of word recognition activity; the occurrence of comprehension activities; and further description of the reading and grouping instruction. Table 4.1 shows samples of the guided questions.

This adapted CCS was also used in general education reading classes (Schumm et al., 2000). Schumm and colleagues (2000) conducted classroom observations of 29 third-grade general education teachers during reading instruction to achieve a better understanding of prevailing

Table 4.1.   Sample guided questions in the qualitative section

1.   What types of adaptations does this teacher make for students in this classroom?
2.   Describe the flow of *transitions* during the lesson observed (e.g., were they quick, quiet, loud, unorganized).
3.   List any phonological, word analysis, phonics, spelling, or fluency instruction that you observed (e.g., a lesson, a workbook, one-to-one instruction).
4.   List any comprehension instruction that you observed (e.g., strategy instruction, main idea, inference, vocabulary, writing in response to reading).

grouping practices for reading instruction. Given the research questions of the study, Schumm and colleagues (2000) focused on items on grouping practices in the quantitative section.

The Adapted Classroom Climate Scale for Use in Reading Classes for Students with EBD

The adapted CCS scale (Moody et al., 2000; Vaughn et al., 1998) was modified for use in resource reading classes for students with EBD (Levy & Vaughn, 2002). Levy and Vaughn (2002) were interested in documenting the current status of reading instructional practices and classroom management practices for students with EBD. Four items that did not specifically address their research questions were removed (i.e., does the teacher communicate expectations to students, do students ask the teacher for help, do students ask other students for help, and do students interact with other students). All items in the descriptive section remained, and three items about fluency instruction, positive feedback, and redirecting off-task behavior were added to the descriptive section.

The Adapted Classroom Climate Scale for Use in Bilingual Education Classrooms

The CCS has also been used to examine the extent to which two elementary bilingual teachers accommodated students with language and learning disabilities (LLD) in their bilingual classrooms. The CCS scale was adapted for this research question by adding a section on bilingual education teacher effectiveness to the original CCS. The newly added bilingual education teacher effectiveness section (13 items) addressed teaching strategies promoting modeling, practice, feedback, active student learning, and integration of first language and culture into the lesson (see Table 4.2). To ensure content validity and inter-rater reliability and to control observer bias, performance indicators (i.e., behavior descriptors) were developed for the bilingual teacher effectiveness

Table 4.2.   Thirteen items on bilingual education teacher effectiveness

1.	Situates and contextualizes the lesson
2.	Orients students to lesson
3.	Gives clear directions
4.	Activates students' background knowledge
5.	Explains and discusses concepts and their relationships
6.	Demonstrates and models
7.	Encourages student discussion
8.	Checks for understanding
9.	Reteaches, re-explains when needed
10.	Provides guided practice
11.	Uses home culture in explanations and discussions
12.	Uses home language for personal and social communication
13.	Integrates language development with academic development

items. The bilingual teacher effectiveness items were measured on the same 5-point Likert-type scale as the original CCS.

FINDINGS

The collection of CCS-informed studies can be divided into two types. The first type of studies focused on within-class comparisons, in which observations focused on the interactivity of a target group in comparison with other students in the class. This includes the McIntosh et al. study (1993), in which the authors examined the educational experiences of students with LD as compared with their general education peers. A similar study looked at the educational experiences of students with LLD as compared with high-, average-, and low-achieving students in bilingual classrooms (Fletcher et al., 1999). These comparative studies were generally interested in determining how students with special needs were accommodated within their classroom.

The second set of studies was descriptive. Vaughn and colleagues (1998) observed elementary resource reading classes for students with LD and analyzed and described reading practices and grouping practices provided in the resource reading classes. The follow-up study was conducted with a subset of the original teachers in the Vaughn et al. study (1998) after the implementation of reading reforms to address the same research questions as the original study (Moody et al., 2000). Similarly, Levy and Vaughn (2002) reported on reading instruction and classroom management practices in resource rooms for students with EBD. Schumm and colleagues (2000) also reported on the prevailing grouping practices that general education classroom teachers used during reading instruction.

Major findings from these studies are organized into six broad categories found on the CCS: 1) grouping patterns, 2) overall classroom climate, 3) teacher-initiated behaviors, 4) student-initiated behaviors, 5) student–teacher interaction or student–student interaction, and 6) reading instruction.

Grouping Patterns

Across all the studies using the CCS, one finding was consistent— teachers used whole-group instruction far more than any other grouping pattern, such as pairing or small groups (Fletcher et al., 1999; Levy & Vaughn, 2002; McIntosh et al., 1993; Moody et al., 2000; Schumm, Moody, & Vaughn, 2000; Vaughn et al., 1998). During whole-group instruction, teachers generally provided the same instruction, same materials, and same activities to all students, regardless of ability, disability, or language. This use of whole-group instruction was observed in a range of classrooms (special education and general education) with different types of students (e.g., students with LD, students with EBD, students without disabilities). In the study of 14 elementary resource rooms for students with LD, the teachers used whole-group instruction and independent activities (in which students work by themselves) significantly more often than small groups, pairs, or individualized activities (a teacher working one to one with a student) (Vaughn et al., 1998). In the follow-up study, the teachers used less whole-group instruction, but it remained the most prevalent grouping pattern (Moody et al., 2000). McIntosh and colleagues (1993) found that across grade levels (elementary, middle, and high school) in general education, the dominant grouping pattern was whole-group instruction. A study by Schumm and colleagues (2000) also confirmed that whole-group instruction was the most frequent grouping format used in elementary general education reading classes.

Following whole-group instruction, the second grouping pattern used most often was independent activity (McIntosh et al., 1993; Moody et al., 2000; Vaughn et al., 1998). As defined by the CCS, independent activities occur when students are engaged individually in an assignment that is the same as the other students. More often than not, independent activities entail the completion of worksheets or assignments listed on the chalkboard that are intended as follow-up instruction or practice. Vaughn and colleagues (1998) revealed that independent activities occurred more often than small groups, pairs, or individualized instruction in the elementary resource classes for students with LD. At follow-up, independent activities were less prominent and more individualization was occurring (Moody et al., 2000). In the other studies, the independent activity was the second most prevalent grouping pattern, but the difference in its frequency of use was not statistically significant from other grouping patterns (i.e., small-group activities, pairing, individualized activities) (McIntosh et al., 1993; Schumm et al., 2000). Levy and Vaughn (2002) revealed a slightly different finding in their study with resource room teachers for students with EBD—the independent activities were the most dominant grouping pattern followed by whole-group instruction.

Overall Classroom Climate

One section of the CCS was intended to estimate the amount of differentiated instruction and the extent to which various accommodations were made for students. Items in this section were answered with a simple yes or no. A "yes" answer on the items reflects a classroom in which students complete the same activities in the same sequence, use the same materials, and sit in the classroom with no differentiation. Analysis of these items was reported in two of the CCS-based studies: McIntosh et al. (1993) and Fletcher et al. (1999).

Both of these comparative studies found that teachers *seldom* changed their instructional practices for students with special needs, and usually they did not treat their students with special needs differently from the general education students. Between 90% and 100% of the time, students were engaged in the same activity, regardless of special needs (McIntosh et al., 1993). This was particularly true at the upper grades. In middle school and high school, students were working on the same activity, following the same sequence of activities, using the same materials, and sitting in similar seating arrangements. There was more differentiation at the elementary school level, but the degree of uniformity was still high, ranging between 73% and 91% (McIntosh et al., 1993).

Similar observations were made in the study of two bilingual classrooms in which students with LLD were included. One classroom followed the pattern as found in the McIntosh et al. (1993) study—students received the same instruction, in the same sequence, with the same materials. In the other classroom, there were more differences, particularly with regard to the sequence of activities and seating arrangements. However, these adjustments were not provided with the intent to single out students with LLD (Fletcher et al., 1999).

Teacher-Initiated Behaviors

The CCS was used to document teacher behaviors during instruction. Teacher-initiated behaviors include responding to the needs of students, monitoring progress, providing positive behavior support, redirecting off-task behaviors, and making negative comments. Vaughn and colleagues (1998) reported that the 14 teachers of students with LD communicated expectations with their students and monitored the students' performance at high levels. These teachers made few negative comments and provided positive feedback. Furthermore, the teachers treated students fairly and successfully redirected off-task behavior. In the follow-up study (Moody et al., 2000), similar findings emerged; six teachers occasionally communicated expectations with their students and redirected off-task behavior. Teachers treated students fairly most of the time and rarely made negative comments.

In a larger study of 29 third-grade classrooms, findings were similar; teachers frequently monitored students' performance and communicated expectations with students. In addition, teachers rarely made negative comments, and they treated students fairly and impartially most of the time. The study conducted with six resource room teachers for students with EBD revealed that progress monitoring, providing positive feedback, and providing negative comments varied among teachers. However, six teachers' responses were average or more than average in responding to students' needs, and five teachers' responses were average or more than average in redirecting students' off-task behaviors. A study by McIntosh and colleagues (1993) revealed that general education teachers frequently monitored students' progress and treated students fairly most of time. The general education teachers also frequently provided positive feedback and seldom provided negative comments to students. These findings were consistent across the grade levels (elementary, middle, and high schools) and for students with and without disabilities.

On one hand, the findings on teacher-initiated behaviors revealed that, overall, teachers used appropriate teaching practices (e.g., monitoring progress, providing positive behavior support, redirecting off-task behaviors) and treated students with disabilities fairly. On the other hand, the findings on grouping patterns and overall classroom climate revealed that teachers primarily used whole-group instruction and provided limited differentiated instruction or materials. This discrepancy may be explained by previous studies on teachers' perceptions about feasibility of accommodating students with disabilities (Schumm & Vaughn, 1991). Items included in the category of teacher-initiated behaviors were similar to the desirable and feasible adaptations identified by the teachers (i.e., adaptations related to social and motivational adjustment of the students and those not requiring any curricular or environmental changes on the part of the teacher). However, providing differentiated grouping practices, instruction, and materials was similar to the least desirable and feasible adaptations identified by teachers (i.e., adaptations requiring changes in the planning, curriculum, materials, and evaluation procedures).

Student-Initiated Behaviors

The CCS provided items and criteria for documenting students' positive and negative behaviors during instruction (Fletcher et al., 1999; Levy & Vaughn, 2002; McIntosh et al., 1993; Vaughn et al., 1998). The positive student behaviors included asking the teacher for help, asking other students for help, and volunteering to answer questions. The negative student behaviors included the extent to which a student interferes with the work and activities of other students, appears frustrated or confused, and makes negative comments.

Students with LD in the general education classrooms engaged in fewer positive student-initiated behaviors, such as volunteering to answer questions, than students without disabilities (McIntosh et al., 1993). These findings were consistent across the grade levels (elementary, middle, and high school). Similarly, students with LD in resource reading classes seldom demonstrated positive student-initiated behaviors (Vaughn et al., 1998). Students with LLD also displayed more frustration and confusion than their peers (Fletcher et al., 1999). Likewise, Levy and Vaughn (2002) found that many students with EBD showed frustration and confusion frequently or most of the time.

Interestingly, students with disabilities did not appear to engage in distracting behaviors more than their peers without disabilities (Fletcher et al., 1999; McIntosh et al., 1993). In fact, students without disabilities were more often observed interfering with the activities of other students, making sarcastic comments, and engaging in personal ridicule than their peers with LD (McIntosh et al., 1993).

Student-Teacher Interaction or Student-Student Interaction

The CCS also measured the frequency of student–teacher interaction or student–student interaction. In general, the items about student–teacher interaction or student–student interaction included engaging in task-related behavior, interacting with the teacher, and interacting with other students.

The McIntosh et al. (1993) study reported that, as compared with the students without disabilities, students with LD were engaged in far fewer classroom activities and were less engaged with their teacher and other students. This lack of engagement held fairly constant across elementary, middle, and high school. The Fletcher et al. study (1999) drew similar conclusions. Students with LLD participated less in class activities and interacted less with the teacher and students than high-, average-, and low-achieving students. Overall, students with special needs were fairly unengaged in classroom activities and somewhat ignored by the teacher and peers.

Reading Instruction

Studies conducted in reading classes revealed that there were limited applications of research-based reading practices such as phonological awareness, phonics, fluency, comprehension, and vocabulary (Levy & Vaughn, 2002; Moody et al., 2000; Schumm et al., 2000; Vaughn et al., 1998).

In a study of 14 resource room teachers for students with LD, 10 of the 14 resource room teachers identified the whole language approach as their primary approach to reading instruction (Vaughn et al., 1998). The teachers were rarely observed providing phonics instruction. In fact, only 3 of the 14 provided ongoing word recognition or decoding instruction. Furthermore, little instruction on comprehension strategies was provided. Of the 41 observations, there was only one record of a comprehension strategy being taught.

In the follow-up study (Moody et al., 2000), the most notable change in teacher perception was the belief that phonics instruction was necessary and valuable for reading instruction for students with LD; however, this change was not seen in observations (Moody et al., 2000). Similarly, teachers talked more about including phonics instruction in reading, but this change was not observed. As in the previous study (Vaughn et al., 1998), there was little or no comprehension instruction, aside from asking students questions about what they read.

In the third-grade study conducted in 29 classrooms, teachers provided little differentiated instruction in word analysis, despite the presence of students who could not decode. Teachers' responses about the need for intensive word analysis instruction for students with reading problems varied. A few were against delivering word analysis instruction; others believed it was necessary but could not find appropriate materials. Most teachers were "neutral" or "unconcerned" about this type of instruction, claiming they taught it "incidentally," but the occurrence of word analysis instruction was not observed (Schumm et al., 2000).

In the study of six resource room teachers of students with EBD (Levy & Vaughn, 2002), only two of the six teachers provided instruction in phonological awareness. Although all teachers had students practice word analysis, they provided students with no or minimal instruction in applying word analysis strategies. Furthermore, the three teachers provided word analysis instruction solely by the use of worksheets. Only two of six teachers provided teacher-led comprehension instruction, but it occurred only once for each teacher. Overall, students with disabilities were infrequently receiving reading instruction associated with improved outcomes in reading.

DISCUSSION AND IMPLICATIONS

This chapter describes the original CCS, its adapted versions, and its use in observational studies and findings from the studies. Major findings from our analysis of the CCS and observational studies using the CCS are that 1) the CCS serves as a research tool that can be used to examine the extent to which teachers provide appropriate and effective instruction for students with and without disabilities in various educational settings and 2) students with disabilities do not receive much differentiated instruction, regardless of the placement (general education or special education), grade levels (elementary, middle, high school), and types of disability (LD or EBD).

The CCS as a Research Tool

The CCS is a comprehensive and flexible classroom observational instrument that can address different research questions and can be used in different educational settings. The original CCS was developed for use in general education classrooms, and it was successfully adapted for use in special education resource rooms and bilingual classrooms. The consistency of findings across the six studies reinforces its reliability. Furthermore, data from the CCS are both quantitative and qualitative, not only providing the researcher with a tool to discover trends and differences but also providing rich descriptive information.

The CCS facilitates understanding of classroom practices by serving as a valid and reliable tool for documenting classroom instructional practices and teacher and student behaviors and interactions. The CCS allows the observers to determine the nature and extent of appropriate and differentiated instruction provided for students. Based on the data obtained with the CCS, the researchers can determine what instructional and curriculum adjustments need to be made in order to ensure the provision of effective instruction for all students.

Although the CCS has a number of positive features, it also has its limitations. One of the limitations of the CCS is that the middle point on the Likert scale (3) is quite broad, ranging from 20% to 69%. This range limits the amount of variance for the ratings, thus perhaps making classrooms seem more static and similar than is actually the case. Conversely, the benefit of this range is the likelihood of achieving high levels of inter-rater reliability.

Summary of Findings from the Studies Using the CCS and Their Implications

A commonality across the six studies, aside from the use of the CCS, is the interest in students with special needs and the extent to which instruction is differentiated and individualized to meet their needs. These studies have considerable variations in settings, grade levels, and types of disability. In spite of these variances, the finding was remarkably similar: Students with special needs did not receive much differentiated instruction.

McIntosh and colleagues (1993) revealed that general education classroom teachers treated students with LD much like other students without disabilities. This may suggest that students with LD were accepted by the teacher and were treated fairly and impartially. This also means, however, that students with LD did not receive differentiated instruction to meet their needs. Students with LD engaged in the same activities and used the same materials as the students without disabilities, and few adaptations were provided. This striking finding was replicated in subsequent studies. Schumm and colleagues (2000) observed lack of differentiated instruction particularly in word analysis instruction in general education reading classrooms. Similarly, students with LLD in bilingual classrooms received undifferentiated instruction (Fletcher et al., 1999). Furthermore, little differentiated instruction and materials were provided in resource reading classes (Levy & Vaughn, 2002; Moody et al., 2000; Vaughn et al., 1998).

Across the studies, teachers relied on whole-group instruction or independent activities during reading instruction (Fletcher et al., 1999; Levy & Vaughn, 2002; Moody et al., 2000; Schumm et al., 2000; Vaughn et al., 1998). Based on the accumulated body of research, however, we know that when students with disabilities are working in pairs and small groups during reading instruction, they improve their reading performance to a greater extent than in whole groups or independent activities (Elbaum, Vaughn, Hughes, & Moody, 1999, 2000; Mathes & Fuchs, 1994; Simmons, Fuchs, Fuchs, Hodge, & Mathes, 1994).

Furthermore, special education teachers in resource rooms seldom applied research-based reading practices (e.g., word recognition, reading comprehension instruction) (Levy & Vaughn, 2002; Moody et al., 2000; Vaughn et al., 1998). Even when there was an incidence of research-based reading practices, the teacher did not provide explicit

Table 4.3. Summary of observational studies using the Classroom Climate Scale (CCS) as a primary measure

Study	Participants	Purpose	Key findings
McIntosh, Vaughn, Schumm, Haager, & Lee (1993)	60 general education teachers in kindergarten through twelfth grade	To compare instruction of general education teachers for mainstreamed students with learning disabilities (LD) with students without LD	Teachers primarily provided whole-group instruction. Teachers provided few adaptations. Students with LD interacted with the teacher, other students, and activities at much lower rates than did other students.
Vaughn, Moody, & Schumm (1998)	14 elementary special education teachers in the resource room for students with LD	To examine reading instruction and grouping practices for students with LD. Teachers primarily provided whole-group instruction.	Little differentiated instruction or materials were provided. Teachers identified the whole language approach as their primary approach, and little instruction on word recognition and comprehension was provided.
Fletcher, Bos, & Johnson (1999)	Two novice bilingual teachers in third grade	To examine how bilingual education teachers accommodate their students with language and learning disabilities (LLD) during language arts and to examine students with LLD as well as a high-achieving, an average-achieving, and a low-achieving student	Teachers primarily used whole-class instruction. Teachers most frequently used undifferentiated instruction.
Moody, Vaughn, Hughes, & Fischer (2000; follow-up study to Vaughn et al. [1998])	Six elementary special education teachers in a resource room for students with LD	To examine the reading instruction, grouping practices, and outcomes for students with LD in resource room settings	Whole-group instruction was the dominant grouping practice. Half of the teachers provided differentiated instruction and materials to match the learning needs of students with LD. Little reading comprehension instruction was provided.
Schumm, Moody, & Vaughn (2000)	29 general education teachers in third grade	To examine the impact of the prevailing grouping practice on academic progress, social progress, and attitudes about reading of students	Teachers primarily provided whole-group instruction. Limited differentiated instruction and materials were provided.
Levy & Vaughn (2002)	Six elementary special educators or teachers for students with emotional/behavioral disorders (EBD)	To examine reading instruction and classroom management practices for students with EBD in the resource room	Independent activities and whole-group instruction were dominant. Use of research-based practices for reading instruction varied by teachers. More attention was placed on behavior than academics.

instruction in application of the reading practices (e.g., word analysis). However, there is substantial evidence to support the importance of providing struggling readers with explicit instruction during reading instruction (National Reading Panel, 2000).

In summary, the current status of special education and general education shows that appropriate education has not been provided for students with disabilities (see Table 4.3). Furthermore, students with disabilities did not benefit from scientific research findings on effective reading practices for struggling readers. The undifferentiated instruction and limited application of research-based reading practices for students with disabilities in both general and special education appeared to be related to teachers' lack of knowledge and skills necessary to provide appropriate adaptations for students with disabilities (Levy & Vaughn, 2002; Schumm & Vaughn, 1995; Vaughn et al., 1998). As many as 70% of general education teachers reported that they did not have sufficient training to adequately equip themselves to teach students with disabilities (Scruggs & Mastropieri, 1996). Similarly, special education teachers were also starving for experiences that prepare them to use research-based reading practices that yield effective outcomes for struggling readers (Levy & Vaughn, 2002; Vaughn et al., 1998).

Thus, the development and provision of professional development training to teachers (both general and special education teachers) is an important task. Luckily, the field has research-based evidence for effective reading practices for struggling readers (National Reading Panel, 2000; Snow, Burns, & Griffin, 1998). To provide appropriate instruction for students with disabilities, general and special education teachers must receive professional development training that delivers knowledge of the effective reading practices and ultimately facilitates effective reading instruction in their classrooms.

REFERENCES

Bailey, G.D. (1984). An evaluator's guide to diagnosing and analyzing teaching styles. *NAASP Bulletin, 68,* 19–25.

Baker, J.M., & Zigmond, N. (1990). Are regular education classes equipped to accommodate students with learning disabilities? *Exceptional Children, 56,* 515–526.

Bryan, T.S., & Bryan, J.H. (1978). Social interactions of learning disabled children. *Learning Disability Quarterly, 1,* 33–37.

Bryant, R., Dean, M., Elrod, G.F., & Blackbourn, J.M. (1999). Rural general education teachers' opinions of adaptations for inclusive classrooms: A renewed call for dual licensure. *Rural Special Education Quarterly, 18*(1), 5–11.

Callaway, R. (1988, April). *A study of teacher's planning.* Paper presented at the annual meeting of the American Educational Research Association, New Orleans, LA.

Dorval, B., McKinney, J.D., & Feagans, L. (1982). Teacher interaction with learning disabled children and average achievers. *Journal of Pediatric Psychology, 7,* 317–330.

Elbaum, B.E., Vaughn, S., Hughes, M.T., & Moody, S.W. (1999). Grouping practices and reading outcomes for students with disabilities. *Exceptional Children, 65*(3), 399–415.

Elbaum, B.E., Vaughn, S., Hughes, M.T., & Moody, S.W. (2000). How effective are one-to-one tutoring programs in reading for elementary students at risk for reading failure? *Journal of Educational Psychology, 92*(4), 605–619.

Fletcher, T.V., Bos, C.S., & Johnson, L.M. (1999). Accommodating English language learners with language and learning disabilities in bilingual education classrooms. *Learning Disabilities Research & Practice, 14*(2), 80–91.

Fox, N.E., & Ysseldyke, J.E. (1997). Implementing inclusion at the middle school level: Lessons from a negative example. *Exceptional Children, 64*(1), 81–98.

Gartner, A., & Lipsky, D.K. (1987). Beyond special education: Toward a quality system for all students. *Harvard Educational Review, 57,* 367–395.

Individuals with Disabilities Education Act (IDEA) of 1990, PL 101-476, 20 U.S.C. §§ 1400 *et seq.*

Levy, S., & Vaughn, S. (2002). An observational study of reading instruction of teachers for students with emotional/behavioral disorders. *Behavior Disorder, 27*(3), 215–235.

Mathes, P.G., & Fuchs, L.S. (1994). The efficacy of peer tutoring in reading for students with mild disabilities: A best-evidence synthesis. *School Psychology Review, 23*(1), 59–80.

McIntosh, R., Vaughn, S., Schumm, J., Haager, D., & Lee, O. (1993). Observations of students with learning disabilities in general education classrooms. *Exceptional Children, 60*(3), 249–261.

Moody, S.W., Vaughn, S., Hughes, M.T., & Fischer, M. (2000). Reading instruction in the resource room: Set up for failure. *Exceptional Children, 66*(3), 305–316.

National Reading Panel. (2000). *Report of the National Reading Panel: Teaching children to read. An evidence-based assessment of the scientific research literature on reading and its implications for reading instruction* (NIH Pub. No. 00–4754). Bethesda, MD: National Institutes of Health.

Schumaker, J.B., Hazel, J.S., Sherman, J.A., & Sheldon, J. (1982). Social skills performances of learning disabled, non-learning disabled, and delinquent adolescents. *Learning Disability Quarterly, 5,* 388–397.

Schumm, J.S., Moody, S.W., & Vaughn, S.R. (2000). Grouping for reading instruction: Does one size fit all? *Journal of Learning Disabilities, 33*(5), 477–488.

Schumm, J.S., & Vaughn, S. (1991). Making adaptations for mainstreamed students: General classroom teachers' perspectives. *Remedial and Special Education, 12*(4), 18–27.

Schumm, J.S., & Vaughn, S. (1995). Getting ready for inclusion: Is the stage set? *Learning Disability Research & Practice, 10*(3), 169–179.

Scruggs, T.E., & Mastropieri, M.A. (1996). Teacher perceptions of mainstreaming/inclusion, 1958–1995: a research synthesis. *Exceptional Children, 63*(1), 59–75.

Simmons, D.C., Fuchs, D., Fuchs, L., Hodge, J.P., & Mathes, P.G. (1994). Importance of instructional complexity and role reciprocity to classwide peer tutoring. *Learning Disabilities Research Practice, 9*(4), 203–212.

Snow, C.E., Burns, M.S., & Griffin, P. (Eds.) (1998). *Preventing reading difficulties in young children.* Washington, DC: National Academy Press.

Vaughn, S., Moody, S., & Schumm, J.S. (1998). Broken promises: Reading instruction in the resource room. *Exceptional Children, 64*(2), 211–226.

Vaughn, S., & Schumm, J.S. (1994). Middle school teachers' planning for students with learning disabilities. *Remedial and Special Education, 15*(3), 152–161.

Classroom Climate Scale

1. Teacher identification number: _____   2. Date: _____

3. Observer: _____   4. Time of observation: _____

5. Number of minutes: _____   6. School: _____

7. Teacher's name: _____   8. Grade(s) taught: _____

9. Subjects taught: _____

10. Teacher information   *Gender* _____   *Ethnicity* _____

11. Total number of students: _____

12. Total number involved in language arts: _____

13. List primary exceptionalities of students involved in language arts:

_____

_____

14. Adults in the classroom and their roles: _____

_____

_____

This is the most recent version of the CCS, which was modified by the Texas Center for Reading and Language Arts in October, 2000. This instrument has been supported by the United States Department of Education, Grant Award H023E900014, Research on General Education Teacher Planning and Adaptation for Students with Handicaps, to the School of Education, University of Miami. Reproduction or use of this document other than for planning grant purposes is prohibited unless expressed permission is given by Sharon Vaughn or Jeanne Schumm, Investigators, P.O. Box 248065, Coral Gables, FL 33124.

Classroom Climate Scale *(continued)*

Directions: The Classroom Climate Scale (CCS) is designed to record in an objective manner a measure of teacher behavior, student behavior, and student–teacher interaction during class activities. The information on the CCS is collected through ratings and observer comments. The observer makes overall judgments for each item. The observer should be as objective as possible, making judgments on observed behavior without evaluation of the teacher's performance. In addition, the observer is encouraged to make comments and describe reactions in the space provided at the end of the observation form.

5 **Most of the time**   If the observed behavior occurs 95% of the time or more during the observation period

4 **Frequently**   If the observed behavior occurs 70% of the time but less than the highest rating

3 **Occasionally**   If the observed behavior occurs between 20% to 70% of the time during the observation period

2 **Seldom**   If the observed behavior occurs less than 20% of the time but more often than the rating of "Rarely"

1 **Rarely**   If the behavior is never observed or occurs so rarely that the behavior cannot be considered part of the observation

Does the teacher

15. Use whole-class activities?

16. Use group activities?

17. Use student pairing?

18. Use independent activities?

19. Use individualized assignments/activities?

20. Respond to the needs of students?

21. Monitor on-going student performance?

22. Appear fair and impartial?

23. Make negative comments, including sarcasm or personal ridicule?

24. Provide positive feedback?

25. Communicate expectations to students?

26. Successfully re-direct off-task behavior?

Classroom Climate Scale *(continued)*
Do students

27. Appear engaged in task-related behavior?

28. Ask the teacher for help?

29. Ask other students for help?

30. Interfere with the work/activity of other students?

31. Appear frustrated or confused?

32. Make comments of sarcasm or personal ridicule?

33. Interact with other students?

Classroom Climate

Answer these questions with yes or no.

34. Is the entire class working on the same activity/assignment?

35. Do all of the students follow the same sequence of activities?

36. Do all of the students use the same materials?

Notes:

Classroom Climate Scale *(continued)*
Classroom Climate *(continued)*

37. What types of adaptations does this teacher make for students in this classroom?

38. Describe the flow of transitions during the lesson observed (e.g., quick, quiet, loud, unorganized).

39. Comment on any behavior or activity that occurred during the observation that was not covered by the items of this observation but that affected the atmosphere of the classroom. Use examples, notes, and anecdotes.
    List any phonological, word analysis, phonics, spelling, or fluency instruction that you observed (e.g., a lesson, a workbook, one-to-one instruction).

40. List any comprehension instruction that you observed (e.g., strategy instruction, main idea, inference, vocabulary, writing in response to reading).

41. Reflect on what you have observed and make a brief summary statement. (If a particular behavior seemed to be associated with any given grouping pattern, please note that here.)

42. Describe the level of teacher expectations for students (low, medium, or high) and how challenging the work is for the students. Give evidence when possible.

43. Are rules posted in the classroom?

44. Is a level system described or written so that it can be viewed in the classroom?

Reminders: Classroom rules, level system, group/individual contingencies, positive reinforcement, response-cost, other punishment

Classroom Climate Scale *(continued)*
Performance Indicators for Teacher Behavior

15. Does the teacher use whole-class activities?

   - The entire class is involved with the same lecture/activity/assignment/ video/discussion/question-and-answer session.
   - Grouping can be double-coded; these do not have to be mutually exclusive.
   - Code only formal structures arranged by the teacher, not informal or incidental grouping.

16. Does the teacher use group activities?

   - The class is working in two or more groups, with three or more students in a group, for a given lecture/activity/assignment.
   - Although the seating arrangement of a classroom may be affected by group activities, this item relates to student interaction in a group, not the seating assignment.

   Note: A class that had been working in groups of two and were then instructed to reform into groups of four would be scored under both item 16 and item 17.

17. Does the teacher use student pairing?

   - The class is divided into groups of two students.
   - One child acts as a peer tutor to another student.
   - Most of the students are working in pairs.
   - Students are in groups of two to share notes, tutor, or work on an assignment/activity.

18. Does the teacher use independent activities?

   - Students are engaged individually on an activity/assignment like the rest of the students in the class. (Help-seeking behaviors may be observed between students, but they are not working in a group.)

19. Does the teacher use individualized assignments/activities? (Can occur simultaneously with independent work)

   - Students are not involved in pairing or group activities and are working individually on differentiated assignments.
   - Individual students are working on individual/differentiated assignments/activities.
   - The teacher works individually with a student for 5 minutes or longer.

Classroom Climate Scale *(continued)*

20. Does the teacher respond to the needs of students? (Alters instruction, not just answering questions [e.g. re-explains concept, finds student having trouble and works with him or her, provides prompts, requestions same student].)

    - Teacher alters assignment for student(s).
    - Teacher develops alternative assignments (e.g., drop or add steps in the assignment).
    - Teacher provides additional practice materials, teacher directed materials, slower or faster paced materials.
    - Teacher reteaches or re-explains new concepts in a different way (not just answering a question but reteaching).
    - During practice, incorrect items are redone with teacher supervision.
    - Teacher provides corrective feedback when necessary (e.g., re-explains, models correct process, provides cues). If students are performing an operation incorrectly, they should be told which parts are correct and which parts are incorrect. (This does not necessarily mean responding to student-initiated questions.)

21. Does the teacher monitor on-going student performance?

    - The teacher checks in with the students during an activity to be sure they are performing correctly.
    - The teacher asks students to demonstrate what they are doing.
    - The teacher has students repeat directions.
    - The teacher checks initial practice items for correctness and provides immediate feedback.
    - The teacher calls on students during class discussion.
    - The teacher assists students on performing assignments correctly.
    - The teacher asks students to raise hands (etc.) if they do or do not understand.
    - The teacher asks students to explain work.

22. Does the teacher appear fair and impartial?

    - Teacher interacts with students in a way that conveys acceptance.
    - Teacher treats all students the same.

23. Does the teacher make negative comments, including sarcasm or personal ridicule?

    - The teacher belittles student(s) in front of the class.
    - The teacher smirks or rolls eyes at class/student.
    - The teacher shows intolerance of a specific student's behavior.
    - The teacher makes sexist, racist, or ethnic remarks.
    - The teacher implies the class/student is not smart enough to complete the assignment.

Classroom Climate Scale *(continued)*

24. Does the teacher provide positive feedback? (Look for physical or verbal evidence.)

    - The teacher says "Well done," "Good," Nice job," That's right," or other similar remarks to students.
    - The teacher uses nonverbal gestures such as winks, smiles, or hand movements to indicate good work or behavior to a student or the class.
    - The teacher uses stars, stickers, or other tangibles to indicate good work or behavior to the class.
    - The teacher praises students publicly and gives reason for praise.
    - The teacher makes affirmative remarks to the whole class.
    - The teacher provides information to students about their progress toward meeting instructional objectives.

25. Does the teacher communicate expectations?

    - The teacher provides a clear and explicit indication of the goals and objectives of the assignment.
    - The teacher provides information about why an assignment is important.
    - The teacher provides step-by-step directions, telling students what task is to be done and how it is to be done.
    - The teacher provides clear and specific indications of expected student performance.

26. Do students appear engaged in task-related behavior?

    - The students work hard, spending little time waiting for help, getting organized, or talking about personal matters.
    - The students seek help from the teacher so that they can continue working on the assignment.
    - The students seek help from another student so that they can continue working on the assignment.
    - Students appear involved in an assignment, demonstration, model, or project.

27. Does the teacher redirect off-task behavior? (Make a note of opportunities, e.g., if one incident occurs and it is addressed, rate a 4 or 5.)

    - If students are off-task, the teacher stands or sits nearer to them.
    - If students are off-task, the teacher indicates to them what activity they should be engaged in.
    - If students are off-task, the the teacher provides individual assistance to them to refocus their attention.
    - The teacher restates objectives or instructions if students appear off-task.
    - Not applicable.

Classroom Climate Scale *(continued)*
Performance Indicators for Student Behavior

28. Do students ask the teacher for help?

  • Students raise hands or call out for assistance.
  • Students request assistance from the teacher.

29. Do students ask other students for help?

30. Do students interfere with the work/activities of other students?

  • Talk is okay if it is task-related and not disruptive.
  • Students talk to or interact with other students in ways that prevent the other students from attending to the teacher's planned activities.
  • Students engage in behaviors or activities that are disruptive or distracting to other students.

31. Do students appear frustrated or confused?

  • Students are frustrated about understanding the task or material.
  • Students are excessively erasing, crumpling paper, or redoing work.
  • Students are grimacing, frowning, or using body language that connotes frustration or confusion.
  • Students say things such as, "This is too hard" or "I don't get it."

32. Do students make comments of sarcasm or personal ridicule?

  • Students make negative comments about other students.
  • Student uses gestures or other body language that denotes negative judgments of others.
  • Students make negative comments about the teacher.

33. Do students interact with other students? (The focus is conversation or physical interaction between students: who is the conduit, the teacher or the student?)

  • Students appear to be talking about or working on a similar project or problem in a constructive manner with other students.
  • Students make eye contact and other gestures that denote striving toward a similar goal as other students.
  • Student shares materials or work on the same project with other students.

Classroom Climate Scale *(continued)*

Comments

Items 34–44 allow for the observer's comments including personal and subjective accounts. The observer may include major patterns or themes about the observation. Include those salient features of the observation that may not have been targeted in the instrument but may be important to the understanding of the overall observation.

5

The English-Language Learner Classroom Observation Instrument for Beginning Readers

DIANE HAAGER, RUSSELL GERSTEN, SCOTT BAKER, AND ANNE W. GRAVES

We now have a reasonably sound research base on critical components for building student literacy in the early grades. Syntheses of reading research conducted by the National Research Council (Snow, Burns, & Griffin, 1998) and the National Reading Panel (2000) provide ample, compelling evidence of the skills, experience, and knowledge that children need to become successful readers in an alphabetic writing system such as English. This research helps clarify how important it is for beginning readers to develop phonemic awareness, alphabetic understanding, and automaticity with the alphabetic code, as well as the foundations of reading comprehension and vocabulary. Yet, virtually all of this research has been conducted with native English-speaking students. There is a lack of ongoing, systematic research investigating the unique learning needs of English-language learners (ELLs) developing reading skills in a second language, which is predominantly English in the United States (Haager & Windmueller, 2001). The United States has experienced the largest wave of immigration in its history, and the academic achievement of ELLs has become a major national concern. Although nearly all states have indicated a strong desire to include ELLs in early reading initiatives created in response to federal legislation (e.g., the Reading Excellence Act of 1998

[PL 105-277], the Reading First Initiative [part of the No Child Left Behind Act of 2001] [PL 107-110]), they are uncertain as to how to proceed (Rhett, 2001).

Although limited, the empirical knowledge base regarding how to effectively teach ELLs to read in a second language was detailed in a report by the National Academy of Sciences (August & Hakuta, 1997) and in a research synthesis by Gersten and Baker (2000b). Knowledge is limited largely because research has focused not on understanding the role of *instructional variables* but rather on evaluating various policy initiatives that in many cases provide only scant evidence of actual classroom practices (August & Hakuta, 1997; Gersten & Baker, 2000a). For example, we have found no empirical studies including classroom observations of specific reading practices for ELLs.

We have consistently argued that principles of effective reading instruction are directly relevant for teaching reading to ELLs (Gersten & Baker, 2000a; Gersten & Jiménez, 1994; Haager & Windmueller, 2001), although significant modulation or adjustment of instruction may be required. One possible adjustment, for example, is that teachers would provide much greater linkage of vocabulary instruction with word analysis instruction for ELLs than for native speakers. Another example is giving additional attention to teaching phonemes and sounds that are prevalent in English but do not exist in a student's native language (be it Korean, Tagalog, Spanish, or other). ELLs may need many more opportunities to practice speaking and reading simple phrases and sentences in the second language than they would if they were native speakers. Though other more substantive adjustments might be needed by ELLs, basic effective instructional practices remain critically important to producing positive student outcomes.

CONCEPTUALIZATION OF THE CLASSROOM OBSERVATION INSTRUMENT

Two years ago, we began a project to explore our hypotheses regarding the critical importance of implementing sound instructional principles and modulation of instruction for ELLs in beginning reading instruction. We decided to focus on the key essential features of reading instruction because of the critical importance of reading in overall academic achievement and the widespread reading achievement difficulties in schools with a high percentage of ELLs. Given the huge gaps in the knowledge base about how to effectively teach ELLs, it made most sense to begin our investigation with systematic observations of beginning reading instruction. We were particularly interested in classrooms attempting to implement research-based principles of instruction and identified key instructional features of beginning reading instruction, including essential curricular features and sound instructional principles.

We worked with a large team of researchers in two states and focused our observations in southern California, an area with a high density of ELLs. California seemed an ideal state for this type of study, in part because the state's Reading and Language Arts Standards were clearly based on contemporary research regarding early reading and because it has the largest ELL population in the nation. We were interested in the key instructional features that would be most associated with growth in reading for this population and used in-depth observations to investigate this relationship. Thus, our goals for conducting observations were to capture both the nature and quality of instruction on key instructional elements. We also intended to explore features of English language development for ELLs that might be integrated into the reading and language arts curriculum.

Early on we had to decide whether the instrument would require low, moderate, or high inference on the part of the observer. We chose a moderate-inference instrument for several reasons. A low-inference instrument, such as those used in the classic studies of beginning reading (Anderson, Evertson, & Brophy, 1979; Foorman, Francis, Beeler, Winikates, & Fletcher, 1997; Stallings & Kaskowitz, 1974), seemed premature because we were still in the early, exploratory stages of identifying instructional variables related to reading outcomes for ELLs. In studies such as these, the coding systems are precisely calibrated and observers are trained to record information about predetermined incidents or types of classroom interactions and the reliability tends to be quite high. However, a precise measure of rates of select classroom interactions such as those used by Anderson et al. (1979) would presuppose the critical elements of effective instruction for ELLs and would also be prohibitive because of lengthy measurement development procedures and intensive training required for this kind of instrumentation. In addition, a low-inference instrument might preclude recording unexpected but important classroom events. Finally, recording rates of behaviors or interactions was not the most compelling research goal. Instead, we were interested in recording the nature and quality of instructional events.

A high-inference measurement system would involve open-ended, qualitative, naturalistic observations, such as we had used in our earlier work with ELL students (Gersten, 1999; Jiménez & Gersten, 1999). In these types of studies, the purpose is to investigate or describe in rich detail existing conditions or events. The observers record detailed descriptions of instructional events in a form such as field notes. Observers record interactions, events, and conditions as they occur naturally. Observers may have some direction as to what types of events to watch for, but generally they do not have a predetermined set of variables in mind and often operate without predetermined hypotheses. In this scenario, there is a certain amount of interpretation on the part of the observer because the classroom events are seen through the observer's eyes and are colored by the observer's past experiences and orientation (Vaughn & Haager, 1994). The advantage to this method is that it yields rich descriptions of complex classrooms. Though we felt that a certain amount of rich description would add to our study, merely conducting open-ended, qualitative field notes did not seem to suit our needs because we had a definite sense of measurable instructional variables that seemed critical to effective instruction, based on earlier research (e.g., Anderson et al., 1979; Foorman et al.,1997; Stallings & Kaskowitz, 1974) and the syntheses of contemporary research on beginning reading (National Reading Panel, 2000; Snow et al., 1998). Based on our own experiences as researchers (e.g., Gersten, 1999; Gersten & Jiménez, 1994: Haager & Windmueller, 2001), we also had some reasonable hunches about specific instructional techniques and modulations that would enhance the reading and language development of ELLs in the early grades.

Strengthening our choice of a moderate inference instrument was earlier research on first-grade reading that found that moderate-inference observational instruments demonstrated satisfactory correlations with reading growth and were far less costly to implement than low-inference instruments (Gersten, Carnine, & Williams, 1982; Gersten, Carnine, Zoref, & Cronin, 1986). A moderate-inference scale would allow the observer to make an informed judgment about the quality or nature of predetermined instructional events without the strict coding structure of a low-inference instrument. Key to using this type of scale would be using observers who had extensive classroom experience, who would understand the complexity and importance of various classroom events, and who could also be objective about what they observed. Finally, moderate-level instruments allow for the simultaneous collection of both quantitative ratings and more open-ended field notes on particularly interesting, perplexing, or evocative classroom observations, thus allowing us to gauge our observations using a predetermined set of variables while being open to capturing the nature of the classroom instruction. After settling on a moderate-inference instrument, we began the process of creating the classroom observation tool.

Sources for the Classroom Observation Instrument

Our goal was to create an instrument that would help us grasp the subtleties and complexities of effective instructional practices for ELLs learning to read. In developing an instrument for the classroom observations, we looked for guidance from various sources representing diverse perspectives on reading and content area instruction.

Four sources were used to generate items for the instrument: 1) studies of effective teaching in beginning reading (Anderson et al., 1979; Foorman, Francis, Shaywitz, Shaywitz, & Fletcher, 1997; Stallings & Kaskowitz, 1974), 2) observational studies of reading instruction for students with significant reading problems (Leinhardt, Zigmond, & Cooley, 1981; Stanovich & Jordan, 1998), 3) descriptive studies of effective instructional environments for ELLs (e.g., Tikunoff et al., 1991), and 4) the research base on components of an effective beginning reading program (e.g., National Reading Panel, 2000).

For items related to effective teaching practices, the instrument developed by Stanovich and Jordan (1998) was a significant starting point. This instrument reflected variables highlighted in many of the earlier observational studies of effective instruction. Stanovich and Jordan's instrument also incorporated important concepts from recommendations of principles of effective instruction discussed by Englert (1984). Englert's recommendations were among the earliest attempts to incorporate advances in comprehension strategies research into a classroom observational system. In addition, more than a decade of work in classroom observations conducted by Stallings (1975) and Anderson and colleagues (1979) was clearly represented in this instrument.

We reviewed the work of researchers focusing on effective instructional practices for teaching academic content to ELLs in the process of acquiring a second language. Tikunoff and colleagues (1991), for example, studied teaching practices in second-language acquisition programs to determine effective and exemplary instructional strategies for ELLs. Elements of their work became the foundation for the section of our observational instrument that addressed modulations and accommodations specific to ELLs. In particular, Tikunoff and colleagues identified an array of common instructional techniques for providing sheltered academic instruction in English (Echevarria, Vogt, & Short, 2000). In addition, we used data from descriptive studies (Baker & Gersten, 2001; Jiménez & Gersten, 1999; Ramírez, 1992) to formulate additional items.

For items related specifically to research-based reading instruction, we turned to syntheses of reading practice such as the National Reading Panel Report (2000) and the National Research Council (Snow et al., 1998). The California Reading and Language Arts Standards (California Department of Education, 1999) provided specific language for describing the early reading curriculum used in the California classrooms. We developed items that allowed us to indicate whether curriculum areas were observed in practice and to rate the quality of instruction.

The procedure used to integrate and collate these disparate sources into a classroom observational instrument was based on the professional work group model (Gersten & Baker, 2000b), involving a group of researchers and teacher educators with somewhat diverse perspectives. By combining the results of our literature search and our own research and professional knowledge of effective ELL instruction with the knowledge and feedback of professionals, we reasoned that we could tease out critical themes and problems in current practice. These themes would become the foundation for our observation instrument. In some cases, we reworked items from previously used scales (e.g., Stanovich & Jordan, 1998; Tikunoff et al., 1991). In other cases, we developed items based on important principles or themes that emerged from our discussions.

DESCRIPTION OF THE INSTRUMENT

The pilot version of the English-Language Learner Classroom Observation Instrument was composed of 45 items rated on a 1–4 Likert scale, with 4 being most effective and 1 being least effective. It is possible to think of the scale as a 7-point scale because observers were given leeway to rate half-points (e.g., a rater could give a 2.5, a score between 2 and 3, on an item). (Items that were not observed received no point value and were excluded in the overall scoring.) On the scale, a 4 indicated "Very effective," 3 represented "Moderately effective," 2 represented "Somewhat effective," and 1 indicated "Not effective." Future work on the scale might include developing descriptive indicators to further define the four levels for each item.

The pilot version included 45 items, several of which were deleted, collapsed, or revised following field-testing due to extremely low base rate (i.e., items that were not observed), low inter-relater reliability, and redundancy. In most cases, items that demonstrated low inter-relater reliability seemed to be poorly phrased and thus subject to interpretation; hence, they were removed from the instrument. Following field-testing and extensive consultation among observers, the instrument was reduced to 32 items. It appears in its current form in the appendix to this chapter. Table 5.1 lists items by cluster.

The ratings are complemented by qualitative notation of activities and responses observed during the period that relates to each item or section. To expand the scope of the data, observers continued to record low base-rate items on a separate sheet attached to the instrument. In addition, field notes regarding the classroom context were recorded, including a description of the reading program, the physical appearance of

Table 5.1. Categories and subcategories from the English-Language Learner Classroom Observation Instrument

Main category	Subcategory
Instructional practice	Models skills and strategies during lesson
	Makes relationships among concepts overt
	Emphasizes distinctive features of new concepts
	Provides prompts and cues
	Teaches difficult vocabulary
	Achieves high level of response accuracy
Interactive teaching	Secures and maintains student attention during lesson
	Gives feedback on academic performance
	Engages in ongoing monitoring of student understanding and performance
	Elicits responses from all students
Adaptations for individual differences	Modifies instruction for students as needed
	Provides extra instruction, practice, and review
	Asks questions to ensure comprehension
	Allots appropriate amount of time for literacy activities
	Makes transitions short and effective
English-language development	Adjusts own use of English to make concepts comprehensible
	Uses visuals or manipulatives to teach content
	Gives oral directions that are clear and appropriate for students' level of English-language development
	Structures opportunities for students to speak
	Selects and incorporates students' responses, ideas, examples, and experiences into lesson
	Provides explicit instruction in English
	Gives students time to respond
	Encourages students to give elaborate responses
	Uses gestures and facial expressions in teaching vocabulary and clarifying meaning of content
Vocabulary development	Teaches difficult vocabulary prior to and during lesson
	Provides systematic instruction to vocabulary development
	Engages students in meaningful interactions about text
Phonemic awareness and decoding	

the room, the role of the adults in the room, and the overall classroom climate.

FIELD-TESTING THE INSTRUMENT

The English-Language Learner Classroom Observation Instrument was field-tested in 1999 and 2000 in 20 California classrooms. Given that beginning reading is the focus of California's reading initiatives and recognizing the effect of the state's Proposition 227 (mandating English-only instruction) on beginning reading instruction in a second language, we focused our observation efforts on the most critical purveyors of beginning reading: first-grade teachers.

The first phase of field-testing consisted of informal, exploratory field-testing, and the second consisted of formal, large-scale field-testing. We began with three members of the research team using the pilot version informally to observe together in one or two classrooms. The researchers then met and discussed the instrument item by item to consider its wording and conceptualization. At this point, several items were reworded, eliminated, or collapsed with other items. Observers consulted with each other to come to agreement about what constituted each level of rating for individual items. Formal field-testing of the instrument was then conducted in seven elementary schools in southern California. Fifty percent of classrooms were mixed, with some native English speakers and a majority of ELLs, while other classrooms consisted solely of ELLs. Although 95% of the classrooms had Spanish-speaking ELLs, 30% of the classrooms also included other ELLs (e.g., students speaking Vietnamese, Somali, Cambodian). Each classroom selected for observation was made up of at least 75% ELLs.

The sample of students for the field-testing consisted of students in 20 classrooms in four urban school districts. Students were assessed with reading instruments, and after removing incomplete data sets due to student attrition or mobility, we had a total of 281 students in the sample. Of these, 159 spoke Spanish as a primary language. Eight other languages were represented: Somali (n = 14), Cantonese dialect (n = 14), Cambodian (n = 12), Vietnamese (n = 12), Hmong (n = 11), Tagalog (n = 3), Lao (n = 2), and Sudanese (n = 1). In the full sample of 281 students, 47 were native English speakers. (Primary-language data were not available for six students.)

Reading outcomes were assessed to assist in establishing criterion-related validity of the observation instrument. We expected that reading outcomes would be higher in classrooms that were rated higher in terms of instructional effectiveness. Students were assessed using the Dynamic Indicators of Basic Early Literacy Skills (DIBELS; Kaminsky & Good, 1996; see also Chapter 8 in this volume), a series of 1-minute reading tasks representing phonemic awareness, alphabetic understanding, and oral reading fluency. An additional reading instrument was adapted from the Reading Results: K–3 Assessment, Reading Comprehension Assessment (California Reading and Literature Project, 1999).

Classrooms were observed during the entire instructional period for reading/language arts. If teachers scheduled an additional time during the day for English language development, the observation was extended to include this time as well. California's reading standards mandate a minimum of 2.5 hours for reading/language arts instruction. Thus, observations ranged from 2.5 to 3 hours per session. Each classroom teacher was observed from two to four times throughout the school year. Observations occurred toward the middle of the school year.

One rating form was completed following at least two complete observation sessions. Additional days were scheduled if an observer felt additional time was required to gather a complete picture of a teacher's typical classroom instruction. In other words, the observer took field notes during a minimum of two visits and then completed the rating form based on the compiled evidence over multiple visits. To reduce the possibility of an interaction effect between the observer and the teacher, observers rotated through the various classrooms and consulted frequently to discuss the meaning of items and how to code different instructional events. Observation was conducted using a continuous time recording schedule.

Multiple observers participated in the piloting of the classroom observational instrument. The observers were six professionals in education (five professors and one doctoral student) who brought somewhat diverse perspectives and professional abilities to the table. Inter-rater reliability was established through joint observations and frequent conferencing following independent completion of rating scales. The median inter-observer agreement was 74%, with a range from 55% to 88%. For a moderate-inference rating system, this was an acceptable level of agreement.

Reliability and Validity of the English-Language Learner Classroom Observation Instrument

To establish reliability of the instrument, we developed six empirically derived subscales based on factor scores. These subscales are described in Table 5.2. The internal consistency was quite high. Cronbach's *alpha* for each subscale ranged from .80 to .95 with a median of .89. (Of course, coefficient *alpha* reliabilities of rating scales are often somewhat high, due in part to the possibility of a small halo effect.)

Criterion-related validity was established by correlating scores from each subscale with residualized growth scores in actual reading performance. The dependent measure for this analysis was a composite of pre- and post-testing of reading comprehension and oral reading fluency, adjusted for pretest differences in letter-naming fluency. Unfortunately, the pretest was given closer to mid-year than the beginning of the year (due to funding issues), and there may actually be an underestimate of growth. Table 5.2 presents the correlations of each subscale with the composite reading score. Here we see the strongest cor-

Table 5.2. Correlations between subscales of observation instrument and composite reading scores

Subscale	Correlation
Instructional practice	.62
Interactive teaching	.57
Adaptations for individual differences	.65
English-language development	.49
Vocabulary development	.51
Phonemic awareness and decoding	.63

relations for Scales 1, 2, and 6 (explicit teaching/art of teaching, instruction geared toward low performers, and phonemic awareness and decoding, respectively). However, the correlations between all of the scales and reading growth were quite strong. The small sample sizes and late pretesting preclude any inferences being drawn from the relatively small differences in Pearson correlations.

The English-Language Learner Classroom Observation Instrument was designed to examine beginning reading instruction in classrooms of students who are primarily ELLs learning to read in English. The scale comprises items representing the research base on effective teaching practices, English language development, and critical factors of beginning reading. The following sections describe two related studies of classrooms included in the field-testing of the instrument. These sections illustrate what we envision as typical usage of this instrument for research purposes.

USE OF THE INSTRUMENT TO RECORD READING
INSTRUCTION IN ENGLISH FOR SPANISH-SPEAKING STUDENTS

A subset of our sample included two schools in southern California with a high percentage of students who spoke Spanish as their primary language but were receiving first-grade instruction in English with minimal primary language support. In this section, we describe the nature and quality of beginning reading instruction in nine first-grade classrooms implementing English reading instruction for students with limited English-language skills who spoke Spanish as their primary language. We also examine student outcomes in each classroom.

The scale yields an overall teaching effectiveness score by averaging a teacher's ratings for the items, but it can be helpful to look at classroom instruction by categories. We used the six empirically derived cluster scores developed in the field-testing phase to examine instruction in the nine classrooms included here. Table 5.3 displays the cluster scores for each teacher. There was a range of ratings within each category of instructional performance on the 4-point Likert scale. There was also a range of ratings across individual teachers.

Our primary aim in this study was simply to document *what* we saw teachers doing in typical beginning reading instruction for Spanish-speaking ELLs in urban schools. A common scenario in urban schools is placing beginning reading instruction in the hands of relatively inexperienced and under-prepared teachers. Table 5.4 divides this teacher sample into two groups: those with less experience (fewer than 3 years) and those with more experience (more than 3 years). Coincidentally, all those in the less experienced category were also working with emergency-waiver status and were working toward earning a teaching credential. There is a distinct pattern of ratings across these two groups. With the exception of Mr. Vallez, teachers' ratings for all clusters in this group were lower than those of teachers in the more experienced group. This supports the notion that teacher preparation *and* experience are important factors in beginning reading.

It is interesting to examine the categories of instruction by cluster. Evidence supports the use of explicit teaching to develop beginning word recognition skills (e.g., National Reading Panel, 2000; Snow et al., 1998). This category was of particular interest to us as we examined what is currently occurring in first-grade classrooms for ELLs. In the explicit teaching/art of teaching cluster, a wide range of scores (1.75–3.92) emerged, with more experienced and prepared teachers providing more effective instruction. The qualitative field notes provide a richer description of how explicit teaching occurred in the classrooms with higher instructional ratings. Many of the observers' notations documented extensive prompting from these more effective teachers throughout instruction:

- "Prompted correct grammar/sentence structure while students wrote"
- "Reiterated to ensure understanding"
- "Rephrased questions and comments as needed"
- "Provided prompts for journal writing"
- "Prompted [regarding] word wall and finger space for handwriting"

Likewise, there were many instances of modeling during instruction, particularly during decoding and writing instruction:

- "Used a variety of words to model the /th/ sound"
- "Let student fix her own error but gave her a model"

Table 5.3. Cluster scores for nine teachers of Spanish-speaking first graders

School	Teacher	Instruction practice	Interactive teaching	Adaptations for individual differences	English-language development	Vocabulary development	Phonemic awareness and decoding
School A	Ms. Rodrigo	2.17	1.4	1.71	1.5	2.25	3.0
	Ms. Miller	3.0	2.6	2.43	1.0	2.5	3.33
	Ms. Moran	1.83	2.2	2.29	2.0	2.25	2.0
	Ms. Linan	2.33	2.0	2.5	0.5	2.0	2.67
	Ms. Gunther	1.75	2.1	1.0	2.5	1.5	2.33
School B	Ms. Coran	3.5	4.0	4.0	4.0	3.25	4.0
	Ms. Herrara	2.0	2.0	1.71	2.25	2.25	2.67
	Ms. Marlow	3.33	3.4	2.86	3.5	3.25	3.33
	Mr. Vallez	3.92	3.4	3.75	3.5	3.5	3.33

Table 5.4. Cluster scores for less and more experienced teachers of Spanish-speaking first graders

Level of experience	Teacher	Instructional practice	Interactive teaching	Adaptations for individual differences	English-language development	Vocabulary development	Phonemic awareness and decoding
Less experienced	Ms. Rodrigo	2.17	1.4	1.71	1.5	2.25	3.0
	Ms. Moran	1.83	2.2	2.29	2.0	2.25	2.0
	Ms. Linan	2.33	2.0	2.5	0.5	2.0	2.67
	Ms. Gunther	1.75	2.1	1.0	2.5	1.5	2.33
	Mr. Valez	3.92	3.4	3.75	3.5	3.5	3.33
More experienced	Ms. Coran	3.5	4.0	4.0	4.0	3.25	4.0
	Ms. Herrara	2.0	2.0	1.71	2.25	2.25	2.67
	Ms. Marlow	3.33	3.4	2.86	3.5	3.25	3.33
	Ms. Miller	3.0	2.6	2.43	1.0	2.5	3.33

- "Showed personal journal to prepare students for writing"
- "Used overhead and board for modeling writing"
- "Modeled blending and dictation activities"

Additional comments documented extensive feedback and clear, explicit explanations of concepts or tasks.

In the category of instruction geared toward low performers, less distinction was evident between the more and less experienced teachers. The qualitative notes provided a description of trends across teachers. First, there were many instances of teachers providing individualized assistance during independent practice or small-group activities such as centers. More effective teachers were observed correcting students' errors and giving specific feedback about tasks. Teachers commented aloud about individual students' performance during practice times. Some teachers asked successful students to help someone who was struggling. Most comments were positive, but in a few cases, teachers missed opportunities for students to respond:

- "Though she was constantly monitoring, I think a few students went through the lesson without direct feedback or opportunity to respond"
- "Not all students had [an] opportunity to respond"
- "[One student] who had behavior problems throughout was never called on, only prompted for behavior"

This area of teaching practice may be one that does not develop naturally for teachers but comes with experience and conscious effort. It is important to note that this cluster is one that correlated highly with reading growth in our larger sample (.65, see Table 5.2).

The next cluster, sheltered English techniques, also yielded a wide range of scores (0.5–4.0), and experience did not necessarily distinguish more skilled teachers. Here, the determining factor may be the reading program used. The teachers in School A generally had lower scores on this cluster than those in School B (see Table 5.3). School A was using a scripted, code-emphasis reading program for the first year. Teachers had received training in how to use the program but were not yet at ease with its structure and expanse. Furthermore, the district had mandated full use of the program, demanding that teachers go through each lesson completely, never varying from the script or the format. This districtwide mandate included extensive monitoring of teachers for compliance. Teachers did not feel free to modulate instruction for English-language support, despite the fact that their principal had given them license to do so. Perhaps the cognitive demand of learning a new program weighed heavily on the teachers, and they simply did not think of modifying instruction for ELLs. Whatever the reason, these teachers seldom clarified vocabulary, used gestures, or provided explicit instruction in English during reading instruction. Though these teachers were supposed to provide a half-hour of English language development during another part of the day, most were using this designated time to catch up on reading activities that did not fit into their earlier 3-hour reading block.

The teachers in School B used an eclectic mix of reading approaches. Most used techniques from a whole language approach, such as extensive journal writing, reading aloud to students, whole-group word study instruction, and center-based activities. There was a great deal of variability in the activities observed across classrooms in School B. One common aspect of instruction across the first-grade classrooms was that they supplemented their self-designed reading programs with a structured phonics program characterized by its use of animals associated with the letter sounds. Each letter had an accompanying animal name, physical gesture, and song to reinforce its sound and shape. Much of the gesturing and prompting (coded under the sheltered English techniques category) observed in these classrooms came from the phonics program. Encouraging elaboration in English was observed mostly during journal writing. To see exemplary sheltered English techniques, we need only to look at Ms. Coran, who received a 4.0 rating on this cluster. Some of the observer comments included

- "Gets down to level of student when working one-to-one, lots of gesturing during phonics instruction"
- "Used many pictorial representations as prompts"
- "Encouraged more elaborate responses during journal writing"
- "Encouraged more complex responses for a paragraph"
- "Encouraged students to include a number of descriptors in their writing"

Interactive teaching is a cluster that also yielded a range of teacher ratings (1.4–4.0). Again, Ms. Coran in School B provides a model for instructing ELLs. Generally, we saw less interactive instruction in School A, where the reading program was very structured and the bulk of the instructional block was devoted to teacher-directed, whole-class instruction. Interactions between teachers and students in School A were primarily of a choral response type, except during independent practice time. Student–student interactions about reading activities were limited in these classrooms. No teacher in School A received higher than a 2.6 in this category. Three teachers in School B received ratings of 3.0 or higher. Regarding securing students' attention, comments from these classrooms included

- "Went over to two students not paying attention and quietly reviewed the instructions"
- "Looked for students sitting quietly to answer a question"
- "Moved student closer to her to help him focus"
- "Teacher is very engaging. Lots of interacting and rewards for engagement"

However, in one classroom, students had difficulty focusing with an unstructured free reading time: "Many kids were off-task during SSR" (sustained silent reading). Regarding incorporating students' responses into literacy activities and encouraging more elaborate oral or written responses, comments from the higher rated classrooms included

- "Students offered sentences with spelling words incorporated"
- "Students select topic to write about"
- "Uses students' examples during opening activity"

Given our predominantly ELL sample, we were very interested in what kinds of teaching practices we would observe regarding the vocabulary development cluster. Our expectation going into this study was that these students receiving instruction in English would have difficulty with decoding and other activities in which they encountered unfamiliar vocabulary words. We were very interested in what teachers did to make the text comprehensible to students. In this category, we again had a wide range of scores (1.5–3.5). There were no apparent differences according to reading program, but the more experienced teachers fared better than less experienced teachers. Most teachers introduced new vocabulary words prior to encountering words in the text. Many teachers reviewed words discussed the previous day and asked students to use new words in sentences. Specific observations in this category from classrooms with ratings of 3.0 or higher included

- "Introduced and defined spelling words"
- "Discussed words with students throughout the lesson"
- "Students individually created sentences for using their spelling words. They would say their sentence (orally), then write a portion of it on the board for everyone to copy"
- "Reviewed vocabulary from a fairy tale presented the day before. Discussed definition of words presented during lesson."
- "Students gave vocabulary definitions in both English and Spanish"

The last category, phonemic awareness and phonics, yielded scores ranging from 2.0 to 4.0. It is apparent that the structured reading program of School A and the structured supplemental phonics program of School B influenced the extent to which teachers included such activities in their daily routine. Within this category, both the quantity and the quality of the specific task or skill observed were rated. The more experienced teachers tended to receive higher ratings on quality of instruction in this area, but the structure of the reading programs certainly helped some of the less experienced teachers. Activities ranged from modeling the blending process to using computer programs to supplement and reinforce concepts. Most teachers went through blending as a whole-group activity, then reinforced it during independent practice time. Teachers in both schools seemed to struggle a bit with having an established routine for teaching decoding. Comments for two classrooms noted that the teacher seemed unprepared, causing a lag in instructional pace. Inconsistencies were noted from day to day over the observation period, raising questions about how systematic the instruction was. One teacher was attempting to teach decoding through onsets and rimes but did not explicitly explain the task. One of the whole language–oriented teachers taught decoding on an individual basis as she met with students during their journal writing.

In the larger study of 20 classrooms, we examined gains in reading achievement in relation to the observed practices, as described previously in this chapter. We did not do a similar analysis with this subset of classrooms because the primary aim here was to provide descriptive information about the classrooms. However, it is helpful to peruse student reading performance in these nine classrooms relative to the expected levels of reading performance. The DIBELS assessment system provides clear first-grade benchmarks for examining student progress, but these benchmarks were developed with native English speakers in mind. We would not expect novices in the English language to meet specific benchmarks at the same time as native speakers. Though we cannot interpret the DIBELS benchmarks with ELLs as we would with native English speakers (Haager & Windmueller, 2001), it is instructionally relevant to know where these ELLs who presumably received typical instruction in urban schools stand in relation to specified benchmarks. The benchmarks are noted in Table 5.5, along with the means and standard deviations for these nine classrooms. We see wide variability both across classrooms and even within each classroom at the midpoint and end of the year, making it difficult to compare the impact of various teaching practices on reading growth in this small sample.

In this sample of classrooms, we observed a range of teaching patterns and were somewhat concerned about the general lack of inten-

Table 5.5. Benchmark scores for nine classrooms of Spanish-speaking first graders (Dynamic Indicators of Basic Early Literacy Skills [DIBELS], Kaminski & Good, 1996)

School	Teacher	Phoneme segmentation fluency (Mid-year)		Nonsense word fluency (Mid-year)		Oral reading fluency (End of year)	
		Mean	Standard deviation	Mean	Standard deviation	Mean	Standard deviation
School A	Ms. Rodrigo	24.1	19.2	30.0	10.5	27.4	21.0
	Ms. Miller	27.2	18.3	31.0	20.7	33.1	20.6
	Ms. Moran	16.6	15.5	18.5	14.7	17.6	17.7
	Ms. Linan	26.0	23.8	18.8	12.4	20.0	16.8
	Ms. Gunther	21.4	14.2	16.7	11.3	15.9	15.4
School B	Ms. Coran	17.2	12.8	27.8	17.3	33.3	29.4
	Ms. Herrara	17.0	15.9	21.8	15.0	30.0	21.1
	Ms. Marlow	20.2	15.9	25.4	13.6	17.9	13.4
	Mr. Vallez	30.6	19.1	23.2	13.8	17.5	10.7

Note: For phoneme segmentation fluency (the number of segmentations of words in 1 minute), the benchmark is 35 by the beginning of first grade. For nonsense word fluency (the number of sounds read correctly in 1 minute), the benchmark is 50 by mid–first grade. For oral reading fluency (the number of words read correctly in 1 minute), the benchmark is 40 by the end of first grade.

sity or explicitness of beginning reading instruction. Furthermore, we were disappointed that there was not a high level of language support in these classrooms of primarily ELLs struggling to read in English, as was evident in the sheltered English techniques observations. We believe that if these teachers had access to texts and teacher's guides to assist them in providing systematic English language development, we might have seen a different picture.

USE OF THE INSTRUMENT TO RECORD READING INSTRUCTION IN ENGLISH IN MULTIPLE LANGUAGE CLASSROOMS

In a different subset of the southern California schools, the English-Language Learner Classroom Observation Instrument was used to examine teaching practices in nine multiple-language, first-grade classrooms in the 1999–2000 school year (Graves, 2003; Haager, Gersten, Baker, & Graves, 2001). Of the 20 or so students in each classroom, students might speak Spanish, Somali, Cambodian, Lao, Vietnamese, Tagalog, Hmong, Chinese, French, or some other language. In most classrooms, five to ten students spoke any one of theses languages. For example, in one room, there were five Spanish speakers, seven Somali speakers, three Cambodian speakers, three Vietnamese speakers, and two native English speakers. Teachers in these classrooms were compelled to teach

Table 5.6. Information about multiple-language classrooms

Teacher	School	Number of years of teaching experience	Teacher speaks language other than English	Languages spoken by students*	Percentage of the class that are English language learners
Ms. Mora	A	21	No	H, L, SP, V	80%
Ms. Darrow	A	25	No	H, C, SP, V	90%
Ms. Caron	A	10	No	H, L, SO, SP, SU, T, V	88%
Mr. Guy	B	2	No	C, SO, SP, V	100%
Ms. Brendan	B	3	Vietnamese	C, SO, SP, V	100%
Ms. Carter	B	3	Korean	C, CH, SP, V	100%
Mr. Jones	C	8	Spanish	Dialects of SP	100%
Ms. Carr	C	9	No	C, SO, SP, V	100%
Ms. Abbot	C	16	No	C, SO, SP, V	100%

*C = Cambodian, CH = Chinese, H = Hmong, L = Lao, SO = Somali, SP = Spanish, SU = Sudan, T = Tagalog, V = Vietnamese

in English because it provided common ground for all students. Native language instruction was a logistical impossibility. Table 5.6 provides information about these classrooms.

With this sample, we first examined the extent to which more students were at risk for reading difficulty in classrooms with low scores on the English-Language Learner Classroom Observation Instrument than in classrooms with moderate to high scores. Second, we wanted to describe specific differences in teaching practices in low- and high-scoring multiple-language classrooms.

Teacher Ratings and Student Outcomes

Teachers were observed according to the procedures described in this chapter. An overall teaching effectiveness score was computed as an average of each teacher's rating on all items. In each of the classrooms, student oral reading fluency was measured using DIBELS subtests (Kaminski & Good, 1996). An easy to understand, readily visible correlation can be determined by simply listing the teacher rating scores and beside those scores, listing the number of students who were reading fewer than 40 words per minute at the end of first grade (see Table 5.7). Kaminsky and Good (2000) have demonstrated that students reading fewer than 40 words per minute can be categorized as at risk for reading failure in later grades.

Of the 115 students in this study, students reading fewer than 40 words per minute by the end of first grade were tallied by classroom and compared against the overall observation rating for each teacher (see Table 5.7). The pattern across teacher and student data is quite striking and supports the notion of the observation instrument as a useful instrument for indicating student outcomes. Teachers with ratings of 3 or higher had 20%–40% of their students reading fewer than 40 words per minute by the end of first grade, and teachers with 2 or lower had 73%–85% of students reading fewer than 40 words per minute.

A second, more dramatic at-risk category emerged after closer examination of the student data. Students reading 18 or fewer words per minute at the end of first grade were obviously well below the benchmark of 40. When the data were examined from that perspective, we saw a pattern linking instruction with student outcomes. Of the two teachers rated 3 or higher on the English-Language Learner Classroom Observation Instrument, one teacher had only two students (in a class of 15) and the other had no students (in a class of 10) reading 18 words or fewer per minute at the end of first grade. In contrast, the four teachers rated 2 or lower on the English-Language Learner Classroom Observation Instrument had 60%–88% of their students reading 18 words

Table 5.7. Observation scale ratings and number of students at risk

Teacher	Rating	0–18 words per minute (WPM)	18–40 WPM	Fewer than 40 WPM/Total in class (Percentage of students reading fewer than 40 WPM)
Ms. Mora	3.75	2	1	3/15 = 20%
Ms. Darrow	3.5	0	4	4/10 = 40%
Ms. Caron	2.5	2	4	6/15 = 40%
Ms. Carter	2.5	5	2	7/14 = 50%
Ms. Brendan	2.5	2	8	10/18 = 55%
Mr. Guy	2.0	9	2	11/15 = 73%
Mr. Jones	2.0	8	0	8/10 = 80%
Ms. Carter	2.0	5	1	6/7 = 85%
Ms. Abbot	1.0	9	0	9/11 = 81%

or fewer per minute at the end of first grade. Though only six teachers were included in this analysis, a remarkable correspondence is evident between teacher ratings on the English-Language Learner Classroom Observation Instrument and students' oral reading fluency outcomes.

Teacher Descriptions

The observation instrument allowed us to examine classroom instruction qualitatively, thus enriching the information obtained with a rating scale. Here are teaching snapshots of the two highest rated teachers, Ms. Mora and Ms. Darrow, who had average scores above 3. In the area of explicit teaching/art of teaching, both teachers modeled skills and strategies, emphasized distinctive features of new concepts, provided prompts, and scheduled literacy activities at an appropriate length. For example, in one reading lesson, Ms. Mora said, "Watch me change this word from *bead* to *bend*. I erased the *a* and wrote an *n*. Now what word do I have? Who can show me *bead*? Who can show me *bend*?" Both Ms. Mora and Ms. Darrow rarely scheduled activities lasting longer than 20 minutes, providing appropriate time for literacy activities.

 Ms. Mora used a structured reading instruction program with particular emphasis on phonological awareness and phonics. She tended to be quite systematic in her approach to teaching language arts, including her consistent assessment and additional instruction for low performers. Her morning began every day with singing, an opening math activity,

and then a structured reading lesson including phonemic awareness and phonics segments. Students listened to words and told the sounds they heard. Demonstrating very high levels of engagement and focusing on maintaining student attention, Ms. Mora asked students to perform tasks such as changing words by retaining the ending and giving the word a different beginning (e.g., she might say, "Pan: Change the /p/ sound to /t/ and now what word do we have?"). Ms. Mora tended to draw pictures of words and give examples of words from the reading lesson. In this way, she demonstrated the cluster sheltered English techniques.

The rest of her typical reading instruction time was spent with individuals and small groups of students. Students engaged in 15 minutes of writing practice and 15 minutes of independent reading time. In these small groups, they wrote and read words from the whole class lesson. Ms. Mora often taught a small homogeneous group of students, guiding their practice with phonemic awareness and phonics at their own level, gearing specialized instruction toward low performers. Other days, she called on students one by one to read independently in decodable text, keeping a record of their speed and accuracy when reading aloud during this time. Spelling words for the weekly tests were consistent with words students were learning to read in the reading program. Students practiced writing their spelling words daily and were asked to generate sentences using the words. Ms. Mora typically read an interesting story to the children, asking them questions about the story as they proceeded through it. She might then ask them to illustrate their favorite part in the story or write about it in their journals.

Both teachers demonstrated skill in maximizing time on task, amount of work produced, time spent reading, appropriate length for teaching segments, specialized small-group instruction, structured daily routines, consistent homework assignments, daily writing tasks, assessment of reading and writing progress, and English language development. Both teachers provided extensive feedback by correcting written work on a daily basis or asking students to self-correct. Both had amassed multiple sets of decodable texts and used them regularly to enhance student reading. Students had their own boxes of books at their desks, including books of different genres and reading levels, and at least 50% of the books in each box were at the student's own level of decoding.

 Ms. Darrow tended to teach reading from an eclectic mix of reading materials. She used leveled readers and assigned students to homogeneous small groups that met on a regular basis and was diligent about assessing the reading and writing progress of all students. The scope and sequence she described when interviewed was part of an oral tradition that she could talk about, but she could not provide an exact written source. Because she did not use a specific reading series, her activities and segments of instruction were often unique and pulled from various sources. She was observed delivering instruction in critical domains for reading instruction such as phonological awareness, phonics, concepts about print, spelling, writing, comprehension, and critical thinking. She was particularly skilled at modeling comprehension and critical thinking skills.

A typical morning in Ms. Darrow's room began with reading aloud a story or factual text on a relevant topic. She methodically explained new vocabulary, questioned students, and explained content. Her highest scores were on the clusters interactive teaching and vocabulary development. During a story she might say, "What do you think Sam was thinking about here? How do you know?" As students answered, always raising their hands and waiting to be called on, Ms. Darrow would say, "Yes, that makes sense. How do you know he was sad?" She would wait for a student to respond and then continue, "Would you be sad if this happened to you?" The observers consistently recognized Ms. Darrow's ability to select and incorporate students' responses, ideas, and experiences into lessons and her tremendous expertise in engaging students in meaningful interactions about text. Each day, students wrote in journals with very structured tasks such as, "Write a letter to Sam's friend in the story we read and tell him why he should listen to Sam." Ms. Darrow asked students to read their journal entries, and she often coached students on developing their thoughts or correcting spelling and grammatical errors. While students were writing, Ms. Darrow took rotations of small homogeneous groups using leveled books. She modeled word attack for those who were reading at lower levels. Ms. Darrow worked with each small group each day. In addition, she often had students take out homework, and she went over the homework item by item, requiring students to correct anything that was misspelled or answered incorrectly.

Thematic teaching was a mainstay in Ms. Darrow's classroom, with written work and readings focusing on holidays and other themes. This was the basis for developing students' English language use. During one observation, the theme was apples. She read a book with beautiful pictures about an apple tree and the phases of the tree throughout the year. Note the teacher–student dialogue below and how it incorporates sheltered English techniques. Ms. Darrow read about the buds turning to flowers in the summer and asked students what they thought would happen next.

Student: "Apples will grow."

Ms. Darrow: "In what season do you think the apples can be picked?" (She reached into the air and pretended to pick an apple from a branch and repeated "picked" slowly while demonstrating the action.)

Student: "Hatween."

Ms. Darrow: "Yes, near Halloween. Does anyone know what season that will be? Let's see. Winter time, we saw the tree bare with no buds or flowers." (She pointed to the picture of the bare tree and pretended to shiver.) "Spring time, we saw the tree with buds, and summer time, we saw the tree with flowers turning into little green apples." (While saying this, her voice gained melodic tones.) "The birds are chirping and everything is fresh and new."

Another student: "In the auusum, I think we will have apples."

Ms. Darrow: "Yes, Araceli. AUTUMN, and what color do you think the apples will be when they are ready to be picked?"

These two snapshots of expert teaching exemplify the clusters of our observation instrument. Though the two teachers have different approaches, they both wove English-language development into their reading lessons fluidly yet explicitly. Both provided ample opportunities for students to respond and discuss the vocabulary and concepts included in the lessons. One teacher provided explicit phonemic awareness and phonics instruction via a structured, scripted reading program designed to move systematically and sequentially through the alphabetic skills. The other taught these skills in the context of thematic reading and extensive student writing activities during whole-group, small-group, and individual tutorial sessions. However, both provided the essential explicit instruction that is critical to student growth at this early stage of reading development. Additional similarities among these two skilled teachers were their years of teaching experience and their tremendous dedication and confidence in their own individual approaches to teaching.

CONCLUSION

The English-Language Learner Classroom Observation Instrument is a flexible tool designed to examine early reading instruction. It may be used to conduct observations across multiple classrooms or to conduct a more in-depth examination with a very small sample. With the ability to record both rating scores and qualitative field notes, it yields systematic information about instructional practice while offering an opportunity for collecting rich qualitative data. Our interest was primarily to document the nature of beginning reading instruction for ELLs, and to that end, one section of the instrument is devoted specifically to English language development and the extent to which it is integrated into reading instruction. It was designed to be used in a research context and may not be very useful as an evaluative instrument.

This observation instrument correlated reasonably well with reading growth in our sample of classrooms; however, we believe more work should be done to fully establish criterion-related validity. Few observation instruments exist that are specifically designed to examine beginning reading instruction, and this instrument was built on factors identified by recent research as critical in beginning reading instruction. Though it was designed for use with ELLs, we believe that with adaptation, such as deleting the sheltered English techniques items, it could be applied to other populations as well.

In summary, we used this instrument to examine instructional factors that are associated with reading growth for beginning readers who are also ELLs. Findings from both quantitative and qualitative analyses highlighted the importance of providing elements of effective classroom instruction (e.g., modeling, giving feedback) and engaging children in English language development activities. Teachers who were rated higher in terms of effectiveness of instruction clearly had greater gains in the reading scores of their students. From our exploratory observations, it appears that teachers who are highly effective may be successful in achieving reading gains regardless of the type of reading program. More specifically, successful teachers who were not using a structured systematic reading program had built into their teaching routine opportunities for systematic work with sounds and decoding, language development, and individual or small-group intensive instruction in basic skills. Factors such as teachers' experience, overall teaching skill, and sensitivity to English language development played a significant role in achieving reading success. Future studies should examine these factors in more depth.

REFERENCES

Anderson, L., Evertson, C., & Brophy, J. (1979). An experimental study of effective teaching in first-grade reading groups. *Elementary School Journal, 79,* 193–223.

August, D., & Hakuta, K. (1997). *Improving schooling for language-minority children.* Washington, DC: National Academy Press.

Baker, S., & Gersten, R. (2001, April). *Instruction and literacy development of English-language learners in English immersion programs: An observational study.* Paper presented at the annual conference of the American Educational Research Association, Seattle, WA.

California Department of Education. (1999). *English-language arts standards for California public schools: Kindergarten through grade twelve.* Sacramento: Author.

California Reading and Literature Project. (1999). *Reading results: K–3 assessment manual.* Sacramento: Author.

Echevarria, J., Vogt, M., & Short, D.J. (2000). *Making content comprehensible for English language learners: The SIOP model.* Needham Heights, MA: Allyn & Bacon.

Englert, C. (1984). Effective direct instruction practices in special education settings. *Remedial and Special Education, 5*(2), 38–47.

Foorman, B.R., Francis, D.J., Beeler, T., Winikates, D., & Fletcher, J. (1997). Early interventions for children with reading problems: Study designs and preliminary findings. *Learning Disabilities: A Multi-Disciplinary Journal, 8*(1), 63–71.

Foorman, B.R., Francis, D.J., Shaywitz, S.E., Shaywitz, B., & Fletcher, J.M. (1997). The case for early reading intervention. In B. Blachman (Ed.), *Foundations of reading acquisition: Implications for intervention and dyslexia* (pp. 103–115). Mahwah, NJ: Lawrence Erlbaum Associates.

Gersten, R. (1999). Lost opportunities: Challenges confronting four teachers of English-language learners. *Elementary School Journal, 100*(1), 37–56.

Gersten, R., & Baker, S. (2000a, May). *Special education research to practice: Ideas that work.* Presentation at the American Youth Policy Forum, Office of Special Education Programs, Office of Special Education and Rehabilitative Services, Washington, DC.

Gersten, R., & Baker, S. (2000b). What we know about effective instructional practices for English-language learners. *Exceptional Children, 66,* 454–470.

Gersten, R., Carnine, D., & Williams, P. (1982). Measuring implementation of a structured educational model in an urban setting: An observational approach. *Educational Evaluation and Policy Analysis, 4,* 67–79.

Gersten, R., Carnine, D., Zoref, L., & Cronin, D. (1986). A multifaceted study of change in seven inner city schools. *Elementary School Journal, 86*(3), 257–276.

Gersten, R., & Jiménez, R. (1994). A delicate balance: Enhancing literacy instruction for students of English as a second language. *The Reading Teacher, 47*(6), 438–449.

Graves, A. (2003, February). *Early reading instruction for English language learners: Research from southern California.* Paper presented at the Pacific Coast Research Conference, La Jolla, CA.

Haager, D., Gersten, R., Baker, S., & Graves, A. (2001, Feb.). *Early literacy instructional practices and student outcomes for English language learners.* Panel presentation at the Pacific Coast Research Conference, La Jolla, CA.

Haager, D., & Windmueller, M. (2001). Early literacy intervention for English language learners at-risk for learning disabilities: Student and teacher outcomes in an urban school. *Learning Disability Quarterly, 24*(4), 235–250.

Jiménez, R., & Gersten, R. (1999). Lessons and dilemmas derived from the literacy instruction of two Latina/o teachers. *American Educational Research Journal. 36*(2), 265–301.

Kaminski, R., & Good, R.H. (1996). Toward a technology for assessing basic early literacy skills. *School Psychology Review, 25*(2), 215–227.

Kaminski, R., & Good, R.H. (1997). Assessing early literacy skills in a problem-solving model: Dynamic Indicators of Basic Early Literacy Skills. In M.R. Shinn (Ed.), *Advanced applications of curriculum-based measurement* (pp. 113–142). New York: The Guilford Press.

Leinhardt, G., Zigmond, N., & Cooley, W.W. (1981). Reading instruction and its effects. *American Educational Research Journal, 18*(3), 343–361.

National Reading Panel. (2000). *Report of the National Reading Panel: Teaching children to read: An evidence-based assessment of the scientific research literature on reading and its implications for reading instruction.* Washington, DC: National Institute of Child Health and Human Development.

No Child Left Behind Act of 2001 (PL 107-100), 20 U.S.C. §§ 6301 *et seq.*

Ramírez, J.D. (1992). Executive summary: Longitudinal study of structured English immersion strategy, early-exit and late-exit transitional bilingual education programs for language-minority children. *Bilingual Research Journal, 16*(1 & 2), 1–62.

Reading Excellence Act of 1998 (PL 105-277), 20 U.S.C. §§ 6601 *et seq.*

Rhett, N. (2001, May). *Synthesis of research on teaching reading in a second language.* Paper presented at the Center for Applied Linguistics Work Group Panel, Washington, DC.

Snow, C.E., Burns, M.S., & Griffin, P. (Eds.). (1998). *Preventing reading difficulties in young children.* Washington, DC: National Academy Press.

Stallings, J. (1975). *Follow-through program classroom observation evaluation.* Menlo Park, CA: Stanford Research Institute.

Stallings, J., & Kaskowitz, D. (1974). *Follow-through classroom observation evaluation, 1972–1973* (SRI Project URU-7370). Stanford, CA: Stanford Research Institute.

Stanovich, P.J., & Jordan, A. (1998). Canadian teachers' and principals' beliefs about inclusive education as predictors of effective teaching in heterogeneous classrooms. *Elementary School Journal, 98*(3), 221–238.

Tikunoff, W.J., Ward, B.A., van Broekhuizen, L.D., Romero, M., Castaneda, L.V., Lucas, T., & Katz, A. (1991). *Final report: A descriptive study of significant features of exemplary special alternative instructional programs.* Los Alamitos, CA: Southwest Regional Educational Laboratory.

Vaughn, S., & Haager, D. (1994). Social assessments with students with learning disabilities: Do they measure up? In S. Vaughn & C. Bos (Eds.), *Research issues in learning disabilities: Theory, methodology, assessment, and ethics* (pp. 276–309). New York: Springer-Verlag.

English-Language Learner Classroom Observation Instrument

Teacher: _____ Date: _____

Observer: _____ Time observation began: _____

School: _____ Time observation ended: _____

Instructional Practice	
Items	*Field notes*
1. Models skills and strategies during lesson 1 2 3 4 Not Partially Moderately Very effective effective effective effective	
2. Makes relationships among concepts overt 1 2 3 4 Not Partially Moderately Very effective effective effective effective	

3. Emphasizes distinctive features of new concepts
  • Broad range of examples and non-examples
  • Examples used to show relevant and irrelevant features
 	
1   2   3   4
Not Partially Moderately Very
effective effective effective effective	

4. Provides prompts and cues in how to use strategies, skills, and concepts (e.g., guided practice, scaffolds, steps, procedures) 1 2 3 4 Not Partially Moderately Very effective effective effective effective	

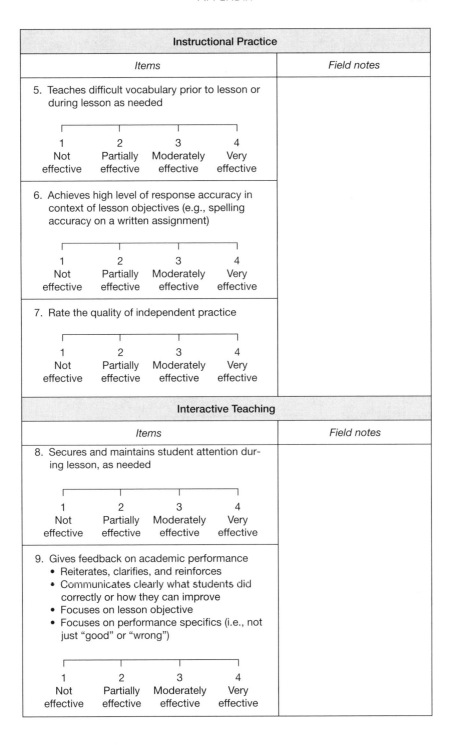

Instructional Practice	
Items	*Field notes*
5. Teaches difficult vocabulary prior to lesson or during lesson as needed 1 — 2 — 3 — 4 Not effective / Partially effective / Moderately effective / Very effective	
6. Achieves high level of response accuracy in context of lesson objectives (e.g., spelling accuracy on a written assignment) 1 — 2 — 3 — 4 Not effective / Partially effective / Moderately effective / Very effective	
7. Rate the quality of independent practice 1 — 2 — 3 — 4 Not effective / Partially effective / Moderately effective / Very effective	

Interactive Teaching	
Items	*Field notes*
8. Secures and maintains student attention during lesson, as needed 1 — 2 — 3 — 4 Not effective / Partially effective / Moderately effective / Very effective	
9. Gives feedback on academic performance • Reiterates, clarifies, and reinforces • Communicates clearly what students did correctly or how they can improve • Focuses on lesson objective • Focuses on performance specifics (i.e., not just "good" or "wrong") 1 — 2 — 3 — 4 Not effective / Partially effective / Moderately effective / Very effective	

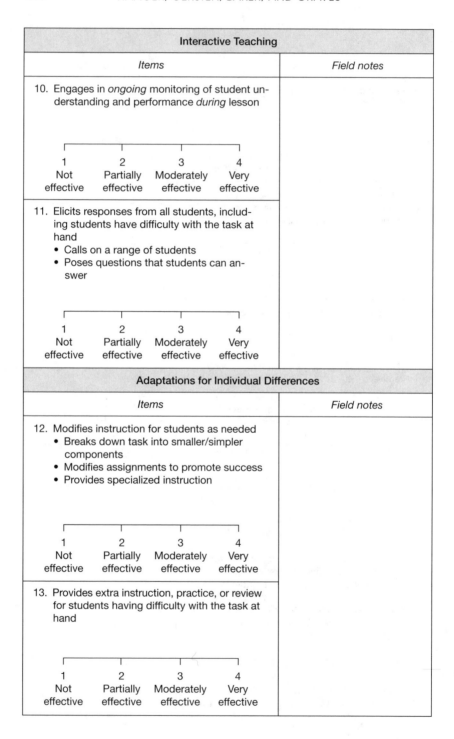

Interactive Teaching	
Items	*Field notes*
10. Engages in *ongoing* monitoring of student understanding and performance *during* lesson 1 2 3 4 Not Partially Moderately Very effective effective effective effective	
11. Elicits responses from all students, including students have difficulty with the task at hand • Calls on a range of students • Poses questions that students can answer 1 2 3 4 Not Partially Moderately Very effective effective effective effective	
Adaptations for Individual Differences	
Items	*Field notes*
12. Modifies instruction for students as needed • Breaks down task into smaller/simpler components • Modifies assignments to promote success • Provides specialized instruction 1 2 3 4 Not Partially Moderately Very effective effective effective effective	
13. Provides extra instruction, practice, or review for students having difficulty with the task at hand 1 2 3 4 Not Partially Moderately Very effective effective effective effective	

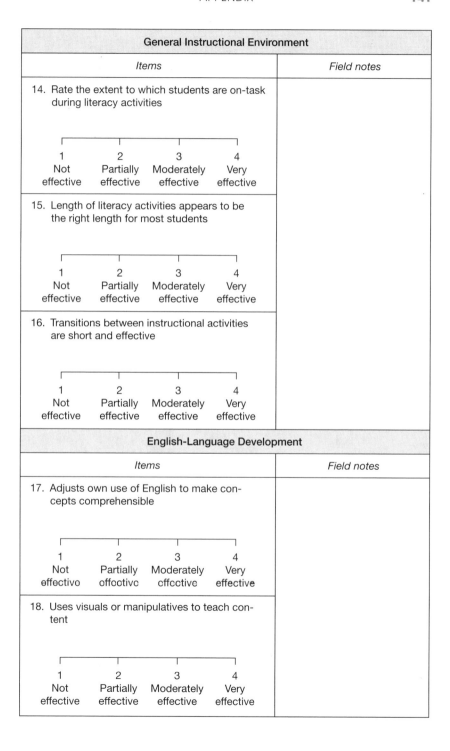

General Instructional Environment	
Items	*Field notes*
14. Rate the extent to which students are on-task during literacy activities 1 2 3 4 Not Partially Moderately Very effective effective effective effective	
15. Length of literacy activities appears to be the right length for most students 1 2 3 4 Not Partially Moderately Very effective effective effective effective	
16. Transitions between instructional activities are short and effective 1 2 3 4 Not Partially Moderately Very effective effective effective effective	
English-Language Development	
Items	*Field notes*
17. Adjusts own use of English to make concepts comprehensible 1 2 3 4 Not Partially Moderately Very effective effective effective effective	
18. Uses visuals or manipulatives to teach content 1 2 3 4 Not Partially Moderately Very effective effective effective effective	

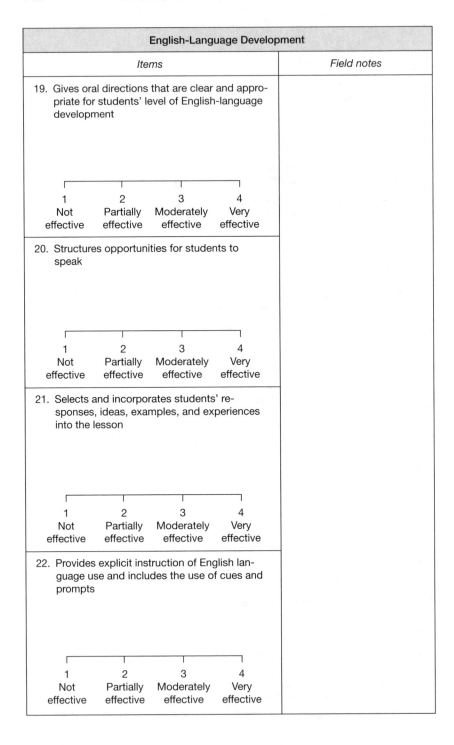

English-Language Development	
Items	*Field notes*
19. Gives oral directions that are clear and appropriate for students' level of English-language development 1 2 3 4 Not Partially Moderately Very effective effective effective effective	
20. Structures opportunities for students to speak 1 2 3 4 Not Partially Moderately Very effective effective effective effective	
21. Selects and incorporates students' responses, ideas, examples, and experiences into the lesson 1 2 3 4 Not Partially Moderately Very effective effective effective effective	
22. Provides explicit instruction of English language use and includes the use of cues and prompts 1 2 3 4 Not Partially Moderately Very effective effective effective effective	

English-Language Development	
Items	*Field notes*
23. Gives students time to respond to questions 1 — 2 — 3 — 4 Not effective Partially effective Moderately effective Very effective	
24. Encourages students to give elaborate responses • Prompts students to expand on one-word answers • Prompts students to provide more information • Prompts students to give more complete answers 1 — 2 — 3 — 4 Not effective Partially effective Moderately effective Very effective	
25. The teacher and/or students strategically use students' native language(s) to help students understand content 1 — 2 — 3 — 4 Not effective Partially effective Moderately effective Very effective	
26. Uses gestures and facial expressions in teaching vocabulary and clarifying meaning of content 1 — 2 — 3 — 4 Not effective Partially effective Moderately effective Very effective	

Content Specific to Reading/Language Arts	
Quality of Instruction	*Field notes*

27. Provides systematic, explicit instruction in
the following areas

Phonemic awareness

1	2	3	4
Not effective	Partially effective	Moderately effective	Very effective

☐ Observed   ☐ Not observed

Letter–sound correspondence

1	2	3	4
Not effective	Partially effective	Moderately effective	Very effective

☐ Observed   ☐ Not observed

Decoding

1	2	3	4
Not effective	Partially effective	Moderately effective	Very effective

☐ Observed   ☐ Not observed

Vocabulary and vocabulary concept development

1	2	3	4
Not effective	Partially effective	Moderately effective	Very effective

☐ Observed   ☐ Not observed

28. Checks student comprehension of text by
asking questions

1	2	3	4
Not effective	Partially effective	Moderately effective	Very effective

29. Engages students in meaningful interactions about text

1	2	3	4
Not effective	Partially effective	Moderately effective	Very effective

6

Conducting Ethnographic Observations of Reading in Elementary Schools

JANETTE KLINGNER, KEITH M. STURGES, AND BETH HARRY

This chapter describes the use of ethnographic observation as a way to learn about reading in elementary school classrooms. We provide examples from a 3-year ethnographic research project in which we examined the special education referral and decision-making processes in 12 south Florida elementary schools. We focus on the lessons learned from four schools implementing Success for All (SFA). This project utilized ethnographic observation techniques so that we could add to our understanding of the interactions between teachers and students and among students in general and special education classrooms. Early observations focused primarily on teachers' actions but over time shifted to specific target students' behaviors. Throughout our research, we also conducted interviews to gain the perspectives of insiders (i.e., participants).

This research was conducted with support from the U.S. Department of Education, Office of Special Education Programs, Grant No. H324C980165. We are indebted to the principals, teachers, students, parents, and other school district personnel who so generously allowed us into their schools and into their lives. We would like to thank our colleague, Robert Moore, and our consultant, Alfredo Artiles, for their invaluable help, and also our research assistants: Aileen Angulo, Iris Campos, Tamara Celestin, Thaissa Champagne, Elizabeth Cramer, Jennifer Dorce, Tony Ford, Sylvia Gutierrez, Christina Herrera, Sharene McKesey, Ailé Montoya, Josefa Rascon, Patricia Stephens, and Cassaundra Wimes.

We define ethnography and give some examples of how this method has been used to study the processes involved in reading instruction. We explain and illustrate the primary features of ethnographic observation techniques, their challenges and drawbacks, and when to use these methods and why. We walk the reader through each stage of ethnographic observations, including training, gaining access to the research setting, obtaining informed consent, locating key informants, determining one's role as an observer, gaining acceptance, building rapport, observing, writing field notes, processing data, and analyzing data. We also discuss ethical issues. Finally, we wrap up with a summary of the emerging hypotheses from our data on the SFA reading program.

OVERVIEW OF THE RESEARCH PROJECT

Our research was part of a larger project that investigated the disproportionate representation of culturally and linguistically diverse students in high-incidence disability categories in special education. This project was called In Search of an Exemplary Special Education Referral and Decision-Making Process for Culturally Diverse Students, or Project SEARCH. As part of the larger project, we investigated instruction in general education classrooms *before* students had been referred for a psychological evaluation. Four of the highest-need urban schools were using SFA as their basic reading program. Thus, we examined the SFA instruction received by struggling readers whose teachers were considering referring them to special education. We wanted to understand the nature of this instruction, as well as students' experiences within the larger school context.

Framework

We observed classroom practices in urban schools to help us understand how these practices might contribute to the disproportionate representation of minority students in special education. Our work was based on the National Academy of Sciences' framework, which stated that disproportionate representation is problematic if any aspect of early instruction or the referral, evaluation, and placement process works against students' success (Heller, Holtzman, & Messick, 1982). We observed instruction in general education classrooms prior to a student's referral, the initial meeting of the Child Study Team, prereferral strategies in general education classrooms, the second meeting of the Child Study Team, the evaluation, the meeting at which a placement decision was made, and instruction in special education classrooms. We were operating from the hypothesis that the events that occur in the general education classroom will ultimately affect student performance and teacher referral decision making.

Our focus on reading instruction was only one aspect of this investigation. Our goal in conducting classroom observations was to develop an understanding of the instructional context, both in general education and special education programs, at each stage of the referral and placement process. Thus, we observed children before they were referred to their school's Child Study Team, during the referral process, and after they had been placed in a special education program. We wanted to determine what reading instruction looked like in these classrooms and how reading instruction and related prereferral strategies may have contributed to students' success or failure.

Four of the schools had adopted SFA as their reading program. SFA is a schoolwide reading program that has been evaluated extensively (for a summary of research on the program, see Slavin et al., 1996). Designed to prevent reading failure, SFA targets low-income populations and requires specialized scheduling to allow small-group instruction at children's skill levels. Program evaluations have focused on assessing student outcomes on standardized achievement measures; however, research on schoolwide interventions indicates that a key aspect of interpreting the success of such models lies in understanding the extent to which they have been implemented with fidelity and in examining the various constraints under which they operate (Herman, Carl, Lampron, Sussman, Berger, & Innes, 2000). Because it was not our purpose to study SFA in particular, we do not claim to be offering any evaluation of its success in the schools in our sample. Nevertheless, our data do raise some interesting questions that would be worthy of further study. For the purposes of this discussion, those data illustrate the power of ethnographic observation to examine social and institutional processes that facilitate or impede such a program.

Participants

The student population at all four of the SFA schools was predominantly Black. At two of the schools, the majority of students spoke Haitian Creole, and at the other two, almost all of the students were African American. Close to 100% of the students received free or reduced-price lunch. Slightly more than a third of the teachers were Caucasian, about a third were Black, and slightly less than a third were

Table 6.1. School demographics, in percentages

School	Ethnicity of students			Free or reduced-price lunch	LEP	Ethnicity of teachers			MS, MA, or more	New to school
	White	Black	Hispanic			White	Black	Hispanic		
1	0+	99	1	97.1	0.5	44	36	20	46	17.1
2	0+	92	8	97.2	43.2	36	34	25	41	8.5
3	0+	89	10	98.9	27.3	36	36	26	41	11.8
4	1	69	29	98.4	13.9	30	25	45	26	17.0

Note: LEP = Students with limited English proficiency; MS, MA, or more = Teachers with master's or specialist's degrees or more advanced degrees

Hispanic. More than 40% of the teachers in three of the schools and 26% of the teachers in the fourth school had master's or specialist's degrees. The percentage of teachers new to the school varied from 8.5% to 17.1% (see Table 6.1).

Data Sources

We observed 21 complete or almost complete SFA lessons by 17 teachers across the four schools. We observed an additional 11 partial lessons, for a total of 32 observations. In addition, we observed Child Study Team meetings and staffing meetings (individualized education program [IEP] meetings) in which children's reading performance and SFA were discussed. We inspected students' work samples, test protocols, evaluation reports, and IEPs.

WHAT IS ETHNOGRAPHY?

Ethnography originated in the field of cultural anthropology in the early 20th century and was adapted by sociologists in the 1920s and 1930s as a way to describe and interpret a cultural or social group or system (Creswell, 1998). Hammersley and Atkinson noted that in many respects, ethnography is the most basic form of social research, with a very long history, "founded on the human capacity for participant observation" (1995, p. 21). The ethnographer participates (either overtly or covertly) in the lives of those he or she is studying—watching, listening, asking questions, and trying to understand all that occurs. This process of data collection is referred to as *fieldwork,* defined as on-site research conducted over a sustained period of time and requiring some degree of researcher involvement (Wolcott, 1995). The fieldworker gathers information through observations, interviews, and artifacts to develop a portrait of life in a social setting as it is experienced and practiced by the people in it (Creswell, 1998). Ethnography is well-suited to answer the question, "What is going on here?" and is most effective when "there is reason to believe that knowing 'what-things-mean-to-those-involved' could conceivably make a difference" (Wolcott, 1988, p. 203). The ethnographic approach is both rigorous and flexible.

Although ethnography began in other disciplines, it has been applied in educational settings since the 1960s. Educational ethnographers examine the processes of teaching and learning, searching for patterns that explain the phenomenon under investigation (Goetz & LeCompte, 1981). They strive to collect rich, descriptive data that document the context, experiences, and viewpoints of teachers, students, administrators, and parents. They explore the relationships among these, seeking to understand interaction patterns and the sociocultural contexts within which these interactions occur. Thus, educational ethnography is well suited to answer questions about complex phenomena, particularly when researchers have sufficient time and resources to invest in their study. We selected ethnography for our research precisely because of its ability to encompass complexity in the study of multifaceted and complicated issues, such as those associated with the disproportionate representation of minorities in special education.

Examples of Ethnographic Studies of Reading in Classrooms

Although not numerous, the ethnographic studies of reading in the classroom are notable in that they have affected practice by influencing how researchers think about the content, context, and dynamics of reading instruction. A handful of these ethnographic reading studies have focused on ability grouping. Others have investigated the influence of cultural and linguistic differences between teachers and students.

Studies of Ability Grouping Rist (1970), McDermott (1976, 1977), Eder (1982), and Borko and Eisenhart (1986) all observed reading groups. Rist observed that students in reading groups in kindergarten, first, and second grades were treated differentially—children in lower groups communicated less frequently with the teacher, were less involved in class activities, and received less instruction than their counterparts in higher groups. McDermott studied the social interactions in two reading groups (one high achieving, one low achieving) in a first-grade classroom for 1 year and documented differences between the groups. Students in the high-achieving group were engaged three times more often than students in the low-achieving group, and interruptions were 20 times as likely to occur in the low-achieving group. In a similar study, Borko and Eisenhart observed high- and low-achieving reading groups in second-grade classrooms for 1 year. They found that readers in the high-achieving groups had more opportunities to read larger segments of text and more chances to read silently and were more likely to discuss and extend the meaning of what they had read than their peers in low-achieving groups. Eder observed reading instruction in a first-grade classroom and examined the teacher's responses to students' interruptions of others' turns at reading. She found differential treatment by the teacher across ability groups—the teacher discouraged interruptions with the top reading groups but responded to interruptions in the lower groups by asking for more information. In each study, the researchers concluded that instruction in low-achieving groups was not as conducive to learning to read as instruction in higher groups.

In a related study, Hart (1982) conducted a participant-observation study of reading, working as a teacher's assistant, as a tutor, and occasionally as a substitute teacher in an elementary school for one semester. Social organization emerged as an important factor influencing reading instruction. Whereas McDermott demonstrated how social organization within the classroom was a foundation for specific interactions that could lead to failure, Hart showed how social organization throughout an elementary school provided a foundation that determined what kinds of people, objectives, and tasks came together in classrooms and influenced the nature and quality of reading instruction.

Cultural and Linguistic Differences   Au (1980); Au and Mason (1981); and Díaz, Moll, and Mehan (1986) are among researchers who have investigated the impact of cultural and linguistic differences on teaching and learning to read and demonstrated the value of culturally relevant pedagogy. Ethnographic observations of reading lessons were one component of the Kamehameha Elementary Education Program (KEEP), a research-and-development program in Hawaii. Lessons were observed while school personnel implemented different reading programs in an effort to improve student performance. When the discourse of reading lessons was allowed to become more like the style of day-to-day Hawaiian conversation, reading achievement improved dramatically (Au, 1980; Au & Mason, 1981).

Díaz and colleagues (1986) used ethnographic methods to analyze a bilingual program in which students were reading well in Spanish but not in English. They found significant differences in the instruction provided in the two languages. Spanish reading instruction included opportunities to learn and apply higher-level thinking skills, whereas the English reading instruction consisted of only lower-level tasks (even for those students who had demonstrated advanced comprehension skills in their first language). When students were given the opportunity to discuss their English stories in Spanish, they were able to demonstrate higher levels of understanding.

What Makes a Research Study Ethnographic?

Although ethnography has been portrayed as little more than storytelling (Walker, 1981, cited in Hammersley & Atkinson, 1995), in fact it is a rigorous research method that relies on meticulous data collection techniques to avoid bias and to ensure accuracy of data (LeCompte & Schensul, 1999). Ethnography requires that the research take place over an extended period of time and in natural settings. Spindler and Spindler (1992) listed several criteria for good ethnography in their chapter in the *Handbook of Qualitative Research in Education*. Among these criteria are the following:

1. Direct, prolonged, on-the-spot observation is essential. "The primary obligation for the ethnographer is to be there when the action takes place and to change that action as little as possible by his or her presence" (p. 64).

2. Observations should be contextualized, both in the immediate setting in which behavior is observed and in further contexts beyond that setting.

3. Observations should be prolonged and repetitive. Chains of events are observed more than once to establish the reliability of the observations.

4. Ethnography evolves. Hypotheses emerge *in situ* (from the data themselves) as the study continues in the setting selected for observation and are tested in the same way. Judgments about what may be significant to study in-depth are deferred until the initial phases of the study have been completed.

5. Good ethnographers are not only good observers but also good collectors of artifacts, products, documents, and anything possibly related to the area of study.

6. The views of the individuals under study are important and attended to through inferences from observations and other forms of ethnographic inquiry (e.g., interviews).

7. Instruments, codes, schedules, and questionnaires are acceptable in an ethnographic study when used for specific purposes, but they must be generated *in situ* as a result of observation and ethnographic inquiry. Ethnographic observation (i.e., with nothing but a pad of paper and pen for notes) must come first.

8. When research reports are written, the presence of the ethnographer is acknowledged and his or her social, personal, and interactional positions in the situation are described.

Many researchers use ethnographic techniques, such as collecting field notes or conducting brief observations, to provide descriptive information for studies that primarily rely on other methodological approaches. Research that incorporates some ethnographic techniques and concepts but combines them with other methods and theoretical frameworks in an interdisciplinary approach are sometimes referred to as *quasi-ethnographies*. In this manner, ethnographers distinguish between doing ethnography and borrowing ethnographic techniques (Wolcott, 1995). The focus of this chapter is on borrowing ethnographic observation techniques.

WHAT IS ETHNOGRAPHIC OBSERVATION?

Ethnographic observation, as a part of what is known as *fieldwork,* is the process of watching and meticulously recording what one sees. It also involves being sharply aware of oneself as an observer and as an interpreter of the data. Thus, field notes must account not only for what was seen and heard but also for the observer's role during data collection and the influence of the social relationships that facilitate or hinder authentic data collection. In the following sections, we explain the key aspects of this entire process, illustrating each point with examples from our data.

Gaining Access

The first steps in entering the field of ethnography are crucial in setting the stage for a successful observational study. Gaining access occurs through *gatekeepers,* individuals who control access to a community, organization, group of people, or source of information and who can provide entrance (LeCompte & Schensul, 1999). Project SEARCH dealt with a sensitive, potentially controversial topic, and if we had not carefully cultivated the trust of school district personnel prior to beginning our work, we easily could have been denied access. Our very first step was to convene an advisory board and ask for guidance. The advisory board included the assistant superintendent in charge of special education for the district, other key district administrators, a high-level representative from the teachers' union, and two representatives from parent advocacy groups. We explained the purpose of our study and asked for input. In this way, we were able to build trust and commitment to the project early on. The assistant superintendent then set up a meeting with the special education directors from all six regions in the district. Again we explained the purpose of our work and asked for input—but with explicit support from the assistant superintendent. Next, we met individually with regional special education directors and asked for input regarding which schools in their region they would recommend we study. (In some cases, we took these recommendations; in others, we did not.) Once we had selected our schools, the special education directors invited the principals and assistant principals to a meeting, and again we explained our research. At each school, the principal or assistant principal walked around with us and introduced us to teachers and other school personnel, letting them know that the administrator supported our work. In every school but one, we felt the doors were wide open to us (and we dropped that one to get to our pre-set limit of 12 schools). We continued to meet regularly with our advisory board throughout the study. We were honest in sharing our intent and careful to emphasize the proactive nature of our work. We explained that we expected to uncover problems but that we would also be looking for exemplary practice and would focus on developing recommendations.

Obtaining Informed Consent to Participate

Acquiring signed permission from participants to proceed is essential with any type of research. With ethnographic research of a sensitive nature, however, acquiring this consent can be particularly problematic. Because ethnography necessitates a detailed description of the context or setting, participants potentially can be recognized by others who read research reports and are familiar with this setting. In our Project SEARCH permission letters, we were required by our university's Institutional Review Board to make it very clear that participants risked the possibility of being recognized, despite our best efforts to camouflage identities, and they could be associated with views others find objectionable. From an ethical perspective, participants should be informed as fully as possible of the nature of the research and the potential benefits and risks of their participation. We had anticipated that because we had included these disclosures in our permission letter, teachers, parents, and others would be reluctant to participate in our research, but in fact we found that the opposite was true. Few teachers or parents declined to participate.

Locating Key Informants

Key informants provide much needed information, without which ethnographic work cannot proceed. They are chosen because they are knowledgeable and are willing to communicate with the ethnographer (LeCompte & Schensul, 1999). In each school, we developed relationships with key informants that proved valuable. We began by interviewing everyone and through this process, connected with some people more than others. These individuals then became our allies, so to speak, and provided further entry into the school. They confided in us, told us what they thought was really going on, and obtained data for us. They also shared insights about who they thought we should observe and which meetings they thought we might want to attend. In some cases, the key informant was a counselor, social worker, or parent liaison. Teachers also became key informants, although generally they did not have access to as much information as school administrators or support personnel did.

Determining the Role of the Observer

The role of the observer and the extent to which he or she is a participant in the research setting can vary along a continuum from that of a complete participant or insider who is fully involved to that of a detached observer who remains uninvolved. Researchers who are participant observers are immersed in the day-to-day lives of those they are studying (Creswell, 1998). In addition to observing, participant observers perform functions and enact roles considered meaningful to the people in the settings they are studying (Vierra & Pollock, 1992). They participate both to develop rapport and also to acquire more of an insider's perspective than would otherwise be possible. The detached observer, on the other end of the continuum, stays in the role of outsider. He or she makes a conscious choice to maintain distance between him- or herself and those he or she is studying, believing that by staying neutral a more objective portrayal of events is possible.

Potential advantages and disadvantages are associated with being a participant observer or a nonparticipant observer. Advantages to participant observation are that the researcher is not perceived to be as much of an intruder (although the participant observer might also be considered an intruder), and more opportunities for interactions are available that can potentially lead to additional data. Pitfalls include the danger of becoming associated with one faction over another (rather than seeming neutral) and role conflict, when participating could mean helping or providing expertise that would interfere with what is being observed. Also, the researcher might go beyond the role needed to conduct research and become unable to maintain the necessary degree of detachment to continue the research (Vierra & Pollock, 1992). Frequent debriefings with fellow researchers and periodic breaks can help maintain an appropriate research stance. One advantage to nonparticipant observation is that it eliminates role confusion—the researcher has one job only, that of observing and recording. Another advantage is that someone thought to be an outsider can be perceived as nonthreatening and impartial. Also, the nonparticipant observer is less likely to alter the setting in some way.

The objectives of the research project should guide the researchers in determining their preferable level of participation. The goal should be to find the best vantage point from which to observe (Wolcott,

1995). It is relevant to ask, "What are my own capabilities for partici-pating and observing?" Every fieldworker must achieve a viable bal-ance. In our research, we found that our roles varied. At times, we were detached and at other times more involved, depending on the situa-tion. We referred to our work in classrooms as participant observation, but in reality we more often observed than participated. We conversed with teachers, students, and others but with rare exceptions, were still clearly perceived to be outsiders. To establish ourselves as friendly and trustworthy outsiders, a central aspect of determining our roles was to take into account issues of acceptance and trust.

Gaining Acceptance and Establishing Rapport

To gain acceptance, at the outset, it is best to be unobtrusive and to blend in, so as not to call unnecessary attention to oneself. If the ob-server has chosen a participant observation role, he or she should do whatever is expected for that role (e.g., in a classroom, to provide ca-sual assistance to a student or two). The objective is to normalize one's presence but not try *too* hard to fit in. It can also help to emphasize the confidential nature of the research (e.g., reminding teachers that real names will not be used when reporting findings).

Rapport goes beyond gaining acceptance (which is neutral) in that it requires participants to have positive feelings toward the researcher. Building rapport necessitates that the researcher gains the *trust* of those involved in the research community (LeCompte & Schensul, 1999). When the investigator and the participant build a trusting relationship, an open atmosphere is created that allows the voices or opinions of the participants to emerge in a more authentic way. This process of build-ing and maintaining rapport is continuous and requires a balancing act because the researcher always wants to know more but cannot ap-pear to be too nosy. The aim is to foster intimacy and closeness rather than distance, as with other methodologies. This closeness is facilitated through active listening and demonstrating concern, empathy, or un-derstanding (Woods, 1992). In some situations, it can be helpful for the researcher to reveal something personal about him- or herself. For ex-ample, after observing a quite frazzled teacher struggle (unsuccessfully) to manage her active, inattentive first-grade class during a reading les-son, one of us commented, "You have so many students! You really have your hands full. I don't know how you do it. I had a hard time with classroom management when I was a teacher." The teacher breathed a sigh of relief and shared her frustrations about what she described as a lack of support from her administration. This interaction significantly strengthened our rapport.

WHAT KINDS OF DATA ARE PRODUCED BY THIS PROCESS?

The outcome of these careful deliberations and actions is a large body of detailed notes and reflections that are referred to as *field notes*. In their most raw form, these are the actual notes recorded during observations. When refined, field notes should read like a smooth narrative that reflects not only the physical aspects of the setting but also evokes the social and emotional qualities that marked the setting as a human endeavor. The term *thick description* is sometimes used to characterize field notes (Geertz, 1973). Denzin (1989) described thick description as providing details and context that evoke emotionality and strong feelings. He noted that with thick description "the voices, feelings, actions, and meanings in interacting individuals are heard" (p. 83). *Thick* means more than merely providing rich details, however. Thick description is theory-rich in that it permits one to evoke the principles and ethos of the community and the cultural theories that guide it (Geertz, 1973).

Writing Field Notes

The main body of the researcher's field notes should carefully and accurately describe what was seen and heard. Thus, field notes have been described as "relatively concrete descriptions of social processes and their contexts" (Hammersley & Atkinson, 1995, p. 175). The goal of the ethnographer is to capture what is witnessed with integrity and alacrity. It is not sufficient to summarize what was done or said—it is important to portray the language and behavior of participants as they actually occurred. The skillful note taker is adept at capturing detail while not losing sight of the whole, going back and forth between each while consistently being cognizant of his or her own feelings, reactions, and impressions. Woods (1992) described these skills as "vision," or the ability to see and absorb a wide range of activity through scanning, and the "power of discernment," or the capacity to select specific aspects of the environment for more concentrated scrutiny. "One's focus moves constantly between figure and ground—like a zoom lens on a camera—to catch the fine detail of what individuals are doing and to keep a perspective on the context of that behavior" (Wolcott, 1988, p. 204).

Field-note writing requires continually making decisions about when and what to record. It would be impossible to document everything, so the ethnographer must choose what is most important at any given point in time. Hammersley and Atkinson (1995) noted that often these decisions take the form of dilemmas concerning depth versus breadth. Detailed notes about one aspect of what is being observed can

only be attained at the risk of missing other important data; yet, specificity must sometimes be sacrificed to gain a broad, descriptive scope.
Following are two descriptions of the same classroom activity by two
different observers. Note that although the details vary somewhat, both
observers captured the same essential information.

Many children seem to have trouble reading the
sentence, "Scott taps the ball with the stick."
They seem to stumble over the word *tap*, and I'm
wondering if they know its meaning. After a couple of tries, the teacher
picks up a long ruler and starts walking down the side of the room with it,
tapping the floor. Then, she takes a large red ball from a box at the back
and taps it with the stick. It rolls under a chair, and she can't pull it out.
She says that it is just like the ball on the pond in the story, this one keeps
rolling away, and Miguel says, "You'll have to swim for it!"

Miguel, a little boy, gets stuck on the sentence,
"Scott tapped the ball with the stick." He is having difficulties with the word *tapped*. Ms. Z gets a
long ruler from the front of the classroom and pretends that it is a stick.
She walks to the back of the room and gets a ball and demonstrates to
the class what Scott is doing so that the kids can visualize the action. She
then asks the class to tell her what she is doing, drawing a parallel between her and Scott to make the connection with the word *tap*. The kids
are fully enthralled with her. She tells them, "Ready, point, read," to continue the story.

How decision-making dilemmas concerning what to focus on and
record are resolved is likely to change over time. During the early days
of a research project, field notes are likely to be fairly general. As the
research progresses and issues emerge, field notes typically become
more focused. Moreover, features that previously seemed insignificant
may take on new meaning and vice versa. As theoretical ideas develop
and change, what is significant and what must be included in the field
notes also changes (Hammersley & Atkinson, 1995). In our observations

of SFA, we started with a broad view of the instruction itself, recording the teacher's actions and to some extent the behaviors of students who stood out as having problems. Over time, our focus narrowed as we paid more attention to target students and their interactions with teachers and other students.

Guidelines for Writing Field Notes   The following set of guidelines for determining what to record in field notes was adapted from LeCompte and Preissle (1993):

1. *Who* is in the group or scene? How many people are there, and what are their identities and relevant characteristics? What are their roles?

2. *What* is happening? What are the people in the scene doing and saying to one another? In what activities are participants engaged? What resources and materials are they using, and how are these allocated? How are activities organized, explained, and justified? What is consumed and what is produced?

    •   How do people behave toward one another? What is the nature of their participation and interaction? How are people connected to one another? What statuses and roles are evident?

    •   What is the content of participants' conversations? What verbal and nonverbal languages do they use for communication? What formats do their conversations follow? Who talks and who listens?

3. *Where* is the scene located? What is the physical setting? How do individuals allocate and use space and physical objects?

4. *When* does the observation take place? How often does this group convene and for how long? How does the group conceptualize, use, and distribute time? How do participants view the past, present, and future?

5. *How* are the identified elements connected or interrelated, either from the participants' point of view or from the researcher's perspective? How does change originate, and how is it managed? What rules or norms govern this social organization? How is power conceptualized and distributed?

6. *Why* does this group operate as it does? What meaning do participants attribute to their activities? What is the group's history? What goals are articulated by the group?

Observers typically write between 5 and 10 handwritten pages of field notes per hour. Ideally, the observer is able to record notes while the observation is taking place. In some settings, however, this might not be advisable (e.g., when the person who is being observed seems intimidated by the process). In such cases, it is important to record notes as soon after leaving the setting as possible when the memory is most fresh. When it is not possible or socially appropriate to record detailed notes on the spot, writing a few key words or an outline helps trigger the memory later. We found ourselves doing this particularly when observing Child Study Team meetings or staffing meetings and during informal conversations. We frequently sat in our parked cars immediately after leaving the school building to record our notes. Some ethnographers use audiotape recorders that they can discreetly speak into as a way of recording information, or they bring laptop computers to the research setting.

Even when the observer can jot down field notes in the observational setting, these notes still must be typed and developed later. As a general rule, it takes twice as much time to type handwritten notes as it does to conduct the initial observation. This process is so time-consuming in part because details should be filled in whenever they are remembered (even though they were not recorded in the initial field notes) and also because the process requires reflection. Kleinman and Copp (1993, cited in Wolcott, 1995) advised that note taking is not complete until the researcher has gone back over his or her notes to make "notes-on-notes"—to reflect about what was observed.

Observer Comments

The process of reflection forms the beginning stages of analysis and is a critical part of doing fieldwork. An established convention in recording field notes is the addition of observer comments (OCs), which may be personal, reflective, analytical, or hypothetical comments or memos inserted into the field notes and usually framed by square brackets to distinguish them clearly from what was actually observed. Although direct observation should note only what was visible or audible in the setting, OCs are a way of recording the researcher's thoughts and reactions. In this way, OCs provide a way to monitor the research process. These reflective responses indicate what the researcher considers noteworthy, problematic, strange, mundane, or obvious. References to personal feelings are of value because they alert the researcher to issues that possibly should be explored further. As comments accumulate, they can lead to preliminary analyses. OCs might be recorded during an observation or added later during the transcription process. Or they might be written separately in a fieldwork journal or d.. vides a running account of the progression of the research (Ha.. ley & Atkinson, 1995). Some researchers leave a column on the rig.. side of the paper for their comments. Wolcott (1995) suggested that the researcher make a practice of recording not only standard information about the day, date, and time of an observation but also reflections about his or her mood, personal reactions, and even random thoughts. These notes can later help the researcher recapture detail and provide a "critical bridge" between what the researcher is experiencing and how that experience is translated into a form in which it can be communicated to others (Wolcott, 1995, p. 99).

Fieldwork, by its very nature, is subjective work. Although researchers must maintain as much objectivity as possible, fieldwork requires some personal involvement and commitment and can be quite subjective. By being aware of his or her emotions and reactions and recording these, the researcher is acknowledging and accounting for this subjectivity (Harry, 1996). Peshkin (1988) defended subjectivity, arguing that it is the basis for the researcher's distinctive contribution to the research. Subjectivities must be made explicit if they are to advance, rather than obscure, the validity of the research (Eisenhart & Howe, 1992; Harry, 1996; Jansen & Peshkin, 1992; Van Maanen, 1988).

Two Success for All Examples

The following field notes are excerpted from observations conducted at different times during the school year, from different schools, and at different grade levels. These observations were selected in part because they are so varied. Each includes observer comments. Ellipses (i.e., " . . . ") indicate that some of the field notes have been deleted for the sake of brevity. All names are pseudonyms.

The first excerpt is an example of field notes taken during SFA story time in a kindergarten class. These abridged notes are from one of our first classroom observations on September 9, 1999, in an urban school with 98% of the students receiving free or reduced-price lunch. Twenty-eight students are present, all but one of whom is African American.

 The teacher calls students to the rug, by group (table). The groups have names like "red hearts," "black triangles," "green circles," and their tables have the corresponding colored shape taped on top. Students get up out of their seats quietly and push their chairs in before walking to the

circle area . . . The teacher does "10 little fingers" with the class to gain their attention. Students all join in and get ready.

> (OC: I'm impressed with this class—they certainly seem to know
> the songs and routines well for only the second week of school.)

Ms. R. introduces the book *Arthur's Eyes*. She asks, "Who is the author? What does the author do?" The dry erase board by her has spaces for the title, author, and illustrator. She fills these in as students respond, with prompting. She tells the students that she has some "super hard" words for them today. Smiling broadly, she says, "I don't know, if you go home and read these words they're going to take you out of kindergarten because they'll say you are too smart for kindergarten." The kids laugh gleefully. The first word is *optometrist*. The kids really are proud of themselves when they are able to "read" the word. She asks what it means, and a student responds, "A doctor who looks at your eyes." (She had introduced the word by saying this, asking who had been to a doctor who looked at their eyes.) "The next word describes someone who takes pictures."

> (OC: The teacher is great; I'm really enjoying observing her and
> this class. I'm sure the kids really believe right now that they are
> smart, that they can read. I can't believe that this is only the sec-
> ond week of school.)

The teacher says, "I need eyes back on me. I need your hands back in your lap." They do "Gramma's Glasses" and finish ready and eager to listen to the story. She tells them that sometimes we read stories, and sometimes we listen to stories. She reads the story to them with enthusiasm and expression—all students listen attentively, their eyes on the teacher or the book, some with their mouths slightly open as if transfixed. Then the teacher asks questions, "Why do you think they might not want to play with him?" She tells them, "I want to see different hands." She regularly reinforces students raising their hands rather than calling out and doesn't call on students who don't raise their hands quietly. To one student who has already responded, she says, "It's okay, my love, I want to hear from someone different." She asks students, "What do you think about that?" "What might happen now?" "What do you think of the book?" "Why did you think it was good?"

> (OC: She uses lots of higher-level questioning. I wonder how
> much of this is SFA and how much of it is this teacher.)

She sends kids back to their seats, again one table at a time. They tiptoe, very quietly . . .

The second excerpt is an example of field notes about an SFA lesson in a third-grade class. These abridged notes are from an observation on March 21, 2000, in a different urban school, with 97% of the students receiving free or reduced-price lunch. About 20 students are in the class. Note what happens to Randy.

 I enter the room at 9:35 and the teacher says, "Good morning, Dr. K. Class, let's say 'good morning' to Dr. K. Remember, she is here to observe us work. Let's be on our best behavior." The students say, "Good morning," and smile. One boy, Randy, stands up as I enter and claps (as if he is happy to see me) and then sits back down. I sit by Randy, but the teacher moves him elsewhere.

The desks are again arranged in clusters of two and four and appear somewhat randomly placed around the room (like before they had been moved into rows for FCAT testing (the state's high-stakes mandatory testing). Students all have their books open, reading in unison. The teacher says, "Excellent, page two." "Excellent, page three." And so on. Students glance at me. Right now they are all doing what they are supposed to be doing. I notice Randy kneeling in his chair, enunciating very clearly, not looking at the book very often, and saying everything correctly.

(OC: I wonder if he has already memorized this book.)
The teacher says, "I love how you guys are reading. Remember what, we are passing our test to go on to Level 21. Mark, sit up nicely." The teacher passes out another set of books (yellow, the others were blue). Randy says, "We are supposed to be on book 17!" Another student says, "This is 16." Randy says with some exasperation in his voice, "But we are supposed to be on 17!" The teacher says calmly, "This is a review book." The students again read in unison—all seem to be reading. The teacher says, "Okay, let's read it again." (. . .) At one point while reading, the students say "stamp" when the word was "stump." They say it correctly the second time. The teacher asks, "What can you do on a stump?" Students say, "Eat a picnic on it." "Stand on it and jump down." "Play with your little cars on it." (. . .) Students continue reading. (. . .)

Randy gets up and goes over to the sink, comes, back, sits, gets up again, and dances around. He had read quite well. Now they have a new book, Level 17. Mark is now lying on his desk, with his book closed.

The teacher comes and opens it. Now he's kneeling on his chair. At 9:57, Randy says in a loud voice, "I'm not reading no more, man." But he does. The teacher says, "Page two." This is the third SFA book like this they are reading in a row. Each is a higher level than the one before it.

> (OC: I'm not sure why they are reading three, because usually with SFA they only read one. I'll have to ask the teacher. Students seem to be getting quite restless reading these books over and over, and I don't blame them. It's clear to me that students are at different levels in this one class, with some, such as Randy, quite able to read the books, and frustrated by having to reread lower books, and others, such as Walter, quite low and frustrated by trying to read books too hard for him.)

Randy goes up to the teacher and points to a word in the book they are reading, saying to her, "This is 'bookbag,' not 'backpack.'" He's right, and the teacher has them read it again. Students are getting more restless. (. . .) They finish, and Randy applauds. He says, "Very, very, very good." Then he gets up and starts collecting books. The teacher says, "Randy, take a seat, please." Her voice is sounding more impatient than before. She collects the books herself. (. . .)

At 10:03 the teacher says, "Yesterday, we started writing our 'Bookstore Cat.' I'm going to give you your papers back." Mark is leaning over his chair, backwards, his head on the floor. The teacher says sternly, "Randy and Mark." (. . .) Mark is now lying over his chair in the opposite direction. Randy is running around his chair, then dancing. The teacher continues passing back papers. "Some people did a good job the last time," she says. (. . .) Sam is now running around the room and also Randy. The teacher tells Randy to sit. Sam says, "He kicking me" (referring to Randy). The teacher says to the class, "Write your first and last name." Randy has now returned to his seat and is sitting, writing. (. . .)

Randy says, "I'm not finished." Several students are talking. The teacher says, "You must have your name, date, and the title." She points to the example she's written on the board. Randy holds up his paper and asks, "Like this?" Now Sam is up walking around. The teacher says, "I'm not chasing you, Sam." Despite the growing chaos around her, the teacher continues the lesson. She holds up a book about a cat and says, "What does this say?" Randy answers correctly. Next she asks another question. Randy answers again, speaking slowly and enunciating clearly. Most kids don't seem to be paying attention. Her voice becoming higher pitched, the teacher says, "I'm waiting. Excuse me, Bernice, we need to get our education." (. . .) Referring to the story, she says, "Something happened outside. What happened outside?" Some students say the answer—Randy and others. They don't raise their hands; they just shout out. Randy gets up and says to the teacher, "Let me see the picture." He tries to look, but she won't let him. A few other kids also get up and try to see. The teacher says, "You guys don't remember." Randy says, "This story too hard." Mark's chair has been knocked over. He picks it up, kneels in his chair, and erases something on his paper. I hear Randy say, "Because you were busy playing." The teacher says, "Randy, pull up at your table." Randy says, "My table is pulled up." The teacher says, "So our first sentence is . . . " and writes on the board: "The kids were watching the puppet show."

Randy is becoming noticeably more agitated. He says, "I not finished, Mommy, Mommy. I not going to catch up." He continues writing. (. . .) It's 10:22. The next sentence on the board that the students are supposed to be copying says: "He run after the bird and catch it."

> (OC: Yes, *run* rather than *ran* and *catch* rather than *caught,* written by the teacher.)

The teacher says, "The book says 'chased' but we aren't going to put that because it's too hard for you." (. . .) Randy is up out of his seat again. The teacher asks him sternly, "What are you doing?" He responds matter-of-factly, "Looking for my pencil." Walter now says, "Look at Mark on the floor!" (. . .) Mark is now doing caterpillar or worm-like dancing movements. Randy asks him, in a tone of admiration, "How you do that?" Mark does it again. The teacher says, "Don't pay attention to Mark because that's what he wants." Now Randy is on the floor, too. (. . .) The teacher calls students to come up to an area on the rug and sit on the floor. Some students comply, but many are fooling around.

> (OC: Although the class seems more and more out of hand, the teacher seems to stay somewhat calm, at least on the surface, and keeps trying to teach.)

One boy is holding another in a headlock. The teacher goes over, separates them, and says, "Thank you." Then she says, "Sam, come here. Your space is right by me." (. . .) "I love the way Christine is ready. Walter, you were nice and you were ready. I liked the way you didn't chase after Mark. You deserve a treat."

Now Sam and Mark are both crawling on the floor. Mark is still doing the worm dance. The teacher says, "Mark, you need to stop. We need to get some work done." Mark gets up and goes and sits at his desk rather than on the floor with the rest of the class. He slouches in his seat and looks defiant. The teacher gets up and goes to the intercom and says, "I need security up here because Mark is doing the worm all over the classroom, and I can't get anything done." To the students on the floor, she says in a clear, strong voice, "It's not all right. We are not going to push and shove. You can go with her, too, when she comes. We need to get our last 30 minutes of work done." Now Mark comes over to the group and sits down. The teacher says, "Now you come over. It's too late." (. . .)

At 10:39, security enters. The teacher says, "Let's go. These two aren't getting any learning done. This one be hitting, can't sit still (referring to Randy). This one wouldn't come to the group; he was crawling around doing the worm." They leave. (. . .)

Later in the day, I found the teacher and asked her about the lesson. She explained that in SFA, it's only supposed to be one level, but she has three because the administration groups students "not by level, it's by the type of kid." She says that she has the students who are behavior problems and that the assistant principal told her to only read one level with them. But she tells me that she wouldn't feel right, couldn't go home at the end of the day knowing that she'd only read one when she has three (or more). So that's why they read three books at the beginning of my observation, one for each level. Some students are still at Level 1–5 and others are 16 or 17. That's why some kids weren't able to read the last two books. Randy is at the highest level—he can read but he's in her class because of his problematic behavior.

ETHNOGRAPHIC OBSERVATION: QUALITY, QUANTITY, STRENGTHS, CHALLENGES, AND ETHICAL ISSUES

In this next section, we discuss issues of quality and quantity. We also point out the strengths and drawbacks of using ethnographic observation techniques. Finally, we consider essential ethical issues.

How Much Is Enough?

How many observations are necessary to fully comprehend a phenomenon? Geertz asserted that it is "not necessary to know everything in order to understand something" (1973, p. 20). Anthropologists traditionally conduct ethnographies over a 2- to 3-year period, residing with the population they are studying and to some extent becoming a member of the community. Educational ethnographers have varied in the extent to which they have immersed themselves in their settings, from one semester to several years. Appropriate length of time depends on the amount of research needed to reach a saturation point, or the point at which continued observation yields no new information and recurring patterns and themes are evident.

Strengths (or When to Use Ethnographic Observation Techniques)

Ethnographic observation techniques are well suited for complex research questions when researchers are either developing grounded theory (essentially starting from scratch, or close to it) or using an analytic induction method to test theory. Strengths include its ability to account for complexity and context, its flexibility, and its use of multiple data sources. A possible research question appropriate for this methodology would be, "What factors contribute to students' success (or failure) with a given reading program?" A research question for which ethnographic observation techniques would not be suitable would be, "How successful are students with a given reading program?"

A hallmark of ethnography is that it examines behaviors and beliefs in context. LeCompte and Schensul defined *context* as "the diverse elements—for example, people groups, institutions, history, economic and political factors, features of the physical environment—that influence the behavior and beliefs of individuals" (1999, p. 18). Wolcott (1988) asserted that "the ethnographic concern for context may be the most important contribution this approach can make."

Ethnography is well suited to address complexity because it strives to account for and understand *all* relevant variables as part of a web. Wolcott (1995) wrote that researchers have a tendency to oversimplify and advised ethnographers to keep probing for more, rather than fewer, factors that may be involved. Rather than trying to rule out or avoid background noise as in quantitative methodologies, the ethnographer tries to do the opposite, building complexity into ongoing analyses.

Flexibility is an essential characteristic of ethnography (Hammersley & Atkinson, 1995). Because it does not entail extensive prefieldwork design, as surveys and experiments generally do, the focus and even the direction of the research can be changed fairly easily, in line with changing assessments of what is required by the process of theory construction. Ethnographers follow leads. When they have a hunch, they can quickly try it out and, if it is promising, follow up. Flexibility applies not only to the direction of the research but also to the data collection methods used.

Ethnographers rely on multiple data sources in a process of cross checking findings. This process is often called *triangulation* and refers to the use of at least three data collection techniques in a study, as well as a practice of layering data across time, informants, and settings. Triangulation of information on the same topic from different data sources is essential to the validity and reliability of ethnographic research (Le-Compte & Schensul, 1999). Observations without interviews and the examination of artifacts would be like a one-legged stool. Much relevant information would be missed. In our work, we gained a great deal by asking questions before, during, or after observations. For instance, in the example of the third-grade SFA class, when we questioned the teacher later in the day, we found out more about how students are grouped. However, we did not stop there. As part of the triangulation process, we also asked other school personnel about SFA grouping practices and checked other observation notes.

Drawbacks (or When Not to Use Ethnographic Techniques)

Ethnographic methods do not provide generalizable results—results apply only to the particular setting in which the research is conducted. When many settings share similar results, however, the results may be used to formulate hypotheses about general patterns. Additional research, using a more structured format, can be completed to test the degree and type of association.

Ethnography is time consuming and labor intensive. It only makes sense to embark on such a huge undertaking if ethnography is clearly the preferable methodology for addressing the researchers' objectives. The choice of method should depend first and foremost on the research question (not the other way around). When the research focuses on understanding the complexity of a broad issue or issues, ethnography is appropriate. When the focus is more predetermined and specific, other methods are preferable.

Ethical Issues

All researchers are bound by a code of ethics that stipulates that they protect the people they study from harm—physical, emotional, and financial harm and harm to their reputations (LeCompte & Schensul, 1999). Ethical issues are a concern with any type of research but can particularly be a concern with ethnography. In part, this is because researchers engage in intensive face-to-face observations and interviews and sometimes observe questionable behaviors. For example, in our research, we observed actions by teachers we knew to be inappropriate (e.g., grabbing a student by the arm and pulling him) and that perhaps should have been reported to the administration. Yet to do so would have betrayed the trust we had established and jeopardized our ability to conduct further research in that setting. We did not observe any behaviors we felt obligated to report, but we would have done so if we had felt anyone was in imminent danger.

In addition, we were acutely aware of the ethical dilemmas we faced as researchers who were knowledgeable about the practices and processes we were observing. We knew how to provide assistance, yet did not want to overly influence or affect the interactions we witnessed. For example, one researcher observed a child's staffing meeting at which she was the only person other than the assistant principal to have also attended the child's Child Study Team meeting, and the new psychologist was saying that the student in question had never received speech and language therapy. The researcher knew that he had and that this was relevant information. She opted to share this information but felt afterward as though it had been a mistake from a research standpoint. We especially experienced role conflict in our relationships with parents who perceived that we could somehow help them, that we would serve as advocates for them and their children and as intermediaries with the school system.

Another issue merits discussion—the importance of giving back to those who participate in a research study. In Project SEARCH, we provided all participants with small gift certificates to a grocery store, teachers' supply store, department store, or fast-food restaurant as a token of our appreciation for their involvement. Yet our perception from the teachers, administrators, and parents we have grown to know well over the years was that the greatest rewards for them in participating were 1) knowing their voices would be heard and 2) feeling that they might be helping in some small way to solve what they perceived to be a real and pressing problem in our society. They are counting on us to come up with recommendations and to improve opportunities for minority children in high-need schools. We know that our report is very important to the school district administrators, who allowed us access into their schools. We took seriously this obligation and made a commitment to share our findings with them before they were released publicly on a broader scale.

DATA HANDLING AND ANALYSIS

Once collected, data must be processed, stored, coded, and analyzed at increasingly finer levels. Grounded theory and analytic induction techniques are applied to make sense of the data. This is a time-consuming and involved process—the strength as well as the bane of ethnography.

Data Processing

The first step in data processing is to type handwritten notes into a computer. It is imperative that the researcher type field notes right away—preferably within a few hours, when details are still vivid. This takes discipline and organization. While typing, some details will probably be recalled that were not recorded at the site and should be included at that time. Observer comments and separate personal notes, theoretical notes, and methodological notes should also be added. This writing task is the beginning phase of analysis.

Storing Data   In large projects with a substantial amount of data, we recommend creating a database for storing, retrieving, and analyzing the data. Various software programs are available to facilitate this process, including NUDIST, The Ethnograph, and ATLAS.ti. We selected ATLAS.ti, which is based on grounded theory and provides researchers with a tool for building emergent theories from the data.

Creating a Coding System   Once the data are entered into the database, they are reviewed for repeating, overarching categories. Textual-level research activities include segmenting documents into passages through coding and "chunking" quotes or important pieces of text according to similar patterns. These categories provide simple descriptive codes. Once all meaningful data are categorized, finer coding can be applied. This process is recursive and continues throughout the life of the research project. As patterns emerge, they become the focus of subsequent data collection efforts. In our early broad coding of SFA data, we categorized relevant chunks of text as pertaining to "SFA grouping," "SFA levels," "SFA scheduling," "SFA content," "SFA activities," "teachers' perceptions," "teachers' instruction (positive, negative, or neutral)," "teachers' classroom management (positive, negative, or neutral)," "students' academics," and "students' behaviors."

Data Analysis

In ethnography, the analysis of data is not a distinct stage of the research that occurs only after all the data have been collected. It begins in the initial stages of fieldwork when research questions are formulated and clarified, continues throughout data collection, and ends during the process of writing results. Formally, it starts to materialize in analytic notes and memoranda; informally, it is manifested in the ethnographer's ideas, hunches, and emergent concepts (Hammersley & Atkinson, 1995). Analysis is tentative and provisional throughout the study and only becomes comprehensive once the data are completely collected. Initially, data are used only for speculating about what might be—possibilities that are likely to be discarded or significantly modified before the research is completed. In this way, the analysis of data informs the evolving research design. This is the core idea of grounded theorizing (Glaser & Strauss, 1967). Theory building and data collection are inextricably linked. The ethnographer is continually looking for disconfirming evidence and contradictory interpretations of findings (Eisner, 1991).

As we continued observing SFA lessons and fine-tuning our analyses, we focused more on the following issues: problems with grouping and mixed levels in the same class, students recycling through the same materials over and over (not enough support for the lowest students), scheduling procedures, students and teachers getting bored, and effects on the Child Study Team process. This process of focusing was accomplished through reflecting about data as we typed our field notes and then discussing our ideas during weekly project meetings. These discussions played an important role in that they assisted us in thinking about what we were finding and helped guide subsequent data collection efforts. For example, after one researcher observed the third-grade class with mixed levels, she brought this up at a meeting, describing the observation and asking if others had witnessed anything similar. Through discussion, it was agreed that the mixed levels phenomenon should be explored further.

Analytic Induction   Analytic induction was originally developed by Znaniecki as a procedure for theory testing (1934, cited in Hammersley & Atkinson, 1995). This process involves the following steps (adapted from Hammersley & Atkinson):

1. An initial definition of the phenomenon to be explained is formulated.

2. Some cases of this phenomenon are investigated, and potential explanatory features are documented.

3. A hypothetical explanation is devised based on an analysis of the data, designed to identify common factors across the cases.

4. Further cases are investigated to test the hypothesis.

5. If the hypothesis does not fit the facts from these new cases, either the hypothesis is reformulated or the phenomenon to be explained is redefined (so that the negative cases are excluded).

6. This procedure of examining cases, redefining the phenomenon, and reformulating the hypothesis is continued until a universal re-

lationship is established, at which point it can be concluded that the hypothesis is valid (though this can never by known with absolute certainty). No analysis can be considered final, since reality is "inexhaustible" and constantly changing.

Analytic induction was

> Developed to cover both necessary and sufficient conditions, and to include the search for negative evidence. . . . [I]n many respects it corresponds to the hypothetico-deductive method. . . . [W]here it differs from this, and most importantly, is in making clear that the testing of theoretical ideas is not the end point of the process of scientific inquiry but is generally only one step leading to further development and refinement of theory. (Hammersley & Atkinson, 1995, p. 236)

Inductive reasoning is involved, allowing for the modification of concepts and relationships between concepts that occurs through the process of doing research, with the goal of most accurately representing the reality of the situation. A benefit of the approach is that findings are more likely to be generalizable because numerous examples must be explained through successively qualified versions of the hypotheses. In summary, the process of data analysis requires discipline, focus, and an ability to consider multiple perspectives. It is tedious and time-consuming when done well. However, it is precisely this rigor that gives the researcher confidence in his or her findings.

EMERGING HYPOTHESES ABOUT SUCCESS FOR ALL

What are we learning about SFA through this stringent process of data collection and analysis? Although we are still analyzing our data, we have formulated tentative hypotheses. Evidence for some interpretations can be found in the SFA observation examples already presented in this chapter. Other conclusions are tied more closely to data we have not shared because of space limitations.

Although we observed some effective SFA instruction, as in the kindergarten observation provided, we did not encounter effective schoolwide programs. We saw some enthusiastic teachers who seemed to teach according to the process and get positive results and other teachers who appeared to be trying to teach as they had been taught to do but struggled. We saw students who clearly were already familiar with the stories they were supposed to read and were bored, acting out, or withdrawn. Classroom management was a considerable problem in some classrooms, even with smaller class sizes. Through our research, we tried to understand why there were problems with overall implementation. One teacher (who preferred SFA to other reading programs, despite its problems) explained that "it wasn't implemented the way it was supposed to have been—some kids were just passed along when they hadn't passed the tests to move to the next level. And they had groups with too many levels and ages mixed together." It intrigued us that something that looked so good on paper was fraught with so many challenges in reality. It is easy for those not directly involved to say (as we have heard), "Well, it is not working because they were not doing it right—if they had just implemented it the way they were supposed to, then they would have achieved better results." Our impression, however, was that these schools faced real dilemmas they were trying their best to solve.

Lowest Achieving Students

It appeared that either SFA did not have enough supports built into it to help with the lowest achieving children or that the supports that had been built in were not feasible enough for the schools to implement as intended. We observed numerous students who appeared to be languishing. For example, a third-grade student named Rex clearly was not making progress. At his staffing, the teacher explained that he was "very eager to learn, but can't learn to read, and can't retain information from one day to the next. We have tried different ways of teaching him. This is his fourth year in SFA, and he is still in Level 6 (an early Kindergarten level)." Also, in the third-grade observation provided, the lower students clearly were not getting reading instruction at the appropriate level. Extra tutoring was provided to first-grade students (by pulling them out of their regular classes during the afternoon) but not children in second grade and above. Thus, some students seemed to fall through the cracks.

Recycling

Students who do not make adequate progress, such as Rex, recycle through the same materials over and over in general and special education classes. After being placed in special education, Rex continued to be taught with SFA (using the same books). We noted that many older students had already memorized the books they were supposed to be reading and had lost interest. In one observation, the teacher told the class they were going to read "the best story" they had read in a long time, "Land of the Midnight Sun." She asked, "How many of you know this story?" All of the older kids raised their hands. These students then ran around the classroom and climbed on desks while the teacher tried to teach the rest of the class. The teacher commented later that students were bored and frustrated. This issue of boredom seemed to be a concern for teachers as well as students. Another teacher told us, "My students already know all of the stories. I keep teaching the same thing over and over, and it's so boring."

Mixed Instructional Levels

Some classes seemed to be dumping grounds for students considered to be troublemakers, even though they were not all at the same level and should not have been together in the same class (as in the field notes example of Randy's class included in this chapter). We observed this in special education classrooms as well as in general education classrooms. One special education teacher told us that the previous year she had had five levels with 4–7 kids each at one time. She said that the class size increased too much, so she got permission to reverse the schedule and teach language arts and math in the mornings and spend the rest of the day on SFA. This was the only way she could get in enough SFA instruction for all of her groups.

Mixed Grade Levels

Not only did we see mixed instructional levels in the same class, but we also observed mixed grade levels. For example, one class with first-through fifth-grade students was a particular challenge for the teacher because the first-grade students were motivated and on task while the older students were turned off and unruly. As the teacher lamented, "It's so bad for the first graders to see those examples." SFA stipulates that students from such a wide range of grade levels not be placed together, but we were told by this teacher that sometimes it occurred because they just did not know where to put the older students who were still so low. These were students who had not been referred to or qualified for special education or who had been referred but whose placement was delayed because the process took so long, "a year and a half or sometimes even 2 years."

Problems with Scheduling

Teachers considered it problematic that they did not have their own students for SFA and that they were assigned different students every 9 weeks, so they were not able "to really get to know their students." This was also a problem in the context of the entire school day because their homeroom students also switched to other teachers later in the day for other subjects (e.g., physical education [PE], Spanish or Haitian Creole, art, music, computers). One teacher complained, "I don't have time to teach. I have them for less than 30 minutes before they go to SFA, and then afterward they go to PE. Just when they have settled down and are working well, it's time for them to leave again. Then they come back for 10 minutes, then they go to lunch. Then they come back and go to Spanish. Then they come back at 2:00. We're the ones that make them hyper. We have them running around all day. I went to the principal and she told me, 'Make the most of it.'" The negative impact of this fragmentation was evident in the fact that a teacher would often not know the reading abilities of homeroom students who were not in the teacher's SFA group. Another teacher summed up the feelings of many by saying,

> With FCAT, SFA, [and] CCC [a required program that necessitated students working at a computer for 30 minutes every day], teachers don't have time to learn more about the teaching profession. Teachers need more flexibility to do things with the students and for themselves. Teachers feel very powerless at times. We are not empowered. They've taken away our flexibility. I can't meet a child's needs if I'm not allowed to be flexible.

Child Study Team Process

SFA affected the Child Study Team process in that SFA test results were used to determine who should be referred. Conversely, the lack of schools' timely placement of students in special education who really seemed to need it affected SFA implementation because this meant that students remained in general education classrooms repeating the same SFA levels again and again. More than one teacher commented that one of the reasons SFA did not work as well as it was supposed to was that some teachers did not refer low students to the Child Study Team. SFA includes a Family Support Team intended to provide assistance, but the extent to which it was used varied by school. In general, school personnel seemed somewhat unsure of their roles and how this team overlapped with the Child Study Team.

CONCLUSION

As stated, the purpose of our project was not to study or evaluate SFA in particular but rather to understand the context within which students are referred to and placed in special education programs. Yet our data do raise some interesting questions about the implementation of SFA that would be worth further exploration. This chapter's goal has been to illustrate the power of ethnographic observation as a way to learn about the content, context, and dynamics of reading instruction in elementary school classrooms. We have described how, why, and when to use ethnographic observation techniques.

REFERENCES

Au, K.H. (1980). Participation structures in a reading lesson with Hawaiian children: Analysis of a culturally appropriate instructional event. *Anthropology and Educational Quarterly, 11,* 91–115.

Au, K.H., & Mason, J.M. (1981). Social organizational factors in learning to read: The balance of rights hypothesis. *Reading Research Quarterly, 17,* 115–152.

Borko, H., & Eisenhart, M. (1986). Students' conceptions of reading and their reading experiences in school. *Elementary School Journal, 86,* 589–611.

Creswell, J.W. (1998). *Qualitative inquiry and research design: Choosing among five traditions.* Thousand Oaks, CA: Sage Publications.

Denzin, N. (1989). *The research act: A theoretical introduction to sociological methods* (3rd ed.). Upper Saddle River, NJ: Prentice-Hall.

Díaz, S., Moll, L., & Mehan, H. (1986). Sociocultural resources in instruction: A context-specific approach. In California State Department of Education, *Beyond language: Social and cultural factors in schooling language minority students* (pp. 187–230). Los Angeles: California State University Evaluation, Dissemination, and Assessment Center.

Eder, D. (1982). Differences in communicative styles across ability groups. In L.C. Wilkinson (Ed.), *Communicating in the classroom* (pp. 245–264). San Diego, CA: Academic Press.

Eisenhart, M.A., & Howe, K.R. (1992). Validity in educational research. In M.D. LeCompte, W.L. Millroy, & J. Preissle (Eds.), *The handbook of qualitative research in education* (pp. 643–680). San Diego, CA: Academic Press.

Eisner, E.W. (1991). *The enlightened eye: Qualitative inquiry and the enhancement of educational practice.* New York: Macmillan.

Geertz, C. (1973). *The interpretation of cultures: Selected essays.* New York: Basic Books.

Glaser, B., & Strauss, A. (1967). *The discovery of grounded theory.* Chicago: Aldine.

Goetz, J.P., & LeCompte, M.D. (1981). *Ethnography and qualitative design in educational research.* San Diego, CA: Academic Press.

Hammersley, M., & Atkinson, P. (1995). *Ethnography: Principles in practice* (2nd ed.). New York: Routledge.

Harry, B. (1996). These families, those families: The impact of researcher identities on the research act. *Exceptional Children, 62*(3), 292–300.

Hart, S. (1982). Analyzing the social organization for reading in one elementary school. In G. Spindler (Ed.), *Doing the ethnography of schooling: Educational anthropology in action* (pp. 410–438). Prospect Heights, IL: Waveland Press.

Heller, R., Holtzman, W., & Messick, S. (Eds). (1982). *Placing children in special education: A strategy for equity.* San Diego, CA: Academy Press.

Herman, R., Carl, B., Lampron, S., Sussman, A., Berger, A., & Innes, F. (2000). *What we know about comprehensive school reform models.* Washington, DC: American Institutes for Research.

Jansen, G., & Peshkin, A. (1992). Subjectivity in qualitative research. In M.D. LeCompte, W.L. Millroy, & J. Preissle (Eds.), *The handbook of qualitative research in education* (pp. 681–725). San Diego, CA: Academic Press.

Kleinman, S., & Copp, M.A. (1993). *Emotions and fieldwork.* Thousand Oaks, CA: Sage Publications.

LeCompte, M.D., & Preissle, J. (1993). *Ethnography and qualitative design in education research* (2nd ed.). San Diego, CA: Academic Press.

LeCompte, M.D., & Schensul, J.J. (1999). *Designing and conducting ethnographic research.* Walnut Creek, CA: AltaMira.

McDermott, R.P. (1976). Achieving school failure: An anthropological approach to illiteracy and social stratification. In H. Singer & R.B. Ruddell (Eds.), *Theoretical models and processes of reading* (pp. 389–428). Newark, DE: International Reading Association.

McDermott, R.P. (1977). The ethnography of speaking and reading. In R.W. Shuy (Ed.), *Linguistic theory: What can it say about reading?* (pp. 153–185). Newark, DE: International Reading Association.

Peshkin, A. (1988). In search of subjectivity—One's own. *Educational Researcher, 17,* 17–22.

Rist, R.C. (1970). Student social class and teacher expectations: The self-fulfilling prophecy in ghetto education. *Harvard Educational Review, 40,* 411–451.

Slavin, R.E., Madden, N.A., Dolan, L.J., Wasik, B.A., Ross, S., Smith, L., & Dianda, M. (1996). Success for All: A summary of research. *Journal of Education for Students Placed at Risk, 1*(1), 41–76.

Spindler, G., & Spindler, L. (1992). Cultural process and ethnography: An anthropological perspective. In M.D. LeCompte, W.L. Millroy, & J. Preissle (Eds.), *The handbook of qualitative research in education* (pp. 53–92). San Diego, CA: Academic Press.

Van Maanen, J. (1988). *Tales of the field: On writing ethnography.* Chicago: University of Chicago.

Vierra, A., & Pollock, J. (1992). *Reading educational research.* Scottsdale, AZ: Gorsuch Scarisbrick.

Wolcott, H.F. (1988). Ethnographic research in education. In R.M. Jaeger (Ed.), *Contemporary methods for research in education* (pp. 187–206). Washington, DC: American Educational Research Association.

Wolcott, H.F. (1995). *The art of fieldwork.* Walnut Creek, CA: AltaMira Press.

Woods, P. (1992). Symbolic interactionism: Theory and method. In M.D. LeCompte, W.L. Millroy, & J. Preissle (Eds.), *The handbook of qualitative research in education* (pp. 337–404). San Diego, CA: Academic Press.

7

"I Can Rite":
Informal Assessment
of Written Language

NANCY MATHER AND NOEL GREGG

Students who struggle with writing experience daily frustration and humiliation when asked to complete writing assessments. One afternoon, Ms. Jaffe, a third-grade teacher, asked her students to write a description of their favorite animal. Edward wanted to write about the giraffe, but because he could not think of how to spell the word, he decided to write about his pet rat. He thought for several minutes and then attempted to write the first sentence. Feeling unhappy with both the content and the appearance of the sentence, he ripped his paper in two. After recess, Edward asked Ms. Jaffe for some tape. Ready to try again, he taped the pieces back together and wrote the following note, presented in Figure 7.1, on the top of his paper: "Sorry I ripped it."

Teachers also feel frustration. Facing a bewildering array of writing samples from students, they often become confused about the most effective ways to assess writing, particularly for struggling students like Edward. Standardized writing assessments may be limited in what they measure and the obtained scores may not coincide with a teacher's judgment of a student's writing abilities. In addition, the majority of standardized instruments typically measure performance only on one topic, in one setting, and at one time. Although standardized measures are useful as screening instruments, additional informal assessments are needed to provide a comprehensive picture of writing abilities.

Figure 7.1. Edward's note to his teacher: "Sorry I ripped it."

Success with written expression requires the orchestration of many abilities, including those needed for lower-level transcription, as well as those essential for higher-level composing. Writing is a recursive process that involves the integration of many different cognitive and linguistic factors at several levels: subword (e.g., phonology, orthography), word (e.g., spelling, vocabulary), sentence (e.g., syntax), and text (e.g., cohesion, type of text structure) (Englert & Raphael, 1988; Gregg, 1995; Gregg & Mather, 2002). These factors then influence the writer's ability to plan, draft, and edit (Englert & Raphael, 1988; Englert, Raphael, Anderson, Gregg, & Anthony, 1989; MacArthur & Graham, 1993).

Berninger (1996) suggested that when evaluating writing, teachers focus on the various "constraints" affecting writing. Understanding the multidimensional impact of constraints such as limited instruction, specific cognitive or linguistic weaknesses, limited cultural experiences, and poor motivation can help inform the type and extent of accommodations and instruction needed as the various constraints affect different aspects of writing skill. Although writing is nonlinear and the processes involved are employed in concert, an informal assessment tool that represents several aspects of writing competence can help depict the writer's strengths, as well the various constraints affecting writing development.

Several important aspects of written language are presented in Figure 7.2. This conceptual framework of written language abilities is organized from lower-level processes (e.g., phonology, orthography) to higher-level processes (e.g., text structure, ideation). Metacognition, placed at the top of the figure, includes self-regulation of the cognitive and linguistic strategies involved in writing, including the abilities to self-instruct, select strategies, and modify performance. These executive processes guide all aspects of writing and are essential for producing effective writing (Englert & Raphael, 1988; Englert et al., 1991). Ideation is next, as the major purpose of writing is communication, the expression of thoughts and ideas. A box is placed around ideation, vocabulary, and text structure to emphasize the interrelationships among these factors. Attitude is shown on the side of the model with a bidirectional

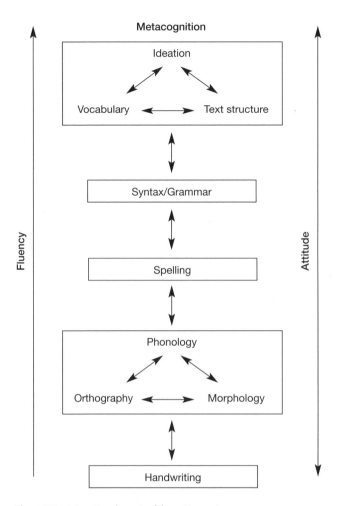

Figure 7.2.   Interactive elements of the writing system.

arrow as poor motivation, lack of interest, or fear of failure can affect any aspect of writing development and performance. Fluency runs along the side of the model with an upward arrow to depict that as lower-level processes become more automatic, the writer produces text with more ease and speed. A box is also placed around phonology (speech sounds), orthography (spelling patterns), and morphology (meaning units) to emphasize their connections to spelling development. The bidirectional arrows within the figure depict the interrelated, interactive features of written language and serve as a reminder that each factor is intermeshed with other writing skills, again demonstrating that the writing process is nonlinear. Performance on one facet of writing can affect performance in another (e.g., poor spelling can influence word choice). Furthermore, the model does not suggest that the factors develop or build in a hierarchical order. Thus, a writer may express ideas clearly, but handwriting and/or spelling may be poor; or a writer may spell accurately but have trouble generating and expressing ideas. This theoretical, conceptual model has not been empirically validated. It was based on theoretical hypotheses that exist in the research literature. It attempts to explain or describe the various factors involved in writing performance.

WRITTEN LANGUAGE PROFILES

This conceptual model was then used to design two profiles: a Written Language Profile, presented in Appendix A, and a Class Written Language Profile, presented in Appendix B. These profiles are designed to provide a procedure for monitoring student writing development. The Written Language Profile has statements that reflect various factors involved in written language. The assessment tool can be used with various teacher-made assessments or through direct observations of a student's written products. To complete the profile, gather several writing samples from students in the class. By analyzing the writing, attempt to determine if performance is more limited (below average) or more advanced (above average) than other students in the class. Also, when completing the profile, consider the age of the student. The expectations for a first-grade student in writing clearly differ from those for a fourth-grade student. The profile may be completed three or more times during the school year monitor a student's writing progress.

Similarly, the Class Written Language Profile can also be compiled across three separate dates to provide an overall summary of the skill levels and progress of all or some class members. This class profile provides a means to summarize written language development. In addition, the Class Written Language Profile allows a teacher to compare one individual's writing progress with overall class proficiency.

Teachers may select and use various portions of both profiles. It is not necessary to complete all items. For example, a teacher may want to use a profile to monitor only those factors related to spelling development or to monitor the factors related primarily to the communication of ideas. Because different skills vary in importance and occur at different developmental levels (e.g., development of legible handwriting usually occurs in the early grades), a teacher may decide to focus on the aspects of writing that are most pertinent to a student's current grade level or level of development. Due to the vast developmental differences in writing competence among children, it is impossible to be prescriptive and provide grade-level starting places or expectations (e.g., a fifth-grade student may still struggle with letter formation, whereas the majority of peers write easily and legibly).

This chapter is organized around a discussion of the informal assessment statements in the Written Language Profile. The goal of evaluating a student, a group of students, or a class is to identify what writers can do and the specific factors or constraints that affect written production. We conclude the chapter with a brief discussion of the importance of voice and the communicative functions of writing.

DISPLAYS A POSITIVE ATTITUDE TOWARD WRITING

Unfortunately, children who struggle with writing often develop a negative attitude toward the process of putting their ideas down on paper. They see little purpose in having to write when they can more easily state what they want to say. Anxiety, attributions, and motivation often influence a writer's performance (Gregg, 1995; Gregg & Mather, 2002). Fear of writing appears to be independent of an individual's sex (Daly & Miller, 1975; Jeroski & Conry, 1981); personality traits (Daly & Miller, 1975; Spielberger, Garsuch, & Lushene, 1970); and subject-specific attitudes (Daly & Wilson, 1983). Academic and social self-esteem, however, do appear to be related to a fear of writing (Daly & Wilson, 1983). Students performing academically below their peers often demonstrate low self-esteem and negative self-concepts about their abilities to write.

For some students, both attitude toward writing and perception of writing competence influence performance (Graham & Harris, 1999). Isha, a sixth-grade student with significant writing problems, was asked whether she liked writing. Her response, presented in Figure 7.3, illus-

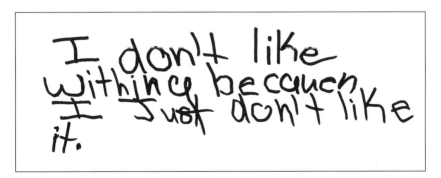

Figure 7.3. Why Isha doesn't like writing: "I don't like writing because I just don't like it."

trates how difficulties with putting her ideas down on paper have affected her attitude toward writing. A negative attitude toward writing, fear of failure and criticism, and limited confidence in abilities can affect all aspects of writing performance. Through direct observation of both the quantity and quality of a student's typical writings, a teacher can assess a student's willingness to write.

FORMS LETTERS EASILY AND QUICKLY

Until recently, handwriting assessment and instruction have received little attention despite the fact that handwriting is an important component of written language (Bain, 2001). Success in early writing development is partially influenced by the development of fine motor skills needed for controlling writing implements and placing letters in an organized way on paper. Edward had difficulty with any task involving fine motor skills. By the time he completed kindergarten, he still could not write his name legibly or cut with scissors. His attempts at drawing in a coloring book consisted of scribbles and a few straight lines drawn through the pictures. He only engaged in these types of activities when required to do so by his teachers or parents. Because writing was so difficult for him, he engaged in lower levels of practice. These types of difficulties lead students to avoid writing, which further arrests writing development (Berninger, Mizokawa, & Bragg, 1991). Thus, skill development is affected by the inherent weaknesses in motor skills, as well as avoidance of the types of tasks that would actually improve skill. Although poor fine motor skills can contribute to several types of difficulties (e.g., tying shoes, buttoning coats, using scissors), the primary impact in a school setting is on handwriting development.

Handwriting is highly related to the linguistic aspects of written language (Abbott & Berninger, 1993; Graham & Weintraub, 1996). Bain (2001) observed that students who struggle with handwriting tend to have four characteristics: 1) an unconventional grip, 2) fingers near to the pencil tip, 3) difficulty with erasing, and 4) trouble aligning letters. For some students, only the motor aspects of writing affect written language production. So much effort is expended in production that attention to other aspects of writing is compromised. In other cases, the problem extends into other domains of writing.

One could easily surmise that Edward's difficulties could be resolved through assistive technology, but when Edward attempts to use a keyboard, his writing is still riddled with spelling errors. For the assignment in Figure 7.4, Edward was given a sheet of paper with several typed, famous quotations. He was asked to retype the quotations to practice his keyboarding skills. Although the motor demands of writing

> We have two eairs and onley one mouth witch indicates
> we shoud listen twice as much as we talk
>
> wen you stop to think don't for get to start again
>
>
> tomorrow is the bysest day of the week
>
> be like a postage stamp stick on to somthing untill the
> job is done
>
> yesterday is gone tommoro is un sertan todayis here so
> use it

Figure 7.4. Edward tries to type sayings his teacher gives him to copy: "We have two ears and only one mouth, which indicates that we should listen twice as much as we should talk. When you stop to think, don't forget to start again. Tomorrow is the busiest day of the week. Be like a postage stamp, and stick to something until the job is done. Yesterday is gone, tomorrow is uncertain, today is here, so use it."

have been reduced, Edward's facility with writing continues to be severely compromised because his problems involve both fine motor skills and spelling.

Developmental Stages

Handwriting proficiency can be described by the following stages (Levine, 1987): 1) imitation (preschool to first grade), in which children pretend to write by copying others; 2) graphic presentation (first and second grade), in which children learn how to form letters and to write on a line with proper spacing; 3) progressive incorporation (late second to fourth grade), in which letters are produced with less effort; and 4) automatization (fourth through seventh grade), in which children write rapidly and efficiently. In the final stages, students develop personalized styles and increase writing proficiency. Students who struggle with handwriting often initially have difficulty learning to form letters and then writing with ease. When compared with their classmates, some students with learning disabilities demonstrate a relatively slow rate of speed (Weintraub & Graham, 1998). As a consequence, these students often have trouble keeping up when taking notes and take longer to complete writing assignments. Weintraub and Graham indicated that on the basis of handwriting alone, students with learning disabilities will accomplish in 50 minutes what peers with typical achievement levels will complete in 30 minutes. To analyze handwriting informally, the two most important considerations are accuracy of letter formation and handwriting speed.

Letter Formation

One major part of a handwriting evaluation is to identify specific errors in letter formation. Although spacing between letters and words and slant affect legibility, accurate letter formation is the most important factor (Quant, 1946). When first learning to write letters, students have more difficulty with some letters. Graham, Berninger, Weintraub, and Schafer (1998) examined the handwriting of 300 children in first through third grades and found that the following six lower-case letters accounted for 48% of the omissions, miscues, and eligibilities: *q, j, z, u, n,* and *k.* In a classic study of specific illegibilities in handwriting, Newland (1932) found that the frequency of illegibilities increased with age and that a failure to close letters was the most frequent illegibility habit. Across the ages, the following four types of difficulties in letter formation caused more than 50% of the illegibilities: 1) failure to close letters, 2) closing looped strokes, 3) looping nonlooped strokes, and 4) using straight up strokes rather than rounded strokes (e.g., writing a *n* like a *u*).

Although most school districts adopt a certain approach to teaching handwriting, research has not demonstrated a clear advantage of one style over another (Graham, 1999; Graham & Miller, 1980). Regardless of approach, the goals are to help students develop legible writing styles so they are able to write quickly and easily without devoting conscious attention to letter formation (Graham, 1999).

Speed

Another central part of an informal evaluation is to observe how quickly and easily a student writes. To do a simple evaluation, provide the student with a copy of a sentence that contains all of the letters of the alphabet, such as "Big oxen, quick zebras, fighting monkeys, and wild pigs have jungle homes" (Tagatz, Otto, Klausmeier, Goodwin, & Cook, 1968). Have the student practice the sentence one time and then copy the sentence as many times as he or she can within 3 minutes. Count the total number of letters written in the 3-minute period, and then divide this number by 3 to get the total letters per minute (lpm). Compare the student's proficiency level to other class members of the same sex.

SEGMENTS SPEECH SOUNDS

As students learn an alphabetic language like English, a critical first step is becoming aware that speech can be divided or sequenced into a series of discrete sounds, syllables, and words. Phonological awareness is an oral language ability that refers to the ability to attend to various aspects of the sound structure of speech. This metacognitive understanding involves the realization that spoken language is made up of a series of sounds (phonemes) that are arranged in a particular order (Clark & Uhry, 1995). Phonological processes are critical for the development of spelling skills (Bailet, 2001) and are related significantly to spelling performance through high school (Calfee, Lindamood, & Lindamood, 1973). Many spelling problems in young adults often reflect specific deficits in the phonological aspects of language (Moats, 2001).

The most important phonological ability for spelling is *segmentation,* the ability to break apart the speech sounds in a word. To become proficient in spelling, students have to develop the understanding that spoken words have segments and that words can be broken down into these discrete sounds. A teacher may use the following sequence to assess segmentation ability informally. Begin with tasks that require the student to segment sentences into individual words. Have the student clap the number of words or push forward markers to represent each word. Next, progress to compound words (e.g., raincoat) and then to the number of syllables with a word. After syllables, see if the student can segment short words into onsets (the beginning part of the syllable) and rimes (the ending part of the syllable, such as –*at* in *cat*). Finally, determine if the student can break words into individual phonemes (speech sounds) by counting the number of sounds (e.g., how many sounds do you hear in the word *eight?* [2]).

Figures 7.5 and 7.6 provide an example of a brief screening tool to assess segmentation abilities, excerpted from the Screening of Early Reading Processes (SERP), developed by Mather, Bos, Podhajski, Babur, and Rhein (2000) and published by Mather and Goldstein (2001). This informal assessment has been widely field-tested. This portion of the screening tool is an adaptation of Sawyer's (1987) *Test of Awareness of Language Segments.*

Segmentation ability may also be inferred by analyzing a student's spellings. Observe whether the writer records a plausible grapheme (letter pattern) for each phoneme in the word. Students with good segmentation ability are able to sequence sounds accurately and their attempted spellings strive to preserve the speech sounds in the words.

RECALLS LETTER STRINGS AND PATTERNS

Some students have difficulty learning and recalling the letter strings and spelling patterns of a language. *Orthographic awareness* is the ability needed to retrieve a whole word unit, a letter cluster unit, or a component letter (Berninger, 1996). In order to spell, a person must have

Instructions for Informal Assessment of Segmentation

Materials

To administer this test, you need a set of 10 colored blocks, chips, or tiles (all the same color), these directions, and a test record form.

Instructions

Examiner instructions are in *italics.* You may rephrase these directions as needed to ensure the student understands the task. Once testing begins, however, do not provide extra help, supports, or additional instructions. Begin each part when the student understands the task. Do not penalize for articulation or sound production errors.

Sentences

Place the 10 colored blocks (or chips or tiles) on the table. Before administering the test items, say, *We are going to use these blocks to say, "My dog barks."* Say each word as you push one block forward for each word. Point to each block as you say, *This block is for "My." This block is for "dog" and this one is for "barks."* After each item, push the blocks back into a group. *Now you do one. Push each block forward to say, "Dan swims."* If the student does not correctly identify the word for each block, say, *Tell me the word for each block.* If the response is correct, say, *Now, do "Dan swims fast."* If the student does not understand the task, use other sentences for additional practice (e.g., "Jane walks to school." "Sue rides her bike.") Remind the student to say each word when pushing the block forward. For a correct response, the student needs to identify the words and the correct number of blocks. If when saying the words of the sentence, the student divides a word into sounds, say, *Try it again but just say the words.* Begin each item with, *Tell and show me with the blocks....*

Syllables

Say, *I'm going to use these blocks to break a word into parts. "Cupcake" has two parts.* Push forward one block for each part as you say it. Then point to each block and say, *This block is "cup" and this one is "cake."* After each item, push the blocks back into a group. Push the blocks in front of the student and say, *Now you do one. Use the blocks to tell and show me the two parts of "football."* If the student does not understand, practice with two or three additional examples (e.g., "raindrop," "popcorn," "toothbrush"). Push forward one block for each part as you say, *Here is a different one. "Doctor" has two parts. This block is "doc" and this one is "tor." Now you do one. Use the blocks to tell and show me the word "paper."* If the student does not understand, practice with two or three additional examples (e.g., "flying," "happy"). For a correct response, the student needs to break the word into parts and identify the correct number of blocks. Begin each item with, *Tell and show me the parts of....*

Sounds

Say, *I'm going to use the blocks to show you all of the sounds in a word. The word "time" would be /t/ /i/ /m/.* Push a block forward as you say each sound. Place the blocks in front of the student. *Now you do one. Show me the sounds in the word "big."* After each item, push the blocks back into a group. If the student does not understand, provide two or three additional examples (e.g., "make," "boat"). For a correct response, the student needs to segment the sounds correctly and identify the correct number of blocks. Begin each item with, *Tell and show me the sounds in....*

Figure 7.5. Instructions for Informal Assessment of Segmentation. (Excerpted from Mather & Goldstein, 2001; reprinted by permission.)

Informal Assessment of Segmentation

Name: _____   Grade: _____   Date: _____

Sentences	Syllables	Sounds
Examples: Dan swims; Dan swims fast	*Examples: foot • ball, pa • per*	*Examples: big /b/ /i/ /g/*
____ 1. Sam runs.	____ 1. hotdog (hot • dog)	____ 1. me /m/ /e/
____ 2. She likes milk.	____ 2. baseball (base • ball)	____ 2. go /g/ /o/
____ 3. Bill got a cat.	____ 3. doorbell (door • bell)	____ 3. bit /b/ /i/ /t/
____ 4. The rose is bright red.	____ 4. funny (fun • ny)	____ 4. red /r/ /e/ /d/
____ 5. I will go to the park.	____ 5. camping (camp • ing)	____ 5. loud /l/ /ou/ /d/
____ 6. The store has lots of things.	____ 6. slowly (slow • ly)	____ 6. food /f/ /oo/ /d/
____ 7. His school is close to his house.	____ 7. carpenter (car • pen • ter)	____ 7. skate /s/ /k/ /a/ /t/
____ 8. She rides her horse each day to school.	____ 8. transportation (trans • por • ta • tion)	____ 8. rust /r/ /u/ /s/ /t/
		____ 9. friend /f/ /r/ /ĕ/ /n/ /d/
		____ 10. napkin /n/ /a/ /p/ /k/ /i/ /n/
Total: ____	Total: ____	Total: ____

Figure 7.6. Informal Assessment of Segmentation. (From Mather, N., & Goldstein, S., [2001]. *Learning disabilities and challenging behaviors: A guide to intervention and classroom management* [p. 198]. Baltimore: Paul H. Brookes Publishing Co.; adapted by permission.)

189

mental images of words stored in memory or word specific memory (Ehri, 2000). Ehri and Wilce (1982) referred to these stored representations as *visual orthographic images.* This ability helps students establish detailed visual or mental representations of words and have rapid, fluent access to these representations. Successful spelling involves the abilities to 1) remember the position of each letter in the word and 2) recall the letters in the correct sequence. Vellutino, Scanlon, and Tanzman (1994) referred to this process as *orthographic coding,* or "the ability to represent the unique array of letters that defines a printed word, as well as general attributes of the writing system such as sequential dependencies, structural redundancies, and letter position frequencies" (p. 314). This knowledge refers specifically to print (Corcos & Willows, 1993).

Knowledge of orthographic structure (the constraints of permissible letter sequences) is evidenced by the ability to sequence common letter strings in the correct order (e.g., *ight*). Although unexpected letters and irregular spelling patterns may be stored in these representations, securing these images is more difficult than securing words that conform to common spelling patterns (Ehri, 2000). Students with weaknesses in orthography have more difficulty with spelling irregular words or exception words than spelling words that have predictable phoneme–grapheme correspondences. Typically, when spelling irregular words, these individuals regularize the element of the word that does not conform to a language's spelling rules. For example, the word *they* will be spelled as *thay,* even though the word has been encountered numerous times in print. Their attempted spellings often violate the underlying rules of English spelling (e.g., spelling *exact* as *egzakt*). In addition, students who have difficulty with orthography have trouble memorizing and spelling words that have multiletter graphemes, such as *tch.* An informal method for assessing orthography is to check to see if the student spells the irregular elements of words correctly.

USES WORD ENDINGS AND AFFIXES CORRECTLY

Morphology refers to the meaning units of language. Just as a phoneme is the smallest unit of sound, a *morpheme* is the smallest unit of meaning. For example, the word *boys* is composed of two morphemes, the meaning unit *boy* and the plural marker *s.* The types of morphological errors that are common in writing include 1) difficulty with word endings, 2) difficulty choosing the correct affixes (prefixes and suffixes) and/or omitting affixes, 3) difficulty using correct inflections (*big* and *bigger*), and 4) difficulty with derivations of a word (e.g., *social* versus *society*) (Moats, 2001).

Knowledge of morphological structures can be observed by analyzing errors in spontaneous writing samples or by using various structured formats. A teacher may review how the writer spells word endings (e.g., *–ed* and *–s*) and prefix and suffix morphemes. In addition, several of the procedures discussed in the section of this chapter on grammar are appropriate for assessing morphology. For example, modified cloze passages can be used where certain parts of words have been deleted (e.g., word endings, prefixes). Students are then asked to complete the blanks with the correct word part.

SPELLS WORDS CORRECTLY

Many children discover the internal structure of words by experiencing numerous opportunities to interact with print (Tangel & Blachman, 1992). Some children, however, do not learn to spell easily or naturally. A lack of automaticity with spelling processes can inhibit content generation and may interfere with both the amount and the quality of writing. If a writer has to stop and think about how to spell a word, an already developed idea may be forgotten (Graham, Berninger, Abbott, Abbott, & Whitaker, 1997). Spelling problems can persist into adulthood (Bruck, 1993; Moats, 2001). Bruck found that although college students with a childhood diagnosis of dyslexia attempted to preserve the phonological structure of words, their knowledge of phoneme–grapheme associations was still limited.

Unfortunately, some words in English are difficult to spell. The English language is described as a deep orthography because of the relationships among phonemes and graphemes. English has approximately 42–44 phonemes but more than 200 graphemes. For example, in English, the speech sound /f/ can be spelled with any of the following graphemes: *f, ph, gh,* or *ff*. Although accurate spelling requires phoneme–grapheme conversion, it is possible to memorize a small core of frequently used words through a mental image or whole-word retrieval strategy rather than mediating the process from the phoneme to the grapheme level.

Figure 7.7 depicts a portion of a writing sample from Charlene, a 15-year-old student. Charlene has managed to memorize the spellings of several commonly used words but does not understand how to apply phoneme–grapheme relationships for spelling. When she comes to a word that is not stored as a whole in her mental lexicon, her attempted spelling bears little resemblance to the target word. She does, however, understand that English spelling is invariant, so once she has decided how to represent a certain word, such as *college* ("commerst"), she maintains that spelling throughout her paper.

Where do I see myself in five year

In five year I see myself at the age of 20 year old. That is very sanatr for me. I will be in Commerst to become a loeaner or like my mom sareb a lar. Ha Ha. The commerst I wol like to go to is mallin or New Yock City. If commerst don't work out for some warths. I will like be a fucharts in New Yock City. I will like to talk Pictarin of Stars and mansta. I will like to put my pictarin in a massat call JIU. So the teen can see my work all over the would. If the fucharts job work out ok. I will caust it and go back to Commerst and talk agin. I will like to become a Scant locaner it is my dust to become one. So I can make my mom and my sister parstar of me.

Figure 7.7. Charlene's writing sample:
Where do I see myself in five years
In five years I see myself at the age of 20 years old. That is very scary to me. I will be in college to become a lawyer, or like my mom says, a liar. Ha ha. The college I would like to go is Miami or New York City. If college doesn't work out for some reason, I would like to be a photographer in New York City. I will like to take pictures of stars and models. I will like to put my pictures in a magazine called J14 so the teens can see my work all over the world. If the photography job works out okay, I will keep it and go back to college to become a trial lawyer. It is my desire to become one so I can make my mom and sister proud of me.

Spelling is a severe constraint for Charlene, and unless she gains an understanding of phoneme–grapheme relationships, her spelling will not improve. Accurate spelling requires an awareness of the internal structure of words (Blachman, 1994), and both lexical and sublexical processes contribute to accuracy (Berninger, 1996). Charlene retrieves words as wholes (lexical retrieval) but does not use phonemes or graphemes (sublexical retrieval) to aid with unknown words.

Spelling ability is based on the integration of fundamental cognitive, linguistic, and motoric processes. As described by Berninger and colleagues (1998) and Berninger and colleagues (2000), spelling requires that the mind's eye, ear, mouth, and hand learn to communicate to process and produce spoken words. In order to understand the possible reasons for poor spelling, consider a writer's phonological, orthographical, and morphological awareness (e.g., knowing that the spelling of the past tense of a verb is -ed even when it sounds like a /t/). In addition, knowledge of word meanings is essential for the spelling of homophones (e.g., *pair* and *pear*). Although interconnected, all of these processes play different roles in spelling development. For children who spell easily, however, awareness of the rules of phonology, orthography, and morphology seem to blend together in a seamless fashion.

Analysis of a student's attempted spellings can help a teacher determine the primary reason for the types of spelling errors. Figure 7.8 presents a binary decision tree to help determine if the student's diffi-

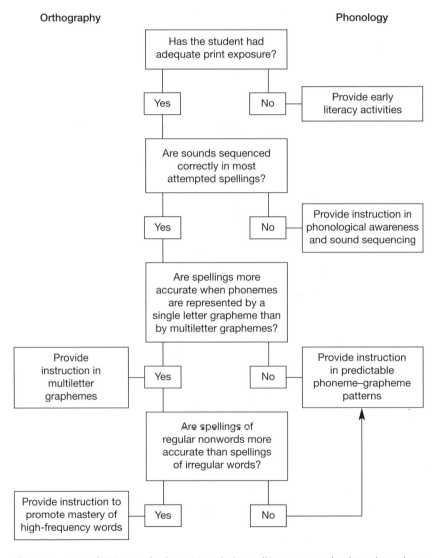

Figure 7.8. Binary decision tree for determining whether spelling errors are related to orthography or phonology.

culties are more related to problems with the mastery of phonology or orthography or with both. Students must first learn to sequence sounds before they can recall specific spelling patterns.

Theories of Spelling Development

Two theoretical approaches have been proposed to explain spelling development: the strategy approach and the stage theory approach. The strategy approach depicts spelling development as continuous, suggesting that children incorporate a variety of strategies when spelling from the beginning of their writing (Treiman, 1998; Treiman & Bourassa, 2000). The stage theorists propose that children appear to progress through several developmental stages when learning to spell (Ehri, 1986, 1989; Gentry, 1982, 1984; Reid, 1988; Weiner, 1994). Even though many children do incorporate varied aspects of linguistic knowledge in their initial spellings and reveal sensitivity to orthographic and morphological influences, the proposed stages of development can help explain a student's performance. For children who struggle with spelling, their difficulties seem indicative of arrest in one of the stages in development (Moats, 2001).

In the prephonetic stage of learning to spell, a child will combine a string of unrelated letters to communicate a message. At the semiphonetic stage, letters are used to represent sounds, but only a few sounds in words are represented. In some instances, students will use the names of letters rather than the letter sounds (Adams, 1990). For example, the word *while* may be written as *yl*. During this stage, the child's spellings may follow logical linguistic patterns, but he or she knows very few correct spellings. A student may know consonant sounds, long vowel sounds, and an occasional sight word. At the phonetic stage, students produce spellings that demonstrate phoneme–grapheme correspondence. When writing, they attempt to record all of the sounds within a word and present them in the correct sound sequence. At the transitional stage, the writer demonstrates awareness of many of the conventions of English orthography. For example, the student spells the past tense of a verb as –*ed* even when the ending sounds like a /t/, such as in the word *trapped*. Operating with chunks of words makes it easier to spell multisyllabic words (Ehri, 2000). At the conventional stage, the writer possesses multiple strategies for determining standard spelling. Although not all words are spelled correctly, the writer regularly employs information from sounds, sight, and meaning as an aid to English spelling.

Similarly, Henderson's (1990) system consists of five stages, progressing from scribbles and pictures (the preliterate stage), to letter-

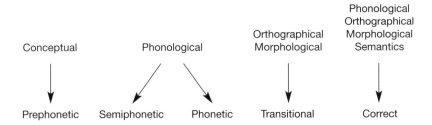

Figure 7.9. Stages of spelling development.

name (letters are used to represent sounds), to within-word patterns (orthographic and morphological patterns are observed), to syllable juncture (consonants are doubled and patterns present in syllables are observed), to derivational constancy (roots and derivations are used). Figure 7.9 illustrates how phonology, orthography, and morphology interact with stages of spelling development.

Assessment of spelling ability requires direct observations of the strategies and knowledge the writer employs. By using information gained from an analysis of spelling performance, techniques can then be identified to help each student increase spelling skill (Graham & Miller, 1979). Students who struggle with spelling require ongoing evaluation, as well as intense, direct, systematic instruction to promote full knowledge of the spelling system (Ehri, 1989; Graham & Miller, 1979).

USES CORRECT GRAMMATICAL FORMS

Grammar includes knowledge of various word forms (e.g., verb tense) and the ability to produce various sentence structures. The ability to produce correct word and sentence forms directly affects the quality rating of writing on high-stakes exams (Gregg, Coleman, Stennett, & Davis, 2002). Common errors associated in producing grammatical structures include omitting words or phrases, reversing word order, substituting related words, overusing simple sentence structures, and using incorrect verb tenses. Research since the 1970s has shown the dramatic impact of context and function (or purpose) on a language user's application of meaning and structure (Gregg et al., 2002). Therefore, when assessing written syntax, one must consider the function of the assigned task, as well as the grammatical forms most appropriate for the type of writing task.

Linguists have encouraged teachers to examine the use of words and sentence structures across different contexts (Chafe, 1982; Chafe &

Danielewicz, 1986; Halliday, 1988). For example, a teacher might assign two different writing assignments, one related to history and one to science. Each of these contexts uses different words and sentence patterns. Because of enhanced knowledge in one domain, a student may be more skilled in writing in one type of context than in another.

Steps in Assessing Written Syntax

The first step in evaluating proficiency to produce word forms and sentence structures is to consider the student's experiences with reading and writing text. The type of reading material a student has been exposed to can influence ability to produce grammatical structures. Although highly decodable text (e.g., *Dan can fan the man*) is useful for increasing phonic skills, this type of text does not provide students with exposure to a variety of sentence structures. In addition, consider whether the student has had experience in writing different types of context (e.g., history, science, mathematics) and whether errors in syntax are consistent across task formats (e.g., structured and nonstructured, timed and untimed).

The next step is to compare a student's oral language competence with written language competence by comparing and contrasting the types of sentences the student produces when speaking and writing. Although written syntax development lags behind oral syntax through middle school or junior high, by eleventh and twelfth grades, the reverse trend occurs (Lobin, 1976). In general, however, students with good syntactic abilities in speaking also employ these same structures in writing unless additional constraints, such as poor spelling, are influencing production. In addition, some delays in syntactic maturity may result from oral language differences (e.g., dialect).

Word class can also affect the ability to manipulate grammatical structures. Open-class words (i.e., verbs, some adverbs, nouns, and adjectives) are usually easier for beginning writers to manipulate in sentence structures than closed-class words (i.e., prepositions, conjunctions, pronouns, and some adverbs). Closed-class words usually represent more abstract concepts and are often used in more complex sentence structures.

The four most basic sentence types used in written expression include simple sentences, compound sentences, complex sentences, and compound-complex sentences. Table 7.1 describes these different sentence types. Use of these sentence types depends on a student's knowledge of independent and dependent clauses. By the time students enter kindergarten, most know many types of clauses (Nippold, 1988). Lobin

Table 7.1.   Four basic sentence types

Sentence type	Requirements	Example
Simple	One independent clause	
	Types	
	Subject (S) verb (V)	Dan runs fast.
	SSV	Dan and Mary run fast.
	SVV	Mary walks and runs fast.
	SSVV	Both Dan and Mary walk and run fast.
Compound	Two independent clauses joined together by a coordinating conjunction	Mary had a hamburger, and Fred had a cheese sandwich.
Complex	Independent clause combined with a dependent clause	After the game, they went out to dinner.
Compound-complex	Two independent clauses combined with a dependent clause	When it was time to go swimming, Martha got her swimming suit, and then she hopped in her car.

(1976) found that 2 or 3 of every 10 sentences spoken by 9-year-olds contained a subordinate clause.

Task Formats   The next step is to determine whether the writer can identify correct grammatical forms and apply them correctly in writing. Several different types of formats can be used to compare grammatical knowledge (identification) with grammatical production. Examples of task formats include identification and judgment, the cloze procedure, scrambled sentences, sentence building and combining activities, controlled stimulus passages, and spontaneous writing. Begin with highly structured tasks focusing on identification of grammatical forms (e.g., cloze, multiple choice) and then move toward less structured tasks requiring grammatical production (e.g., sentence combining, sentence building, controlled stimulus passage). Finally, consider a student's proficiency with grammar in spontaneous text in both timed and untimed settings across different contexts. No single task or test can determine proficiency with word form and grammatical structures. Instead, instructional goals should be determined from a collection of writing samples on different topics.

Identification and Judgment   The purpose of using recognition and judgment tasks is to determine if the writer can identify correct grammatical forms. A student may be able to identify when grammatical forms are incorrect but not be able to produce the form in writing. One commonly used format is referred to as recognition and judgment of grammaticality tasks (Wiig & Semel, 1984). For example, the student would be presented the following sentence: *Yesterday the girl go to shop.* Then the writer would identify whether the grammar is correct in the sentence by indicating simply yes or no. A variation or extension of this task is to ask the student to correct sentences that are not grammatically correct.

Classification and Categorization   These types of tasks are also excellent means to assess a writer's understanding of grammatical structures (Wiig & Semel, 1984). On this type of task, the student is given two sentences (*He will walk his dog. He walked his dog*). Then the student is asked to determine which sentence would be identified with the word *yesterday* and which with *tomorrow*.

The Cloze Procedure   The cloze procedure is another way to assess word choice, morphology, and written syntax. The writer is presented with a single sentence, several sentences, a paragraph, or complete writing sample in which target words have been deleted. The student then selects and writes specific words that will maintain the sentence meaning.

Scrambled Sentences   The words in a sentence may also be rearranged to assess a writer's knowledge of the rules for word order (Wiig & Semel, 1984). The student is presented sentences in which words, phrases, or clauses are grammatically correct and incorrect and then asked to identify the correct sentence (e.g., *The bird red tiny is* or *The tiny bird is red*), or the student may be given only incorrect sentences and asked to rewrite and correct the sentences.

Sentence Building and Combining   Sentence building and sentence combining activities allow a teacher to observe a writer's attempts to manipulate language in order to improve the maturity of syntactic structures (Strong, 1983). For sentence building activities, provide the student with single words or a set of words to use in constructing a sentence. With sentence combining tasks, give the writer sets of short sentences that are to be combined into a single sentence. Sentence combining activities are also useful for assessing morphology, spelling, punctuation, capitalization, vocabulary, and flexibility with style.

Controlled Stimulus Passage   A controlled stimulus passage (CSP) allows the teacher to control such writing variables as topic, style, and length while requiring the student to manipulate more text than possible with sentence combining tasks (O'Donnell & Hunt, 1975). On a

CSP task, the writer is asked to rewrite a paragraph that contains short, choppy sentences. Therefore, the writer must decide which sentences, clauses, and words to combine, eliminate, and change. The teacher would note syntax, punctuation, organization, and spelling errors. As noted previously, the context of the paragraph could affect the performance outcome. Therefore, a teacher would want to provide the student with several CSP tasks that require different contents (e.g., narrative, history, mathematics, science).

Spontaneous Writing   Analysis of spontaneous writing samples provides a way to evaluate the student's ability to construct connected discourse in the least structured manner. Therefore, the writer must simultaneously manage all of the components of writing (e.g., handwriting, spelling, vocabulary, text structure). A teacher may want to compare syntactical competence across types of assignments (e.g., narrative, expository) and the complexity of the task. The length of the writing sample, the age of the student, the type of context, and the knowledge that the student has about the topic can all influence the syntactical structures produced.

One way to determine the number of errors a student is making in syntax is to calculate the percentage of errors on specific words to the total number of words produced. Or count the number of errors in sentence structures, and compare it with the total number of sentences. Using Part One of the Syntax Coding Sheet (see Figure 7.10), a teacher could count the number of sentence types (e.g., simple, complex) and calculate how often certain structures are used. Ideally, a writer should use a mix of different types of structures, rather than only one type. In Part Two, a teacher can record various types of sentence errors (e.g., fragments, run-ons, misplaced modifiers) and then determine the ratio of the number of errors to the total number of sentences in the sample. In addition, a teacher may want to listen to a student read a paper aloud (or into a tape recorder) to assess the writer's ability to recognize and correct errors. Part Three of the Syntax Coding Sheet provides examples of observations to note as a student reads a writing sample aloud.

Punctuation   Correct use of punctuation helps a writer to structure meaning at both the sentence and text level. Awareness and use of punctuation are developmental processes dependent primarily on the amount of exposure to and instruction with print. Invented punctuation (Martens & Goodman, 1996) is as normal a stage of development for beginning writers as invented spelling (Bissex, 1980; Read, 1975). Ferreiro and Zucc

Syntax Coding Sheet for Spontaneous Writing Sample

Student: _____ Completion time: _____

Grade: _____ Topic: _____

Part One: Sentence Patterns

Pattern	Count		Number of errors / Total number of sentences
	Correct	Incorrect	
Simple			
Compound			
Complex			
Compound-complex			

Part Two: Sentence Errors

Pattern	Count	Number of errors / Total number of sentences
Fragment		
Run-on sentence		
Misplaced modifier		
Faulty reference		
Sentence meaning unclear		

Part Three: Taped Reading of Written Text

Reads exactly as printed	Yes	No
Alters content to enhance meaning	Yes	No
Recognizes sentences that do not make sense	Yes	No
Corrects for missing periods, question marks, and commas through voice inflection and rhythm	Yes	No
Corrects word usage errors	Yes	No
Adds omitted words	Yes	No
Deletes inserted words	Yes	No

Figure 7.10. Syntax coding sheet for analyzing spontaneous writing samples.

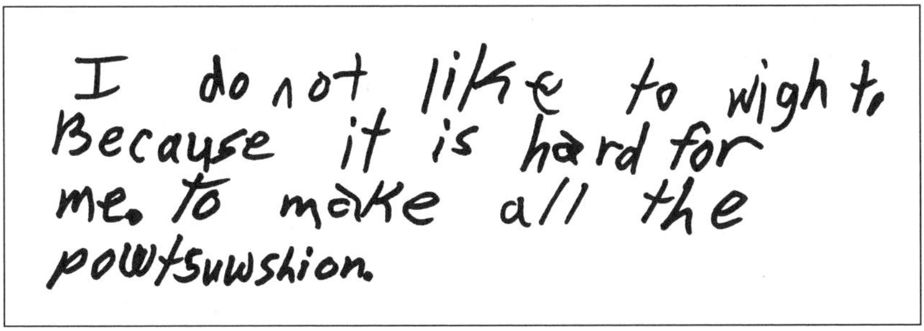

Figure 7.11.   Jamal's note about punctuation: "I do not like to write because it is hard for me to make all the punctuation."

as an alternative means to their lexical and textual solutions" (1996, p. 204). Some students have trouble mastering the rules of punctuation. When asked if he likes writing, Jamal noted that punctuation is difficult (see Figure 7.11).

Assess knowledge of punctuation by conducting brief assessments of editing skill and by analyzing punctuation use in spontaneous writing samples. The types of tasks described for assessing grammatical knowledge are also useful for evaluating a student's ability to apply correct punctuation (e.g., identification, sentence combining, controlled stimulus passage). Difficulty with punctuation often occurs when writers are learning new grammatical structures, such as those involved in sentence combining exercises. Understanding the reason for an error (e.g., lack of understanding of what constitutes a complete sentence, misunderstanding of the use of quotation marks) is essential for planning intervention.

USES A VARIETY OF WORDS

Vocabulary or word-level knowledge is integral to success with written expression. As Vygotsky noted, "Thought may be compared to a cloud shedding a shower of words" (1962, p. 56). Words and the concepts they represent are the building blocks of written expression (Bell & Perfetti, 1994; Cunningham, Stanovich, & Wilson, 1990). A student may understand the meaning of a word but have difficulty using the word correctly in a sentence. A very simple word, such as *when*, conceptually represents the abstract construct of time. Difficulty using such a word can be at either the conceptual or the grammatical level.

A writer's vocabulary is influenced by three main factors: 1) familiarity with words, 2) the depth of conceptual understanding of those words, and 3) the ability to retrieve words as needed (Gould, 2001). In general, many students demonstrating writing difficulties produce fewer words (fluency) and less sophisticated word choices than their peers. As a first step in assessing word choice, evaluate if discrepancies exist between the vocabulary words produced in speaking and writing. For some students with writing problems, knowledge of word meanings is low and they do not have the breadth of word choice that is needed for good writing. An impoverished vocabulary may be the result of limited exposure, limited experiences, or limited time spent reading. Also, the type of text that the student is asked to read (i.e., predictable, decodable, high-frequency, or authentic literature) may influence vocabulary development.

For other students, a lack of automaticity at the subword level (i.e., phonology, orthography, morphology, motor) and word level (spelling) inhibits the quality and fluency of written vocabulary. Depending on the nature of their learning difficulties, their speaking vocabulary may be age-appropriate or even more advanced than their peers. Students with writing difficulties often demonstrate difficulty with retrieving and spelling the words they wish to use, therefore devoting excessive amounts of time and energy to low-level tasks. Word choice is then governed by the words a student can spell rather than the best choice of ideas. Figure 7.12 provides a portion of a story written by Gilbert. Gilbert finally learned how to spell the word *police,* so the word was present in every story he wrote. When asked why he always included the word *police,* he responded: "I just feel comfortable with the word because I finally know how to spell it." Note that Gilbert also spells the word *again* four different ways within one sentence.

USES APPROPRIATE ORGANIZATIONAL FORMATS

Although several types of text structures exist, the two most frequently required of writers during the school years are narrative and expository. *Narrative text* refers most often to fictional passages, whereas *expository text* refers to events and nonfictional passages. In early elementary school, the most predominate type of writing is narrative. As children progress through school, the majority of assignments are expository in nature (e.g., essays, reports).

Narrative Writing

Narrative writing includes such forms as scripts, story telling, and event telling. The ability to produce narrative structures requires adequate

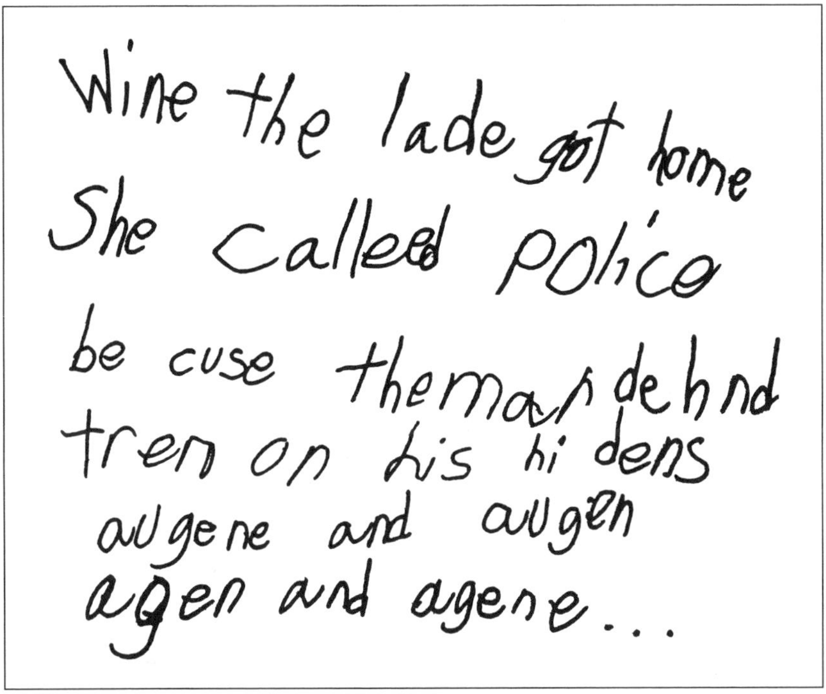

Wine the lade got home
She called police
be cuse theman dehnd
tren on his hi dens
augene and augen
agen and agene...

Figure 7.12.   Gilbert's story: "When the lady got home, she called the police because the man behind turned on his high beams again and again and again and again."

word-level skills (vocabulary and spelling), syntax (sentence structure), and knowledge of story structure (organization). Story structure or story grammar is the underlying framework for the story, which includes elements such as the setting, description of the characters, a problem, attempts to solve the problem, a solution, and an ending. When analyzing stories, consider whether a student has included all elements of a story and the depth of the description (e.g., the external features and internal responses of the characters).

The writer attempting to produce narrative text is required to integrate thought and language, requiring higher-level thinking abilities. Recognizing the need to consider how a writer's thought and language abilities affect text comprehension and production, Applebee (1978) applied Vygotsky's (1962) theory of concept development to narrative-level analysis. His six major narrative structure patterns provide a simple way to analyze children's use of structure in producing text. These six structures include heaps, sequences, primitive narratives, unfocused chains, focused chains, and narratives. Table 7.2 provides an adaptation

Table 7.2. Analysis of narrative typologies

Level	Description	Sample
Heaps	Unrelated statements	I like goldfish. I like teacher. I like candy.
Sequences	One central idea	If I were a dog. I wud go and bark. And to see my frins. I wud like dog bones.
Primative narrative	Co-occuring events	Wen I was a little puppy I did no better and I was messing wif a cat and I ran in the woods to get the cat and ate the cat.
Unfocused chains	Temporal relationships linking to each other	My life in the day of a sandwich. I was put together in the morning. I was bred and jam. Then I was taken to school. My little boy friend ate me at lunch.
Focused chains	Chain of events Central idea present	Win I wint to the mon I deskoverd craud desiason of a alina and lots of roks ther was a D.N.A. of an alan. So the oter sintis ask I are working on a cloning mich.

Sources: Applebee, 1978; Gregg & Hafter, 2000; Hedberg & Westby 1993.

of these typologies in a format for informal assessment with examples of children's writing at each of these stages.

Expository Writing

A major requirement of the elementary, secondary, and postsecondary curriculum is to be able to write expository text. Expository writing includes such forms as explanations (sequences), comparisons and contrasts, descriptions, and opinion essays. Students with writing disabilities demonstrate difficulty with producing the structures required in expository text (Englert et al., 1989; Englert & Thomas, 1987). These writers appear to be less sensitive to text structure, and to organizing, categorizing, revising, and monitoring ideas on the basis of text structure (Englert et al., 1989).

Each type of expository text (e.g., opinion, compare and contrast, descriptive) has a slightly different organizational scheme. Thus, a student may be able to write a descriptive passage but may struggle with the organization required in a compare and contrast structure. The first step for assessing the ability to produce expository text is to understand the writer's awareness of various text structures. Next, analyze fluency and cohesion. For example, did the student write limited text (low fluency) or have difficulty organizing ideas within the text? Finally, evaluate cohesion to determine whether the problem is more within and between sentences or within the organization of the total text structure. A scale can be used to assess a writer's use of an introduction, steps in explanation, use of key words, and overall organization for the purpose of evaluating different types of expository text structures.

Englert's (1990) Cognitive Strategy in Writing (CSIW) curriculum provides a comprehensive methodology for evaluating and providing instruction in expository text. Underlying CSIW is the premise that writers experiencing difficulty with producing expository text do not know the strategies used for planning, organizing, writing, editing, and revising. The curriculum material includes think-sheets designed to heighten a writer's awareness of expository writing strategies. (For a complete description of CSIW curriculum, see Englert, 1990.)

EXPRESSES IDEAS CLEARLY

Several factors influence a student's ability to express ideas in writing. One major consideration is the writer's background knowledge related to the topic. If one does not know much about a topic, the resulting product often lacks substance and detail. Thus, prior knowledge is a critical element for effective writing, and prewriting activities are important for ensuring that a writer has something to say and share about the selected topic. Other factors to consider are cohesion and sense of audience.

Cohesion

Shaughnessy described cohesion as the "grammar of passages" (1977, p. 72). The goal of writing is the construction of a coherent form (Scinto, 1982). Test coherence results when the words within and between sentences provide relevant and connected information for the reader to construct meaning. Halliday and Hasan (1976) explained that cohesion refers to the semantic bonds between words in a text (e.g., *John* is my friend. *He* is very smart.)

The three basic types of cohesive ties that are used most frequently in beginning writer's text are grammatical, transitional, and lexical. Grammatical ties include any pronominal, demonstrative, or comparative words that refer to a noun or pronoun in another sentence or paragraph (e.g., *Alberto* got a ride to his soccer game. *He* was the first one to arrive.) Transitional ties are words and phrases that show relationships between and among statements (e.g., The book was overdue at the library. *In addition,* Martha owed a late fee on another book.) Lexical ties include repeated words, synonyms, and superordinate ties (e.g., In the evening, the children spotted both *mice and raccoons.* They had never seen these *animals* in the wild before.) The cloze procedure can also be used to assess a student's flexibility in using cohesive ties. Delete the first words in sentences and ask the student to add words that will make the text stay together.

Young writers go through a transition from writing lists of single words to producing unconnected complete sentences and finally generating connected sentences or paragraphs. This lack of cohesion between sentences is often still present in the writing of older students with writing difficulties and can arise from "problems with the linguistic devices themselves, the writer's sense of audience, or the cognitive demand of the text structure" (Litowitz, 1981, p. 84).

Sense of Audience

Writing is a social activity involving the construction of meaningful communication between the writer and the reader. Vygotsky (1962) discussed the complex process of writing, stressing that writing involves mastery of cognitive skills within the development of new social understanding. Writers categorize and synthesize their experiences through inner speech, the language of thought. To transform inner language to written text requires that one integrate thought with consideration for the needs of the reader. As Vygotsky (1962) stressed, writing is a dialogue between the writer and reader. The writer must realize that the reader may have a different perspective and that language must be tailored to engage and maintain the reader's interest.

Some students have difficulty perceiving and maintaining the needs of the reader (Englert, 1990; Englert et al., 1988; Graham & Harris, 1999). Other students have a good awareness of the audience needs, but because of so many spelling and mechanical errors, their messages are lost (Gregg & McAlexander, 1989; Gregg, Sigalas, Hoy, Wisenbaker, & McKinley, 1996). Understanding the perspective of the reader requires social inference, critical to communicating specific messages across different audiences (e.g., writer to teacher, writer to peer, writer to trusted adult). Writers vary in their writing competence depending on the audience they are addressing (Britton, Burgess, Martin, McLeod, & Rosen, 1975). To assess sense of audience and its relationship to writing competence, provide many opportunities for evaluating writing across audiences. Some children produce better writing when

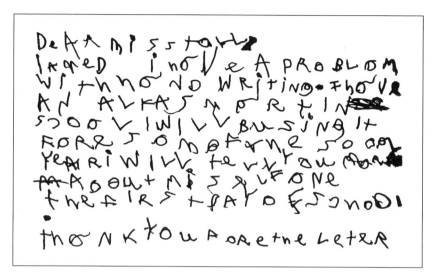

Figure 7.13. Ed's note to his teacher: "Dear Miss Stall, I am Ed. I have a problem with handwriting. I have an Alpha Smart for school. I will be using it for some of the school year. I will tell you more about myself on the first day of school. Thank you for the letter."

asked to write to their peers than when asked to write to an authority figure (e.g., letter to the principal).

Although his writing had evolved by fifth grade, Edward still struggled with writing. He was, however, able to maintain a strong sense of audience when composing. Prior to the start of fifth grade, he received a letter from his teacher-to-be requesting that he write a letter back telling her something about himself. Figure 7.13 illustrates his letter. He decided to tell her about his difficulties with writing and to let her know that he would be using an Alpha Smart device for many writing activities.

COMPOSES TEXT EASILY

Fluency in writing is often referred to as *verbosity* or *length* and is measured by the total number of words that a student writes within a given time frame. As skill in writing improves, the ease and speed of production increase. As an increasing number of school districts are requiring a writing examination for promotion, the use of impressionistic quality scores is increasing. Students with writing disabilities are often less fluent in their writing and often receive lower ratings than writers who generate more text (Gregg et al., 2002). Coleman, Gregg, Davis, and Stennett (2001) found that word complexity and fluency make a significant contribution to impressionistic quality writing scores. Students with writing problems scored significantly below their peers in all areas measuring fluency, word choice, and spelling. These writing constraints had a significant impact on the overall quality scores.

In 2002, Gregg and colleagues reported high correlations among fluency, quality, and the complexity of word choice, suggesting that they are measuring similar constructs. A high correlation between fluency and lexical complexity is not surprising because the number of words is a factor in each index. The extremely high correlation between fluency and quality does, however, suggest that writers who access words and syntactical structures easily are better equipped to produce high-quality writing than those who do not. Gregg and colleagues observed that writers with cognitive and linguistic difficulties affecting fluency or lexical complexity are also likely to have poor basic writing skills (i.e., spelling, handwriting, punctuation), as well as poor quality.

Fluency and quality are not separate constructs but are co-occurring functions during the writing process. To informally assess fluency, collect several measures across samples in a student's portfolio. Perform frequency counts on a variety of factors, such as the total number of words; number of different types of words; words greater than one syllable, two syllables, and three syllables; and the frequency of types of words generated (e.g., common and uncommon words).

USES STRATEGIES WHEN COMPOSING

Metacognitive processes are involved from the beginning stages of writing until the final product. The gradually increasing awareness of the writing process is developmental and influenced by a variety of cognitive and language competencies. For example, successful first-grade writers quickly learn that writing is a tool to express ideas and influence the thinking of others, whereas struggling writers communicate that the purpose of writing is to write letters, rather than ideas. As the demands of the school curriculum increase, students struggling with reading and writing often do not employ strategies. When a writer is involved in the planning of writing, self-questioning strategies are necessary, such as "Who is the audience?" "What do I know about them?" and "How do I organize this information?" (Englert & Raphael, 1988). Before and during composing, the writer must select an organizational format and a type of text structure (e.g., narrative, expository), access knowledge of text scheme, monitor for completeness of ideas, and revise to adhere to the meaning (Englert et al., 1989).

Students who struggle with writing tend to be less knowledgeable about the processes involved in writing than their peers without writing difficulties (Englert & Mariage, 1991; Englert & Raphael, 1988; Graham & Harris, 1989; MacArthur & Graham, 1993). The central reason for their difficulties is limited knowledge of how to plan and monitor the processes involved in writing (Englert & Raphael, 1988; Englert et al., 1989; MacArthur & Graham, 1993). When compared with competent writers, poor writers are often less sensitive to organizing, categorizing, revising, and monitoring ideas on the basis of text structure (Englert et al., 1989; Englert et al., 1988; Graham, Harris, & Sawyer, 1987; Hallenbeck, 1996). They demonstrate little advanced planning when writing (Englert & Raphael, 1988), rely on external criteria (Graham, Schwartz, & MacArthur, 1993), and produce poorly organized written products (de la Paz, Swanson, & Graham, 1998). In addition, Graham (1999) found that students with writing disabilities focused more on the mechanical aspects of text (e.g., spelling, handwriting, word substitutions) when editing and revising rather than on the ideational or organizational aspects.

Metacognition also encompasses an individual's goals, beliefs, and attitudes about the writing process (Westby & Clauser, 1999). Peter clearly expressed that he did not like writing although he understood the importance of writing for communicating ideas (see Figure 7.14).

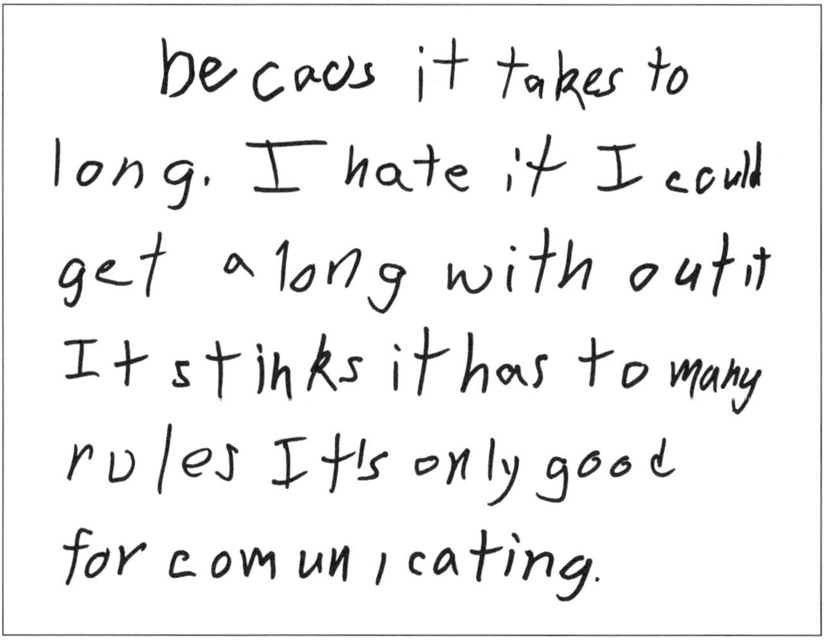
be caus it takes to long. I hate it I could get a long with outit It stinks it has to many rules It's only good for comunicating.

Figure 7.14. Peter's note about why he doesn't like writing: "Because it takes too long. I hate it. I could get along without it. It stinks. It has too many rules. It's only good for communicating."

One effective method for assessing an individual's metacognitive awareness of the writing process is an interview (Englert et al., 1989; Gregg, 1995). Interview questions, such as those listed in Figure 7.15, may be used to obtain information about the writer's motivation, goals, and beliefs about writing. Zainaldin (2001) found that elementary-age children who struggle with writing had less metacognitive awareness of the organization and revision of text structure than their peers but were similar in regard to their feelings toward writing. This finding may suggest that for some young struggling writers, the aversion to writing is not as firmly entrenched as it is in older writers. Children must have continued positive experiences with writing with the focus placed on what the developing writers can do, rather than what they cannot do.

Comments Recorded from an Oral Interview
Interveiw topic: Favorite story

1. How do you feel about writing?	*I hate it.*
2. Do you write at home?	*No, I talk.*
3. What are your favorite things to write about?	*Animals*
4. What is the hardest thing about writing for you?	*It hurts my hand.*
5. What is the easiest thing about writing for you?	*Finding my pencil*
6. What is your favorite instrument to write with (e.g., pen, pencil, computer, crayon)?	*Everything*
7. Does it matter if it is noisy or quiet while you are writing?	*Yeah, quiet I like. No one makes noisy. Teacher won't yell at us.*
8. Does it matter if the room where you are writing is messy?	*I like neat.*
9. Do you ever write letters? Who do you write them to?	*Yeah, birthday card*
10. What is writing?	*Write words*

Figure 7.15.   A metacognitive interview with a first-grade female writer with learning disabilities placed in a class for students with behavior disorders.

By watching children as they write, a teacher can directly observe the types of strategies the writers employ when producing text.

Voice

A critical consideration in evaluating writing is the importance of helping students find and preserve their voices. Students who have difficulty with writing early in their academic careers begin to lose confidence in their abilities to express their opinions and beliefs. Many reasons contribute to this loss of voice. The cognitive and language-based problems discussed throughout this chapter are important contributors. For example, Edward, who ripped up his paper in a moment of intense frustration, is at risk for losing his writing identity. For some students, failure to become automatic with basic writing skills hampers their willingness to express their ideas in writing. Struggling writers have a fear of making errors and putting their ideas down on paper if the initial product will be criticized. A teacher who struggles to decipher a student's writing may inadvertently convey the belief that form (e.g., spelling) is more important than content.

Other students with different cultural experiences or viewpoints may be afraid to express diverse opinions. Stephen, a ninth-grade student, was asked to write about a time where he had either witnessed or experienced prejudice. His first draft, presented in Figure 7.16, is

I consider my slef as T.O. when I was in 5 or 6 grade my teacher mis . . . iwent to the story and got somting to drenk. Wll shen I got to school iwent strait tomy classroom because I was running light. i sat my drenk on the table where I sat some kid rickey spild it. My teacher got mad and stared to call me names Like you stupid yaqui then she was also telling don't you know anting. She is agenc yaquie people because she was colling me yaqui when she was colling namesi was not paing no atticion to what she was saining. She went to for abowt the yaqui people I finolcy got mad and tould hoair to come dowen and quit hating.

Figure 7.16. Stephen's first draft of an essay about one of his experiences with racism: "I consider myself as T.O. When I was in fifth or sixth grade, my teacher Miss . . . I went to the store and got something to drink. Well, when I got to school, I went straight to my classroom because I was running late. I set my drink on the table where I sat. Some kid Ricky spilled it. My teacher got mad and started to call me names like "you stupid Yaqui," [and] then she was also telling [me], "Don't you know anything?" She is against Yaqui people because she was calling me Yaqui. When she was calling names, I was not paying attention to what she was saying. She went too far about the Yaqui people. I finally got mad and told her to calm down and quit hating."

filled with numerous errors, but the message is clearly expressed. An important part of the evaluation process is to first and foremost acknowledge the message that the writer is attempting to share.

CONCLUSION

The primary goal of a writing assessment is to provide a direct link to instruction. The more writing strategies and skills students develop, the more confident they will be in letting us hear their voices. By including many samples from students with writing problems, we have attempted to let these young people speak for themselves about the writing process, particularly how difficult it is for them. Teachers working with students play an integral role in nurturing and developing the voices of these struggling writers. Despite significant difficulties with either the lower-level transcription and/or the higher-level composing skills, all students should be encouraged to express their ideas in writing. As one young adolescent wrote, "I can rite. I finole can rite something. Sumone helpt me find my sol. You no dat wuz my teesher."

REFERENCES

Abbott, R.D., & Berninger, V.W. (1993). Structural equation modeling of relationships among developmental skills and writing skills in primary and intermediate grade writers. *Journal of Educational Psychology, 85,* 478–508.

Adams, M.J. (1990). *Beginning to read: Thinking and learning about print.* Cambridge, MA: MIT Press.

Applebee, A.N. (1978). *The child's concept of a story.* Chicago: University of Chicago Press.

Bailet, L.L. (2001). Development and disorders of spelling in the beginning school years. In A.M. Bain, L.L. Bailet, & L.C. Moats (Eds.), *Written language disorders: Theory into practice* (2nd ed., pp. 1–41). Austin, TX: PRO-ED.

Bain, A.M. (2001). Handwriting disorders. In A.M. Bain, L.L. Bailet, & L.C. Moats (Eds.), *Written language disorders: Theory into practice* (2nd ed., pp. 77–101). Austin, TX: PRO-ED.

Bell, L.C., & Perfetti, C.A. (1994). Reading skill: Some adult comparisons. *Journal of Educational Psychology, 86,* 244–255.

Berninger, V.W. (1996). *Reading and writing acquisition: A developmental neuropsychological perspective.* Oxford: Westview Press.

Berninger, V., Abbott, R., Rogan, L., Reed, L., Abbott, S., Brooks, A., Vaughan, K., & Graham, S. (1998). Teaching spelling to children with specific learning disabilities: The mind's ear and eye beat the computer or pencil. *Learning Disability Quarterly, 21,* 106–122.

Berninger, V., Mizokawa, D., & Bragg, R. (1991). Theory-based diagnosis and remediation of writing disabilities. *Journal of School Psychology, 29,* 57–97.

Berninger, V., Vaughan, K., Abbott, R., Brooks, A., Begay, K., Curtin, G., Byrd, K., & Graham, S. (2000). Language-based spelling instruction: Teaching children to make multiple connections between spoken and written words. *Learning Disability Quarterly, 23,* 117–135.

Bissex, G. (1980). *GYNS AT WRK: A child learns to write and read.* Cambridge, MA: Harvard University Press.

Blachman, B.A. (1994). Early literacy acquisition: The role of phonological awareness. In G.P. Wallach & K.G. Butler (Eds.), *Language learning disabilities in school-age children and adolescents* (pp. 253–274). New York: Merrill.

Britton, J., Burgess, T., Martin, N., McLeod, A. & Rosen, H. (1975). *The development of writing abilities.* London: MacMillan Education.

Bruck, M. (1993). Component spelling skills of college students with childhood diagnoses of dyslexia. *Learning Disability Quarterly, 16,* 171–184.

Calfee, R.C., Lindamood, P., & Lindamood, C. (1973). Acoustic-phonic skills in reading: Kindergarten through twelfth grade. *Journal of Educational Psychology, 64,* 293–298.

Chafe, W.L. (1982). Integration and involvement in speaking, writing, and oral literature. In D. Tannen (Ed.), *Spoken and written language: Exploring orality and literacy* (pp. 35–54). Norwood, NJ: Ablex.

Chafe, W.L., & Danielewicz, J. (1986). Properties of spoken and written language. In R. Horowitz & S.J. Samuels (Eds.), *Comprehending oral and written language* (pp. 82–113). New York: Academic Press.

Clark, D.B., & Uhry, J.K. (1995). *Dyslexia: Theory and practice of remedial instruction* (2nd ed.). Timonium, MD: York Press.

Coleman, C., Gregg, N., Davis, J.M., & Stennett, R. (2001). *Knowledge in the expository essays of college students with and without disabilities.* Paper presented at the meeting of the Society for the Scientific Study of Reading, Boulder, CO.

Corcos, E., & Willows, D.M. (1993). The processing of orthographic information. In D.M. Willows, R.S. Kruk, & E. Corcos (Eds.), *Visual processes in reading and reading disabilities* (pp. 163–190). Mahwah, NJ: Lawrence Erlbaum Associates.

Cunningham, A.E., Stanovich, K.R., & Wilson, M.R. (1990). Cognitive variation in adult college students differing in reading ability. In T.H. Carr & B.A. Levy (Eds.), *Reading and its development: Component skills approaches* (pp. 129–159). San Diego: Academic Press.

Daly, J.A., & Miller, M.D. (1975). Apprehension of writing as a predictor of message intensity. *Journal of Psychology, 89,* 175–177.

Daly, J.A., & Wilson, D. (1983). Writing apprehension, self-esteem, and personality. *Research in the Teaching of English, 7,* 327–341.

de la Paz, S., Swanson, P., & Graham, S. (1998). The contribution of executive control to the revising of students with writing and learning disabilities. *Journal of Educational Psychology, 89,* 203–222.

Ehri, L.C. (1986). Sources of difficulty in learning to read and spell. In M.L. Wolraich & D. Routh (Eds.), *Advances in developmental and behavioral pediatrics* (pp. 121–195). Greenwich, CT: JAI Press.

Ehri, L.C. (1989). The development of spelling knowledge and its role in reading acquisition and reading disability. *Journal of Learning Disabilities, 22,* 356–365.

Ehri, L.C. (2000). Learning to read and learning to spell: Two sides of a coin. *Topics in Language Disorders, 20*(3), 19–36.

Ehri, L., & Wilce, L. (1982). Recognition of spellings printed in lower and mixed case: Evidence for orthographic images. *Journal of Reading Behavior, 14,* 219–230.

Englert, C. (1990). Unraveling the mysteries of writing through strategy instruction. In T.E. Scruggs & B.Y.L. Wong (Eds.), *Intervention research in learning disabilities* (pp. 186–223). New York: Springer-Verlag.

Englert, C., & Mariage, T. (1991). Shared understandings: Structuring the writing experience through dialogue. *Journal of Learning Disabilities, 24,* 330–342.

Englert, C., & Raphael, T. (1988). Constructing well-formed prose: Process,
structure, and metacognitive knowledge. *Exceptional Children, 54,* 513–520.

Englert, C.S., Raphael, T.E., Anderson, L.M., Gregg, S.L., & Anthony, H.M.
(1989). Exposition: Reading, writing and the metacognitive knowledge of
learning disabled students. *Learning Disabilities Research, 5,* 5–24.

Englert, C., Raphael, T., Fear, K., & Anderson, L. (1988). Students' metacognitive knowledge about how to write informational reports. *Learning Disabilities Quarterly, 11,* 18–46.

Englert, C., & Thomas, C.C. (1987). Sensitivity to text structure in reading and
writing: A comparison between learning disabled and non-learning disabled
students. *Learning Disabilities Quarterly, 10,* 93–105.

Ferreiro, E., & Zucchermaglio, C. (1996). Children's use of punctuation marks:
A case of quoted speech. In C. Pontecorvo, M. Orsolini, B. Burge, & A.L.
Resnick (Eds.), *Children's early text construction* (pp. 177–208). Mahwah, NJ:
Lawrence Erlbaum Associates.

Gentry, J.R. (1982). An analysis of developmental spelling in GNYS AT WRK.
Reading Teacher, 36, 192–200.

Gentry, J.R. (1984). Developmental aspects of learning to spell. *Academic Therapy, 20,* 11–19.

Gould, B.W. (2001). Curricular strategies for written expression. In A.M. Bain,
L.L. Bailet, & L.C. Moats (Eds.), *Written language disorders: Theory into practice*
(2nd ed., pp. 185–220). Austin, TX: PRO-ED.

Graham, S. (1999). Handwriting and spelling instruction for students with
learning disabilities: A review. *Learning Disability Quarterly, 22,* 78–98.

Graham, S., Berninger, V.W., Abbott, R.D., Abbott, S.P., & Whitaker, D. (1997).
Role of mechanics in composing of elementary school students: A new methodological approach. *Journal of Educational Psychology, 89,* 170–182.

Graham, S., Berninger, V., Weintraub, N., & Schafer, W. (1998). The development of handwriting fluency and legibility ingredients 1 through 9. *Journal
of Educational Research, 92,* 42–52.

Graham, S., & Harris, K.R., (1989). Improving learning disabled student's skills
at composing essays: Self-instructional strategy training. *Exceptional Children,
56,* 201–214.

Graham, S., & Harris, K.R. (1999). Assessment and intervention in overcoming
writing difficulties: An illustration from the self-regulated strategy development model. *Language, Speech and Hearing Services in Schools, 30,* 255–264.

Graham, S., Harris, K.R., & Sawyer, R. (1987). Composition instruction with
learning disabled students: Self-instructional strategy training. *Focus on Exceptional Children, 20*(4), 1–11.

Graham, S., & Miller, L. (1979). Spelling research and practice: A unified approach. *Focus on Exceptional Children, 12*(2), 1–16.

Graham, S., & Miller, L. (1980). Handwriting research and practice: A unified
approach. *Focus on Exceptional Children, 13*(2), 1–6.

Graham, S., Schwartz, S., & MacArthur, C. (1993). Knowledge of writing and
the composing process, attitude toward writing, and self-efficacy for students

with and without learning disabilities. *Journal of Learning Disabilities, 26,* 237–249.

Graham, S., & Weintraub, N. (1996). A review of handwriting research: Progress and prospects from 1980 to 1994. *Educational Psychology Review, 8,* 7–87.

Gregg, N. (1995). *Written expression disorders.* Dordrecht, The Netherlands: Kluwer Academic Publishers.

Gregg, N., Coleman, C., Stennett, R.B., & Davis, M. (2002). Discourse complexity of college writers with and without disabilities: A multidimensional analysis. *Journal of Learning Disabilities, 35,* 23–38, 56.

Gregg, N., & Hafer, T. (2001). Disorders of written expression. In A.M. Bain, L.L. Bailet, & L.C. Moats (Eds.), *Written language disorders: Theory into practice* (2nd ed., pp. 103–136). Austin, TX: PRO-ED.

Gregg, N., & Mather, N. (2002). School is fun at recess: Informal analyses of written language for students with learning disabilities. *Journal of Learning Disabilities, 35,* 7–22.

Gregg, N., & McAlexander, P. (1989). The relation between sense of audience and specific learning disabilities: An exploration. *Annals of Dyslexia, 39,* 206–226.

Gregg, N., Sigalas, S.A., Hoy, C., Wisenbaker, J., & McKinley, C. (1996). Sense of audience and the adult writer: A study across competence levels. *Reading and Writing: An Interdisciplinary Journal, 8,* 121–137.

Hallenbeck, M.J. (1996). The cognitive strategy in writing: Welcome relief for adolescents with learning disabilities. *Learning Disabilities Research & Practice, 11,* 107–119.

Halliday, M.A.K. (1988). On the language of physical science. In M. Ghadessy (Ed.), *Registers of written English: Situational factors and linguistic features* (pp. 162–178). London: Pinter.

Halliday, M.A.K., & Hasan, R. (1976). *Cohesion in English.* London: Longman.

Hedberg, N.L., & Westby, C.E. (1993). *Analyzing storytelling skills: Theory to practice.* Tucson, AZ: Communication Skill Builders.

Henderson, E.H. (1990). *Teaching spelling* (2nd ed.). Boston: Houghton Mifflin.

Jeroski, S.F., & Conry, R.F. (1981). *Development and field application of the attitude toward writing scale.* Paper presented at the annual conference of the American Educational Research Association, Los Angeles.

Levine, M. (1987). *Developmental variations and learning disorders.* Cambridge, MA: Educators Publishing Service.

Litowitz, B. (1981). Developmental issues in written language. *Topics in Language Disorders, 1*(2), 73–89.

Lobin, W. (1976). *Language development: Kindergarten through grade twelve* (Research Report No. 18). Urbana, IL: National Council of Teachers of English.

MacArthur, C., & Graham, S. (1993). Integrating strategy instruction and word processing into a process approach to writing instruction. *School Psychology Review, 22,* 671–682.

Martens, F., & Goodman, Y. (1996). Invented punctuation. In N. Hall & A. Robinson (Eds.), *Learning about punctuation* (pp. 104–117). Portsmouth, NH: Heinemann.

Mather, N., Bos, C., Podhajski, B., Babur, N., & Rhein, D. (2000). *Screening of early reading processes.* Unpublished manuscript. University of Arizona, Tucson.

Mather, N., & Goldstein, S. (2001). *Learning disabilities and challenging behaviors: A guide to intervention and classroom management.* Baltimore: Paul H. Brookes Publishing Co.

Moats, L.C. (2001). Spelling disability in adolescents and adults. In A.M. Bain, L.L. Bailet, & L.C. Moats (Eds.), *Written language disorders: Theory into practice* (2nd ed., pp. 43–75). Austin, TX: PRO-ED.

Newland, T.E. (1932). An analytical study of the development of illegibilities in handwriting from the lower grades to adulthood. *Journal of Educational Research, 26,* 249–258.

Nippold, M.A. (1988). *Later language development: Ages nine through nineteen.* Boston: College Hill Press.

O'Donnell, R.C., & Hunt, K. (1975). Syntactic Maturity Test. In W.T. Fagan, C.R. Cooper, & J.M. Jensen (Eds.), *Measures for research and evaluation in the English language arts* (pp. 22–37). Urbana, IL: National Council of Teachers of English.

Quant, L. (1946). Factors affecting the legibility of handwriting. *Journal of Experimental Education, 14,* 297–316.

Read, C. (1975). *Children's categorization of speech sounds in English* (NCTE Research Report No. 17). Urbana, IL: National Council of Teachers of English.

Reid, D.K. (1988). *Teaching the learning disabled: A cognitive developmental approach.* Needham Heights, MA: Allyn & Bacon.

Sawyer, D.J. (1987). *Test of Awareness of Language Segments.* Austin, TX: PRO-ED.

Scinto, L.F.M. (1982). *The acquisition of functional composition strategies for text.* Hamburg, Germany: Helmut Bushe.

Shaughnessy, M.P. (1977). *Errors and expectations: A guide for teachers of basic writing.* New York: Oxford University Press.

Speilberger, C., Garsuch, R., & Lushene, R. (1970). *Manual for the state-trait anxiety inventory.* Palo Alto, CA: Consulting Psychological Press.

Strong, W. (1983). *Sentence combining: A composing book.* New York: Random House.

Tagatz, G.E., Otto, W., Klausmeier, H.J., Goodwin, W.L., & Cook, D.M. (1968). Effect of three methods of instruction upon the handwriting performance of third and fourth graders. *American Educational Research, 5,* 81–90.

Tangel, D.M., & Blachman, B.A. (1992). Effect of phoneme awareness instruction on kindergarten children's invented spelling. *Journal of Reading Behavior, 24,* 233–261.

Treiman, R. (1998). Why spelling? The benefits of incorporating spelling into beginning reading instruction. In J.L. Metsala & L.C. Ehri (Eds.), *Word recognition in beginning literacy* (pp. 289–313). Mahwah, NJ: Lawrence Erlbaum Associates.

Treiman, R., & Bourassa, D.C. (2000). The development of spelling skill. *Topics in Language Disorders, 20*(3), 1–18.

Vellutino, F.R., Scanlon, D.M., & Tanzman, M.S. (1994). Components of reading ability: Issues and problems in operationalizing word identification, phonological coding, and orthographic coding. In G.R. Lyon (Ed.), *Frames of reference for the assessment of learning disabilities: New views on measurement issues* (pp. 279–332). Baltimore: Paul H. Brookes Publishing Co.

Vygotsky, L.S. (1962). *Thought and language.* Cambridge, MA: MIT Press.

Weiner, S. (1994). Four first graders' descriptions of how they spell. *Elementary School Journal, 94,* 315–332.

Weintraub, N., & Graham, S. (1998). Writing legibly and quickly: A study of children's ability to adjust their handwriting to meet common classroom demands. *Learning Disabilities Research & Practice, 13,* 146–152.

Westby, C., & Clauser, P. (1999). The right stuff for writing: Assessing and facilitating written language. In H.W. Catts & A.G. Kamhi (Eds.), *Language and reading disabilities* (pp. 259–324). Needham Heights, MA: Allyn & Bacon,

Wiig, E.H. & Semel, E. (1984). *Language assessment and intervention for the learning disabled.* Columbus, OH: Merrill.

Zainaldin, I. (2001). *Metacognitive knowledge of writing: A comparison of elementary students with and without learning disabilities.* Unpublished manuscript, University of Georgia.

Appendix A: Written Language Profile

Name: _____

Date 1: _____ Date 2: _____

Date 3: _____ Date 4: _____

Directions: Rate the writer's mastery from below average to above average.

Item	Below average		Average		Above average
Attitude Displays a positive attitude toward writing	1	2	3	4	5
Handwriting Forms letters easily and quickly	1	2	3	4	5
Phonology Segments speech sounds	1	2	3	4	5
Orthography Recalls letter strings and patterns	1	2	3	4	5
Morphology Uses word endings and affixes correctly	1	2	3	4	5
Spelling Spells words correctly	1	2	3	4	5
Syntax/Grammar Uses correct grammatical forms	1	2	3	4	5
Vocabulary Uses a variety of words	1	2	3	4	5
Text Structure Uses appropriate organizational formats	1	2	3	4	5
Ideation Expresses ideas clearly	1	2	3	4	5
Fluency Composes text easily	1	2	3	4	5
Metacognition Uses strategies when composing	1	2	3	4	5

Appendix B: Class Written Language Profile

Date 1: _____ Date 2: _____ Date 3: _____

Student's name	Attitude	Handwriting	Phonology	Orthography	Morphology	Spelling	Syntax/Grammar	Vocabulary	Text Structure	Ideation	Fluency	Metacognition

8

Reviewing Outcomes

Using DIBELS to Evaluate
Kindergarten Curricula and Interventions

ROLAND H. GOOD III, RUTH A. KAMINSKI, SYLVIA B. SMITH,
DEBORAH C. SIMMONS, ED KAMÉENUI, AND JOSHUA WALLIN

School-based data on basic early literacy skills can shape and define the application of research-based principles, strategies, and materials in classrooms (Baker & Smith, 2001; Good, Kaminski, Simmons, & Kaméenui, 2001; Good, Simmons, & Kaméenui, 2001; Simmons, Kuykendall, King, Cornachione, & Kaméenui, 2000). Assessment systems and technology, such as the Dynamic Indicators of Basic Early Literacy Skills (DIBELS; Good & Kaminski, 2002), can be critical catalysts in changing early literacy practices. At a time when attention is being drawn to the performance of students on statewide high-stakes tests, teachers and administrators want to know how best to change beginning reading outcomes. By using an outcomes-driven model to analyze school-based data on basic early literacy skills, a school team can evaluate and plan components of effective beginning reading programs, including professional development, instruction, curriculum materials, and supplemental materials.

DYNAMIC INDICATORS OF BASIC EARLY LITERACY SKILLS

The DIBELS assessments are intended to provide school-based data for use in informing quality of instruction and reviewing school-level outcomes. The measures are intended to be brief and repeatable. Each measure is available in 20 alternate forms and is designed to take approximately 1 minute to administer. For a benchmark assessment, two to four measures are administered. Additional information about the DIBELS measures and a free download of the measures are available at dibels.uoregon.edu/.

Important Caveats for the DIBELS Data System

This chapter draws heavily on the information available from schools and districts participating in the DIBELS Data System. The DIBELS Data System enabled us to analyze school and student performance in the context of more than 300 school districts, more than 600 schools, and more than 32,000 students during 2001–2002. The DIBELS Data System also allowed us to examine current information about student performance and outcomes. The DIBELS measures focus on the direct assessment of skills. As curricula and instruction in participating schools focus increasingly on critical early literacy skills, the performance of students in participating schools can be expected to change. Although this chapter primarily uses information from the 2001–2002 academic year, across-year outcomes are examined; in those cases, information from the 2000–2001 and 2001–2002 academic years is summarized.

Several caveats are appropriate when interpreting information from the DIBELS Data System. First, participating schools may not be representative of all schools in the country. They are likely to emphasize phonemic awareness, phonics, and fluency in their curricula and instruction. Participating schools are likely to teach toward established benchmark goals in early literacy, monitor progress toward early literacy goals, and modify their instruction and curricula on the basis of student progress and outcomes. They also are likely to have adopted a research-based core reading curriculum. They may be more likely to have a history of poor academic performance and may be more motivated to make curricular and instructional changes. In each of the aspects, participating schools may not be representative of all schools.

Second, the scores that participating schools enter into the DIBELS Data System are the product of the school's administration procedures and training. The DIBELS assessments are provided with detailed standardized administration and scoring directions. A web-based tutorial on administration and scoring is available, and many trainers are available around the country. However, no measures are in place to guarantee that schools using DIBELS and the DIBELS Data System are adhering to standardized procedures. If the accuracy of administration and scoring of the DIBELS measures is compromised, then interpretation of the scores is not possible.

Third, scores from the DIBELS Data System affect outcomes and are not simply inert ingredients. Rather, DIBELS results may actively affect future outcomes. DIBELS scores may be used by schools to identify students who are at risk of poor reading outcomes and help them using powerful and effective interventions. If the interventions result in successful outcomes for the students who were at risk for reading difficulties, then the predicted risk has been eliminated. In all trainings and web support, the importance of addressing skill deficits with effective interventions is stressed. For example, a student who scores low on DIBELS Initial Sound Fluency (ISF) measure with a concomitant indication of at-risk status in the DIBELS Data System may achieve the end of kindergarten goal on DIBELS Phoneme Segmentation Fluency (PSF) measure. In this case, the prediction of the student's at-risk status may have been inaccurate, or it may have been thwarted by an effective intervention that was implemented to mitigate the student's risk.

Format for School-Based Reports

A proposed format for school reports is provided in the appendix to this chapter. The school-based report is intended to provide a means for a school's early literacy team to appraise the school's early literacy outcomes, to form a judgment about the effectiveness of their core curriculum and system of additional intervention, and to begin to plan improvements in their curriculum and intervention if indicated. Because research-based early literacy instruction occurs within the complex host environment of schools, a school's early literacy team should match resources with needs to form a system that works in the local context. Important participants on the school's early literacy team include the principal, kindergarten and first-grade general education teachers, remedial reading teachers, school psychologist, speech-language pathologist, and other support personnel as available in the school. Each member of the team brings a different combination of skills, expertise, and background that are essential to a schoolwide system.

ELEMENTS OF AN EFFECTIVE BEGINNING READING PROGRAM

An analysis of school-based data on basic early literacy skills can help a school's early literacy team evaluate and plan components of an effective beginning reading program. These components include effective professional development, informed instruction, well-chosen curriculum materials, supplemental materials, and a system of additional intervention. Each part is critical for ensuring that all children learn basic early literacy concepts.

Professional Development

One of the primary goals of professional development is to help develop reflective practitioners (Bowman, Donovan, & Burns, 2001). Research that links professional development, the realities of the classroom, and the use of student data gives teachers new ways of reflecting on their teaching and choice of materials (Baker & Smith, 1999, 2001; Smith, Baker, & Oudeans, 2001). School-based reports from the DIBELS Data System provide a basis on which to periodically evaluate the professional development needs of a school. The reports can become vehicles for teacher change by operationalizing four principles of effective professional development (Baker & Smith, 1999). First, a clear focus is created with concrete, realistic, and challenging goals for improved child performance on critical basic early literacy skills—labeled *benchmarks* and validated by large-scale studies (Good, Gruba, & Kaminski, 2001). Second, professional development is focused on both technical and conceptual components of instruction with clear, unambiguous links between critical basic early literacy skills and DIBELS measures (Good, Kaminski, Simmons, & Kaméenui, 2001). Third, change is enhanced through grade-level discussion of teacher reports in which collegial relationships and necessary support systems are created to help make instructional and programmatic decisions based on data. Finally, compelling visual representations in the teacher reports help teachers immediately see the effects of their instructional changes on student performance.

Instruction

The performance of children not meeting benchmarks prompts teachers to examine factors over which they have control, such as instructional strategies. For example, increasing the explicitness of teacher talk and frequency of review and practice produced noticeable differences in the springtime for children who had not met the winter benchmark for the DIBELS ISF measure (Baker & Smith, 1999).

Curriculum

DIBELS school-based reports indicate the percentages of students needing additional intervention. A high percentage of children needing intensive intervention indicates a concern about the core curriculum provided to all kindergarten students. The *core curriculum* is the curriculum or program used with all children in the general classroom setting. For example, in the fall, a high percentage of very low scores indicates inadequate early literacy experiences before entering kindergarten. In the winter or spring of kindergarten, high percentages of low scores indicate that the general curriculum in the first half of kindergarten is not working for most of the children. In either case, a high percentage of children requiring intensive intervention highlights the need to use the most effective curriculum available as the core curriculum (Simmons et al., 2000).

Supplemental Materials and Programs

In order to meet kindergarten benchmarks, many kindergarten curricula require supplemental materials and programs. For example, some programs, such as *Ladders to Literacy* (Notari-Syverson, O'Connor, & Vadasy, 1998; O'Connor, Notari-Syverson, & Vadasy, 1998), *Road to the Code* (Blachmann, Ball, Black, & Tangel, 2000), and *Phonemic Awareness in Young Children* (Adams, Foorman, Lundberg, & Beeler, 1998) can be integrated into a variety of kindergarten programs and provide teachers with suggestions for additional supports in every lesson. School reports can assist a school-based early literacy team in evaluating their kindergarten curriculum and determining whether additional supplemental materials and programs are needed to increase the effectiveness of the core program with respect to the core components of early literacy.

System of Additional Intervention

Even with high-quality implementation of effective core curriculum and strategies, some children need more instructional support or additional intervention. For example, *Phonological Awareness Training for Reading* (Torgesen & Bryant, 1994) was created as an additional intervention for children in kindergarten through second grade to be delivered in small groups. Interventions for children needing intensive support are characterized by careful attention to instructional design issues such as careful example selection, explicit instruction, and scaffolding of instructional support. Although research-based programs are readily available, evidence of a program's effectiveness does not guarantee that the program will work for every child with substantial and intensive needs. The progress of children needing intensive support should be monitored frequently to evaluate and modify the instructional support to meet every child's needs. The ongoing process of implementing, evaluating, and modifying the modification is described in Good, Gruba, and Kaminski (2001).

School-based reports can assist in evaluating the system of additional intervention. The school-based early literacy team can then evaluate whether students at risk for poor reading outcomes are being identified early enough and provided with interventions effective enough to change their learning trajectories. The school can also evaluate whether sufficient resources are invested in the prevention of learning difficulties and whether selected interventions are effective enough and implemented with sufficient integrity.

In addition, the documentation of positive and consistent progress for children who are at risk can be used to validate and justify the school's allocation of resources for prevention. For example, in order to meet the kindergarten early literacy goals, one school provided an additional 40 minutes in an extended day program, called the K Plus program, for children who were not making adequate progress in the regular classroom program. Institutionalizing the model required allocation of instructional, transportation, and space resources in the school district. DIBELS documentation of the effectiveness of the K Plus program not only provided a justification to central administration for the use of the resources, the school-based reports also prompted use of the model by other schools in the district to meet the needs of children with intensive instructional needs (Baker & Smith, 1999). A supplemental curriculum, Early Reading Intervention, was developed by another project to be used within a K Plus program to meet the needs of children requiring strategic or intensive levels of instructional support (Simmons et al., 2000). In short, a school-based assessment system provides frequent and sensitive information on how well children are progressing in learning critical basic early literacy concepts to guide professional development, inform instruction, allocate resources, and select materials and programs.

USING THE OUTCOMES-DRIVEN MODEL

The Outcomes-Driven Model is based on a problem-solving model and the initial application of the problem-solving model to early literacy skills. The model was developed to provide a prevention-oriented assessment and intervention decision-making system designed to preempt early reading difficulty and ensure adequate progress, step by step, toward outcomes that eventually result in established, adequate reading achievement. The Outcomes-Driven Model accomplishes steps to outcomes through a set of five educational decisions: 1) identifying need for support, 2) validating need for support, 3) planning instructional support, 4) evaluating support, and 5) reviewing outcomes, as depicted in Figure 8.1. Each educational decision corresponds with a step in implementing the model.

Five Decision-Making Steps in the Outcomes-Driven Model

The first step in the Outcomes-Driven Model is focused on identifying children early who may need additional instructional support to meet a benchmark goal. To identify a need for support, a benchmark assessment using selected DIBELS probes is administered to all children in the school three times per year: at the beginning, middle, and end of

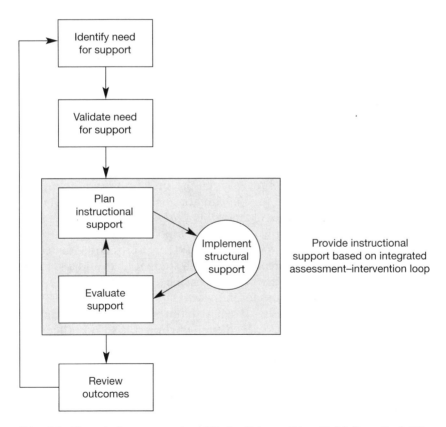

Figure 8.1. The reviewing outcomes step within the Outcomes-Driven Model. (From Good, R.H., Gruba, J., & Kaminski, R.A. [2002]. Best practices in using Dynamic Indicators of Basic Early Literacy Skills (DIBELS) in an outcomes-driven model. In A. Thomas & J. Grimes [Eds.], *Best practices in school psychology IV* [pp. 699–720]. Bethesda, MD: National Association of School Psychologists. Copyright 2002 by the National Association of School Psychologists. Reprinted with permission of the publisher.)

the school year. The benchmark assessment identifies individual students who are at risk for reading difficulty and may need additional instructional support to achieve the next benchmark goal. The benchmark assessment also provides information regarding the performance of all children in the school with respect to benchmark goals that can be used in the final step of reviewing outcomes.

The second step in the Outcomes-Driven Model is to validate that an individual student needs additional instructional support and that some other factor is not the reason for low performance. To validate need, an examiner conducts brief, repeated assessments of the target skill using alternate forms of the assessment under different conditions.

The third decision-making step in the Outcomes-Driven Model is to plan instructional support for those students whose need for support has been validated. A variety of research-based interventions and instructional strategies are available for teachers to choose from to provide additional instructional support for each of the foundational early reading skills. The school-based early literacy team can establish a plan for additional intervention based on the review of outcomes. To determine if the instructional strategies are appropriate, however, the fourth step of the Outcomes-Driven Model, evaluating support, is necessary. For students who need additional instructional support, progress is monitored weekly or monthly, using alternate forms of the appropriate DIBELS measure. If the student is making adequate progress to achieve the benchmark goal, the instructional supports are continued. If, however, evaluation of progress reveals that the student is not making sufficient progress to achieve the benchmark goal, a modification in the student's instruction to provide more support is indicated.

The final step of the Outcomes-Driven Model is to review outcomes. The purpose of this step is to review the structure of supports the school has in place to achieve outcomes at both a student level and a systems level. The review of outcomes occurs at each benchmark assessment period. The review of outcomes for individual students provides information about a student's status with regard to the benchmark and indicates whether the student has achieved the benchmark and no longer requires additional instructional support. At a systems level, which is the focus of this chapter, a review of outcomes addresses the overall effectiveness of the core curriculum and system of additional intervention in promoting the achievement of important reading outcomes for all children.

The Outcomes-Driven Model is intended to be a continuous, recursive model. At an individual level, an assessment–intervention feedback loop is embedded in the planning instructional support and evaluating and modifying instructional support steps of the model. Based on the student's progress toward an important goal, the instructional plan is changed, the implementation of instructional support is changed, the changes are evaluated, and the instructional plan is modified accordingly. The assessment–intervention feedback loop is satisfied when the student is making adequate progress toward the goal.

At a systems level, a recursive process occurs as the outcomes of the instructional support system are reviewed from one benchmark period to the next and the system is thereby modified. A first concern is the core curriculum and instruction that serves as the educational foundation for the school. The educational system should have 1) an effective core curriculum and instruction, 2) procedures to identify students who need additional intervention, 3) a mechanism to deliver additional intervention (time, personnel, curriculum, space), and 4) procedures to escalate the amount of instructional support, if needed, to achieve benchmark goals.

Because of the recursive and cyclical nature of the model, this last step is important throughout the year. Assessment at one point in time serves to inform recommendations for subsequent instruction at the same time that it provides information to review outcomes of instruction and learning opportunities that have come before. Thus, the beginning of the kindergarten benchmark assessment provides a basis for recommending the amount of instructional support that is likely to be needed in the first half of kindergarten and for reviewing preschool and community outcomes for the children's preschool learning opportunities. In this way, on a systems level, the first and fifth decision-making steps in the Outcomes-Driven Model are directly related.

Instructional Recommendation at the Beginning of Kindergarten

At the beginning of kindergarten, the DIBELS ISF and DIBELS Letter Naming Fluency (LNF) tasks are administered to all students in the school. At the beginning of kindergarten, an ISF score below 4 would be below the 20th percentile, and a score below 8 would be below the 40th percentile. For LNF, a score below 2 would be below the 20th percentile, and a score of 8 or higher would be at the 40th percentile or above. A student scoring below the 20th percentile on either measure would indicate the child as at risk for difficulty with learning to read. A student scoring at or above the 40th percentile would be considered at low risk of difficulty with learning to read. In between the 20th and 40th percentiles, a student would be considered at some risk. Of course, the core premise of a prevention system is that these judgments of risk can be changed with appropriate intervention. The cutoff points for at-risk and low-risk status are presented in Table 8.1.

Table 8.1. Descriptive levels of performance in beginning of kindergarten on Dynamic Indicators of Basic Early Literacy Skills (DIBELS) measures

Variable	Performance	Descriptor
ISF	< 4	At risk
	4–7	Some risk
	≥ 8	Low risk
LNF	< 2	At risk
	2–7	Some risk
	≥ 8	Low risk

Key: ISF = Initial Sound Fluency, LNF = Letter Naming Fluency

Note: At risk for reading difficulty is based on performance below the 20th percentile and some risk is based on performance below the 40th percentile using systemwide percentile ranks.

The possible combinations of risk status are enumerated in Table 8.2. For each combination of risk indicators, the percentile rank, conditional percentage achieving subsequent goals, relative incidence, and instructional recommendation are provided. The fundamental purpose of the DIBELS assessment at the beginning of kindergarten is to identify children who may need additional intervention to achieve subsequent literacy goals. Thus, the primary information to consider is the student's risk reported as the conditional percentage achieving subsequent literacy goals. Each literacy goal represents a level of skill on a core component of early literacy that predicts successful reading outcomes. Each percentage is referred to as a conditional percentage because it is the percentage of children with similar risk status who achieved the early literacy goal. That is, the percentage is conditional on or given that the student has the particular pattern of risk. The early literacy goals include the percentage of children with similar risk status who achieve 1) the middle of kindergarten goal of 25 on ISF, 2) the end of kindergarten goal of 35 on DIBELS PSF, 3) the middle of first grade goal of 50 on DIBELS Nonsense Word Fluency (NWF), and 4) the end of first grade goal of 40 or more on DIBELS Oral Reading Fluency (DORF).

For example, a student who scores below 4 on ISF and below 2 on LNF would be identified as *at risk* on both indicators. His or her performance would be at the third percentile, meaning that 3% of students were at similar or greater risk of reading difficulty. Of the students who are at risk on both indictors, 9% meet the middle of kindergarten goal of 25 on ISF, 44% meet the end of kindergarten goal of 35 on PSF, 24% percent meet the middle of first grade goal of 50 on NWF, and 34%

Table 8.2. Instructional recommendations for individual patterns of performance on Dynamic Indicators of Basic Early Literacy Skills (DIBELS) benchmark assessments at the beginning of kindergarten

ISF	LNF	Percentile	Percentage of students meeting later goals					Incidence	Instructional support recommendation
			Middle of kindergarten ISF	End of kindergarten PSF	Middle of first grade NWF	End of first grade DORF	Average		
At risk	At risk	3	9	44	24	34	27	More common	Intensive—substantial intervention
Some risk	At risk	9	13	48	27	31	30	More common	Intensive—substantial intervention
At risk	Some risk	13	13	53	32	44	35	More common	Intensive—substantial intervention
Some risk	Some risk	19	18	58	33	45	39	More common	Strategic—additional intervention
Low risk	At risk	25	26	57	30	43	39	More common	Strategic—additional intervention
Low risk	Some risk	33	35	68	43	56	51	More common	Strategic—additional intervention
At risk	Low risk	42	23	59	50	74	51	More common	Strategic—additional intervention
Some risk	Low risk	50	30	71	51	75	57	More common	Strategic—additional intervention
Low risk	Low risk	76	62	83	69	87	75	More common	Benchmark—at grade level

Key: ISF = Initial Sound Fluency. LNF = Letter Naming Fluency. PSF = Phoneme Segmentation Fluency. NWF = Nonsense Word Fluency, DORF = DIBELS Oral Reading Fluency.

Note: Percentage of students meeting goals is the conditional percentage of children who meet 1) the middle of kindergarten goal of 25 on Initial Sound Fluency, 2) the end of kindergarten goal of 35 on Phonetic Sound Fluency, 3) the middle of first grade goal of 50 on Nonsense Word Fluency, and 4) the end of first grade goal of 40 or more on Oral Reading Fluency.

meet the end of first grade goal of 40 or more on the DORF. The average percentage achieving subsequent early literacy goals was obtained by averaging the four conditional percentages (i.e., 9, 44, 24, and 34). The average percentage achieving subsequent early literacy goals for students identified as at risk on both indicators at the beginning of kindergarten was 27%. Thus, the average percentage provides an overall indicator of degree of risk.

Although the DORF goal represents the most crucial early literacy outcome for kindergarten and first grade, the intermediary goals represent teaching targets in route to the outcome. For students achieving the intermediary goals, the odds of reaching the DORF goal at the end of first grade improve as follows: 1) 87% of children achieving the ISF goal become readers, 2) 80% of children achieving the PSF goal become readers, and 3) 91% of children achieving the NWF goal become readers. Each early literacy benchmark goal achieved increases the odds of achieving subsequent early literacy goals. However, achieving only one of the early literacy goals is not sufficient. It is necessary to achieve all goals to be on track for successful reading outcomes.

The incidence column of Table 8.2 indicates whether the pattern of risk is relatively common, unusual, or extremely rare. If more than 2% of children display a particular pattern of risk, it would be considered more common. If 0.9% to 2% of children display a pattern of risk, it would be considered unusual. If fewer than 0.9% of children display a pattern of risk, it would be considered extremely rare.

The instructional recommendation for students with each pattern of risk is reported in the final column of Table 8.2. For students who are unlikely to achieve subsequent goals unless provided with an appropriate, effective intervention, the recommendation is "Intensive—substantial intervention." For students with even odds of achieving subsequent goals unless provided with an appropriate intervention, the recommendation is "Strategic—additional intervention." Finally, for students who are likely to achieve subsequent early literacy goals, the recommendation is "Benchmark—at grade level," indicating that continuing instruction with an effective, research-based core curriculum should be sufficient for those students to achieve subsequent early literacy goals.

The decision utility of the instructional recommendations provided in the beginning of kindergarten is reported in Table 8.3. For students with a "Benchmark—at grade level" recommendation, 62% achieve the middle of kindergarten goal of 25 or more on the DIBELS ISF measure, and only 2% have severe difficulty with initial sounds. The fundamental conclusion to be drawn is that recommendations of inten-

Table 8.3. Decision utility for beginning of kindergarten Dynamic Indicators of Basic Early Literacy Skills (DIBELS) benchmark assessments of Initial Sound Fluency, used to identify phonemic awareness health and severe phonemic awareness difficulty in the middle of kindergarten

DIBELS instructional recommendation	Conditional percentage achieving 25 or more	Conditional percentage achieving less than 10
Intensive—substantial intervention	11	46
Strategic—additional intervention	27	19
Benchmark—at grade level	62	2

sive, strategic, and benchmark are meaningfully different. The number of children entering kindergarten who receive recommendations of intensive or benchmark for a school provides an indication of the challenge the school faces in supporting children to achieve early literacy outcomes.

ORGANIZING QUESTIONS FOR REVIEWING OUTCOMES

There are several organizing questions for the final decision-making step of the Outcomes-Driven Model—reviewing outcomes.

1. How do the beginning kindergarten skills of students in our school compare with students' skills in other schools participating in the DIBELS Data System?

2. How do the early literacy skills of mid-year kindergarten students in our school compare with students' skills in other schools participating in the DIBELS Data System?

3. How effective is our core curriculum and instruction in supporting students who are entering kindergarten with benchmark skills to achieve the DIBELS ISF goal in the middle of kindergarten?

4. How effective is our system of additional intervention in supporting students who are entering kindergarten at risk for reading difficulty to achieve the DIBELS ISF goal in the middle of kindergarten?

5. How do the early literacy skills of end of year kindergarten students in our school compare with students' skills in other schools participating in the DIBELS Data System?

6. How effective is our core curriculum and instruction in supporting students who are on track in the middle of kindergarten to achieve the DIBELS PSF goal by the end of kindergarten?

7. How effective is our system of additional intervention in supporting students who are at risk for reading difficulty in the middle of
kindergarten to achieve the DIBELS PSF goal by the end of kindergarten?

The following sections address these questions in order. Although the
sections follow a sequential order, from the end of preschool to the end
of kindergarten, assessments of each stage serve as a basis to review the
outcomes for previous learning opportunities and recommend the
amount of instructional support needed at the next stage. For example,
the benchmark assessment at the beginning of kindergarten provides a
basis for recommending the amount of instructional support that is
likely to be needed in the first half of kindergarten in addition to reviewing preschool and community outcomes for children's preschool
experiences.

Reviewing Preschool and Community Outreach Outcomes

The first issue to examine is how the entry-level skills of kindergarten
students compare with scores of kindergarteners in other schools participating in the DIBELS Data System. The entry-level skills of students
can be an indication of the community context, effectiveness of preschools in the community, and emphasis on early literacy skills in the
community. In addition, entry-level skills can reflect cultural and language factors within the larger community, such as home language
other than English, the degree of similarity or difference between the
other language and English, the diverse levels of the child's and family's levels of proficiency in the other language and English, and differences between the language conventions and dialect spoken at home
and the formal English used at school. In a sense, skills at the beginning
of the kindergarten instructional sequence represent the outcome of
the preschool instructional sequence.

DIBELS ISF of 8 or more and DIBELS LNF of 8 or more represent
critical preschool goals that enable children to enter kindergarten with
the odds in their favor of achieving subsequent early literacy goals. This
is not to say that these are the only goals of preschool experiences, just
that they should represent at least one goal of preschool and community experiences. Preschool materials and supports are published and
available on-line (e.g., the *Ladders to Literacy* model, www.wri-edu.org/
ladders/; *Reading Rockets,* www.readingrockets.org/). Schools can assist
in serving as a liaison with preschool and parent organizations to support preschool and community learning opportunities so that children
enter kindergarten with the level of literacy skills predictive of success-

ful reading outcomes. A reasonable goal for preschool and community outreach efforts is for all students to enter kindergarten with a benchmark instructional recommendation. But, regardless of whether children enter kindergarten with benchmark skills or with intensive instructional support needs, our responsibility is to provide a core curriculum and a system of additional intervention that are sufficient to support their achievement of crucial early literacy skills.

A school with a very high percentage of children entering kindergarten with a benchmark recommendation has an easier challenge in supporting all students' achievement of subsequent early literacy goals. A school with a high percentage of children entering kindergarten with intensive instructional needs must adapt and adjust its core curriculum and system of additional intervention to address the challenge. With a high percentage of children with intensive instructional needs, the most effective core curriculum and the most carefully designed system of additional intervention are necessary. Table 8.4 provides a normative context for comparing the skills of students beginning kindergarten with the skills of students in other schools.

In Table 8.4, the first column provides a school-based percentile rank. Other columns provide the corresponding percentage of students in each instructional recommendation category. The row corresponding to the 50th percentile provides an indication of pattern of performance in a typical (median) school. In a typical school, 44% of children entering kindergarten are likely to achieve crucial early literacy goals and a benchmark instructional recommendation. For 39% of children in a typical school, the likelihood of achieving early literacy goals cannot be clearly stated, and a strategic instructional recommendation is made. Fourteen percent of children entering kindergarten in a typical school are at risk for difficulty with learning to read. Children with an intensive instructional recommendation are unlikely to achieve subsequent early literacy goals—unless the school provides intensive interventions to change children's reading trajectory early. However, there is substantial school-to-school variability in the entry skills of kindergarten students.

Table 8.4 can be read by locating a school's percentage of children in an instructional recommendation category and identifying the corresponding school-based percentile rank. A percentile rank is interpreted as the percentage of schools with as many or fewer students in the instructional recommendation category. For example, if 63% of children in a school have a benchmark instructional recommendation at the beginning of kindergarten, then the school is at the 80th to 85th percentile, compared with other schools in the DIBELS Data System. In other words, the school has more students in the benchmark category

Table 8.4. School-based normative context for evaluating percentage of students in each instructional recommendation category in the beginning of kindergarten

School-based percentile	Percentage of students in instructional recommendation category		
	Intensive	Strategic	Benchmark
5	2	22	13
10	3	26	19
15	5	28	24
20	6	30	27
25	8	32	31
30	9	33	34
35	10	35	37
40	11	36	40
45	13	38	42
50	14	39	44
55	15	41	47
60	17	42	50
65	18	43	52
70	20	45	54
75	22	46	57
80	24	49	60
85	27	50	65
90	31	53	68
95	43	56	72
99	55	63	85

Note: Based on 382 schools with at least 40 students in kindergarten in 2001–2002.

than 80% to 85% of schools in the system. Similarly, if 40% of students have an intensive instructional recommendation in the beginning of kindergarten, the school has more students with intensive instructional needs than 90% to 95% of schools in the DIBELS Data System.

Instructional Recommendation for the Middle of Kindergarten

Reading risk and health indicators for the middle of kindergarten are summarized in Table 8.5. In the middle of kindergarten, students are expected to have established awareness of the initial sounds in words with a score of 25 or more on DIBELS ISF measure. Additional indicators of adequate early literacy progress and low risk are LNF scores of 27 or more, a PSF score of 18 or more, and an NWF score of 13 or more. Students with ISF scores below 10 may be experiencing significant difficulty in learning the sound structure of English and are at risk of not achieving subsequent early literacy goals—unless substantial intervention support is provided in the second half of kindergarten. Additional

Table 8.5. Descriptive levels of performance in the middle of kindergarten as measured by Dynamic Indicators of Basic Early Literacy Skills (DIBELS)

Variable	Performance	Descriptor
ISF	< 10	Deficit
	10–24	Emerging
	≥ 25	Established
LNF	< 15	At risk
	15–26	Some risk
	≥ 27	Low risk
PSF	< 7	At risk
	7–17	Some risk
	≥ 18	Low risk
NWF	< 5	At risk
	5–12	Some risk
	≥ 13	Low risk

Key: ISF = Initial Sound Fluency, LNF = Letter Naming Fluency, PSF = Phoneme Segmentation Fluency, NWF = Nonsense Word Fluency

risk indicators are an LNF score below 15, a PSF score below 7, and an NWF score below 5.

The conditional percentage of children achieving subsequent early literacy goals for each pattern of risk indicators is summarized in Table 8.6. In general, students with risk indicators in two or more areas may require intensive intervention to achieve early literacy goals. A recommendation for intensive intervention is made when a student is unlikely to achieve subsequent early literacy goals without substantial support. For example, of the students in the DIBELS Data System who had a deficit in ISF, were at risk on LNF, and who were at risk on PSF, only 14% achieved the first-grade DORF goal of 40 or more words correct per minute. Patterns characterized by some risk or emerging skills received an instructional recommendation for strategic support. In general, students with a strategic support recommendation had even odds of achieving subsequent early literacy goals. Patterns characterized by established skills and low risk received a benchmark instructional recommendation. Students who are achieving benchmarks are on track for crucial literacy outcomes and are likely to achieve subsequent benchmark goals.

Unusual and rare patterns may indicate either measurement error on the particular assessment or a problem with the integrity of the assessment process, in which case retraining of the tester may be necessary. For example, a student with a deficit on ISF, at risk on LNF, but low

Table 8.6. Instructional recommendations for individual patterns of performance on Dynamic Indicators of Basic Early Literacy Skills (DIBELS) benchmark assessments at the middle of kindergarten

ISF	LNF	PSF	Percentile	Percentage of students meeting later goals				Incidence	Instructional support recommendation
				End of kindergarten PSF	Middle of first grade NWF	End of first grade DORF	Average		
Deficit	At risk	At risk	3	18	14	19	17	More common	Intensive—substantial intervention
Deficit	At risk	Some risk	7	34	13	21	23	Unusual	Intensive—substantial intervention
Emerging	At risk	At risk	9	28	20	28	25	More common	Intensive—substantial intervention
Emerging	At risk	Some risk	11	41	17	22	27	More common	Intensive—substantial intervention
Deficit	Some risk	At risk	13	24	28	48	33	More common	Intensive—substantial intervention
Deficit	At risk	Low risk	15	60	21	25	35	Unusual	Intensive—substantial intervention
Deficit	Some risk	Some risk	16	37	30	40	36	Unusual	Strategic—additional intervention
Established	At risk	At risk	17	45	32	31	36	Extremely rare	Strategic—additional intervention
Emerging	Some risk	At risk	18	37	30	49	38	Unusual	Strategic—additional intervention
Deficit	Low risk	At risk	20	30	37	58	42	Unusual	Strategic—additional intervention
Established	Some risk	At risk	21	42	38	49	43	Extremely rare	Strategic—additional intervention
Emerging	Some risk	Some risk	22	47	36	51	45	More common	Strategic—additional intervention
Established	At risk	Some risk	24	52	38	47	45	Extremely rare	Strategic—additional intervention

Emerging	At risk	Low risk	26	75	29	36	47	More common	Strategic—additional intervention
Deficit	Low risk	Some risk	28	43	42	68	51	Unusual	Strategic—additional intervention
Deficit	Some risk	Low risk	29	66	41	55	54	Extremely rare	Strategic—additional intervention
Emerging	Low risk	At risk	31	42	50	70	54	More common	Strategic—additional intervention
Established	Some risk	Some risk	33	55	44	64	54	Unusual	Strategic—additional intervention
Established	At risk	Low risk	34	82	34	47	54	Unusual	Strategic—additional intervention
Emerging	Low risk	Some risk	38	53	53	80	62	More common	Strategic—additional intervention
Emerging	Some risk	Low risk	44	82	47	59	63	More common	Strategic—additional intervention
Established	Low risk	At risk	47	51	58	89	66	Extremely rare	Benchmark—at grade level
Established	Low risk	Some risk	49	58	62	87	69	More common	Benchmark—at grade level
Deficit	Low risk	Low risk	52	74	60	75	70	Unusual	Benchmark—at grade level
Established	Some risk	Low risk	54	88	56	69	71	More common	Benchmark—at grade level
Emerging	Low risk	Low risk	64	88	68	83	80	More common	Benchmark—at grade level
Established	Low risk	Low risk	86	93	80	93	89	More common	Benchmark—at grade level

Key: ISF = Initial Sound Fluency, LNF = Letter Naming Fluency, PSF = Phoneme Segmentation Fluency, NWF = Nonsense Word Fluency, DORF = DIBELS Oral Reading Fluency

Note: Percentage of students meeting goal is the conditional percentage of children who meet the end of first grade goal of 40 or more on Oral Reading Fluency. Based on approximately 32,000 students, 638 schools, and 255 school districts.

risk on PSF represents an unusual pattern of performance and one that is implausible. In order to obtain a score of 18 or more on PSF, students need to have an emerging understanding of the sound structure of English. It is implausible for them to experience severe difficulty in identifying the initial sounds of words. Even though students with this pattern are likely to achieve the spring of kindergarten PSF goal, they are unlikely to achieve the middle of first grade NWF goal or the end of first grade DORF goal without additional intervention. If a school finds many children with this pattern, it may be indicative of a need to retrain the testers. Perhaps, for example, testers are mistakenly giving credit to children who are saying words slowly but not explicitly elongating each individual phoneme in the word. If there is confusion about this scoring rule, review and practice with the PSF scoring rule on elongating sounds in words would be appropriate. (PSF Rule 8 in the *DIBELS Administration and Scoring Guide* is available at dibels.uoregon.edu/.)

The decision utility of the DIBELS instructional support recommendations with respect to the end of kindergarten PSF goal is summarized in Table 8.7. The crucial conclusion from examination of Table 8.7 is that students who achieve the middle of kindergarten goals in ISF, PSF, and LNF are very likely to achieve the end of kindergarten goal and are unlikely to experience severe difficulty with phonemic awareness skills at the end of kindergarten.

Reviewing Middle of Kindergarten Outcomes

The second organizing question addresses how the early literacy skills of mid-year kindergarten students in one school compare with students' skills in other schools participating in the DIBELS Data System. The purpose of reviewing outcomes in the middle of kindergarten is to take stock of the total effects of the learning opportunities experienced in preschool, the community, and the first half of kindergarten. Three bases for evaluation are important to consider: 1) current middle of kindergarten outcomes compared to middle of kindergarten outcomes

Table 8.7. Decision utility for middle of kindergarten Dynamic Indicators of Basic Early Literacy Skills (DIBELS) benchmark assessment of Phoneme Segmentation Fluency to identify phonemic awareness health and severe phonemic awareness difficulty in the end of kindergarten

DIBELS instructional recommendation	Conditional percentage achieving 35 or more	Conditional percentage achieving less than 10
Intensive—substantial intervention	29	31
Strategic—additional intervention	57	9
Benchmark—at grade level	88	1

from prior years, 2) middle of kindergarten outcomes compared with the middle of kindergarten outcomes achieved by other schools participating in the DIBELS Data System, and 3) middle of kindergarten outcomes compared with school-based, desired middle of kindergarten outcome goals.

Comparison with Prior Middle of Kindergarten Outcomes   A first basis of comparison for a school to evaluate its middle of kindergarten outcomes is to compare the current year outcomes with outcomes achieved in prior years. Good, Gruba, and Kaminski include an example of using the DIBELS Data System to generate a histogram of 1998–1999 academic year literacy outcomes for comparison with a histogram of 1999–2000 academic year outcomes for the same grade and time of year (2001, p. 692). Another means of comparing outcomes from the current year with those of prior years is the cross-year box plot also available from the View/Create Reports section of the DIBELS Data System. Differences in early literacy outcomes that are large, dramatic, and important are visually apparent using both approaches.

Comparison with Middle of Kindergarten Outcomes for Other Schools   A second basis for comparison is to evaluate middle of kindergarten outcomes compared with other schools participating in the DIBELS Data System. A normative context for middle of kindergarten outcomes is provided in Table 8.8. The middle of kindergarten outcomes for a typical school are represented by the 50th percentile row. At the 50th percentile, half of all participating schools achieve poorer outcomes, and half of all participating schools achieve better middle of kindergarten outcomes. In a typical school, 54% of students are at benchmark, strategic support has been recommended for 32% of students, and intensive support has been recommended for 14% of students. Most schools achieve better outcomes than schools with fewer than 54% of students at benchmark in the middle of kindergarten. For example, if only 40% of children at a school are at benchmark in the middle of kindergarten, then the school would be at the 25th percentile. Most schools (75%) have as many or more children achieving the middle of kindergarten goal. A similar interpretation is possible for intensive and strategic recommendations. For example, a school in which 40% of students receive a strategic support recommendation would be at the 80th to 85th percentile. In other words, it would have more students who need strategic support than 80%–85% of schools. In general, a high-performing school would obtain a high percentile rank for benchmark and low percentile ranks for the number of students requiring strategic and intensive intervention.

Table 8.8. School-based normative context for evaluating the percentage of students in each instructional recommendation category in the middle of kindergarten

School-based percentile	Percentage of students in instructional recommendation category		
	Intensive	Strategic	Benchmark
5	2	14	22
10	3	18	28
15	4	20	32
20	6	21	37
25	7	23	40
30	8	25	43
35	10	27	46
40	11	29	49
45	12	30	51
50	14	32	54
55	15	33	56
60	17	34	59
65	19	35	61
70	21	36	64
75	23	38	67
80	25	39	70
85	29	41	73
90	32	44	78
95	40	48	81
99	51	56	89

Note: Based on 404 schools with at least 40 students in kindergarten in 2000–2001 and first grade in 2001–2002.

Comparison with Desired Middle of Kindergarten School Outcomes All evaluations of middle of kindergarten outcomes should include a focus on the desired goal: All kindergarten children, regardless of initial risk status, should be at benchmark and on track for early literacy outcomes. By getting children on track for successful reading outcomes and keeping them on track, we turn the concept of "no child left behind" into reality.

Once a school has identified its middle of kindergarten early literacy outcomes and how its outcomes compare with prior years and other schools, the next step is to examine the factors that contribute to those outcomes, especially factors that can be altered to improve outcomes. One consideration is the entry-level skills of kindergarten students. Another is the effectiveness of the core curriculum and instruction provided in the first half of kindergarten, with respect to early literacy skills in general and phonemic awareness skills in particular. A third consideration is the effectiveness of the system of additional intervention that is in place in the first half of kindergarten to support children at risk of poor reading and literacy outcomes to achieve benchmark goals.

Reviewing Core Curriculum
Outcomes in First Half of Kindergarten

This section explores the third organizing question: How effective is our core curriculum and instruction in supporting students who are entering kindergarten with benchmark skills to achieve the DIBELS ISF goal in the middle of kindergarten? Effective core curriculum and instruction should support most students who are on track to achieve the next benchmark goal. That is, most students who are at benchmark at the beginning of kindergarten should achieve the benchmark goals set for the middle of kindergarten with an effective core curriculum and high-quality instruction. A normative context for evaluating a school's core curriculum and instruction in the first half of kindergarten is provided in Table 8.9. In Table 8.9, the percentage of children in each instructional recommendation category at the beginning of kindergarten who achieve the middle of kindergarten ISF goal is compared across schools. For example, a typical school at the 50th percentile supports 62% of the children who were on track at the beginning of kindergarten to achieve the ISF goal. It is important to keep in mind that these outcomes are for those students who were on track at the beginning of kindergarten. In a typical school, 54% of children are on track at the beginning of kindergarten, and of those children, a typical school supports 62% to achieve the ISF goal. In comparison, if a school's core curriculum and instruction supports 90% of its students who were on track to achieve the middle of kindergarten ISF goal, the school would be at the 95th to 99th percentile. However, if a school supports only 30% of the students who were on track to achieve the middle of kindergarten ISF goal, the school would be at the 10th percentile, compared with other schools, in the effectiveness of its core curriculum and instruction.

A different perspective on the school-based normative context is provided in Figure 8.2. In Figure 8.2, the solid bars show the distribution of middle of kindergarten outcomes for children who were at benchmark at the beginning of kindergarten. The horizontal axis shows the percentage of children achieving the middle of kindergarten ISF goal. The vertical axis shows the number of schools that supported that percentage of children to achieve the ISF goal. Consistent with the school-based percentile comparison, most schools supported 61%–70% of at-benchmark students to achieve the middle of kindergarten ISF goal.

Table 8.9. School-based normative context for evaluating the conditional percentage of each instructional recommendation category achieving the middle of kindergarten Dynamic Indicators of Basic Early Literacy Skills (DIBELS) Initial Sound Frequency goal

School-based percentile	Percentage of students in instructional recommendation category		
	Intensive	Strategic	Benchmark
5	0	4	22
10	0	7	30
15	0	11	38
20	0	13	43
25	0	15	47
30	0	17	50
35	0	19	54
40	0	21	57
45	0	22	60
50	3	24	62
55	7	26	64
60	8	28	66
65	10	32	68
70	14	35	70
75	17	38	72
80	20	40	75
85	25	44	79
90	33	50	83
95	43	57	89
99	75	76	96

Note: Based on 382 schools with at least 40 students in kindergarten in 2001–2002.

The variability between schools is remarkable, however. Fourteen schools supported 91%–100% of their at-benchmark students to achieve the ISF goal. Ten schools supported 0%–10% of their at-benchmark students to achieve the ISF goal.

Two reasons for the dramatic differences between schools in its middle of kindergarten outcomes for at-benchmark students should be examined by the school's early literacy team. One explanation that should be considered and ruled out before examining other possible explanations is that there may have been systematic errors in administration and scoring of the DIBELS ISF measure. If the scores are not accurate, further interpretation is not appropriate. The *DIBELS Initial Sound Fluency Assessment Integrity Checklist* in the *DIBELS Administration and Scoring Guide* (available at dibels.uoregon.edu/) should be used to evaluate the accuracy of administration and scoring of each tester in the school. In addition, a random sample of 10% of students can be retested to ensure that scores display adequate reliability.

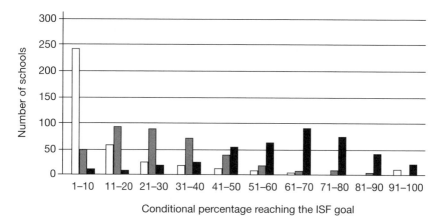

Figure 8.2. Distribution of schools with respect to the conditional percentage of children achieving 25 or more sounds correct per minute on the middle of kindergarten Initial Sound Fluency (ISF) given instructional recommendation category in the beginning of kindergarten. (*Key:* ☐ = Intensive, ▨ = Strategic, ■ = Benchmark)

If the scores are accurate, the most plausible explanation for school differences in middle-of-kindergarten outcomes for at-benchmark students is differences in the effectiveness of the core curriculum and instruction. The school differences are not attributable to the skills or background of the students in the school because the solid bars in Figure 8.2 only refer to those students who were entering kindergarten with benchmark skills predictive of successful early literacy outcomes. The school differences are also not attributable to differences in the system of additional intervention. It is the role of the core curriculum and instruction to support students who are on track to achieve crucial early literacy outcomes.

When reviewing middle of kindergarten outcomes, the early literacy team may determine that their school outcomes are typical and frequently occurring. However, the team must still ask, "Is typical good enough?" The key feature of the DIBELS assessments is its focus on core components of early literacy that are teachable. Many published, research-based curricula and supplemental materials are readily available to support instruction. As schools change the focus of their core curriculum and instruction, the distribution of middle of kindergarten outcomes in Figure 8.2 can be expected to change as well. Perhaps the most important conclusion to draw from examination of Figure 8.2 is that most schools do not have an adequate focus on phonemic awareness in general and initial sounds of words in particular in the first half of kindergarten. For most schools, the core curriculum and instruction are not as effective as they could be.

Of course, an alternative explanation to consider is that the DIBELS middle of kindergarten benchmark goal is too high. However, the DIBELS benchmark goals are established not based on norms but based on the likelihood of achieving subsequent literacy outcomes. For students identified as needing intensive intervention, only 26% achieved 40 or more words read correctly on the end of first-grade DORF assessment. For students identified as needing strategic intervention, 59% achieved the first-grade goal. Most important, for students meeting the middle of kindergarten benchmark goals, 88% achieved the first-grade goal of reading 40 or more words correct per minute.

A number of published supplemental materials are available with a variety of activities that can be used in the first half of kindergarten to teach and practice initial sounds in words. Selected materials and activities are described in Table 8.10. These activities range from game-like, engaging activities that combine movement and song to teach and practice initial sounds in words to carefully designed instruction that can help children who are struggling with phonemic awareness skills to understand the sound structure of English.

Reviewing the System of Additional Intervention in First Half of Kindergarten

The fourth question to explore is how effective the system of additional intervention is in supporting students entering kindergarten who are at risk for not achieving the DIBELS ISF goal in the middle of kindergarten. For students who are at risk for severe difficulty in learning to read, a system of additional intervention is necessary to help them achieve subsequent early literacy benchmark goals. An effective system of additional intervention supports more students who are at risk for not achieving literacy goals.

A normative context to evaluate the effectiveness of the school's system of additional intervention is provided in Table 8.9. In particular, the column reporting the percentage of children with intensive intervention recommendations and the corresponding school-based percentile provide a basis with which to evaluate a school's system of additional intervention. A typical school in the DIBELS Data System supports only 3% of children with an intensive instructional recommendation at the beginning of kindergarten to achieve the ISF goal for the middle of kindergarten. A school that supports no students with an intensive instructional need to achieve the ISF goal would be at the 45th percentile. A school that supports 75% percent of students with an intensive instructional recommendation to achieve the ISF goal would be at the 99th percentile.

Table 8.10. Examples of initial sound activities in commercially available curricula with research support

Curriculum	Activities	Pages	Comments
Ladders to Literacy (O'Connor, Notari-Syverson & Vadasy, 1998)	Sound Isolation Pretend Play Sound of the Week First Sound Song Word to Word First Sound Bingo	113 116 119 124 134 140	Game-like activities Phonemic awareness activities are not grouped by skill Appropriate for benchmark and strategic level support Three levels of instructional supports provided for every activity
Phonemic Awareness in Young Children (Adams, Foorman, Lundberg, & Beeler, 1998)	Unit 7. Initial and Final Sounds: 4 initial sounds activities	7a, 7b, 7c, 7d	Game-like activities. First sound activities are grouped together Appropriate for benchmark and strategic level support
Phonological Awareness Training for Reading (Torgesen & Bryant, 1994)	Segmentation of initial phoneme Matching words by similar beginning sounds Production of initial phonemes in words	Wordset 1 Wordsets 2–5	Repeated use of skills across different sets of words with games Systematic use of Lindamood technique of feeling how sounds are produced Appropriate for all levels of support in small groups
Road to the Code (Blachmann, Ball, Black, & Tangel, 2000)	Embedded first sound instruction in segmentation activities	Every lesson	Emphasis on segmentation and letter–sound correspondence Appropriate for all levels of support in small groups
Sound Foundation Kit (Byrne, & Fielding-Barnsley, 1993b)	The entire program focuses on first and last sounds.	Every lesson	Matching words by initial or ending sounds. Uses eight phonemes Appropriate for benchmark and strategic support

The distribution of school outcomes for students with an intensive intervention recommendation is provided in Figure 8.2, shown as white bars. These findings highlight a general need for a greatly improved system of additional intervention in the first half of kindergarten. With an effective system of additional intervention, these outcomes can be changed dramatically. In Figure 8.2, there are four schools that are effective in supporting 91%–100% of their students with an intensive intervention recommendation to achieve the middle of kindergarten ISF goal.

Instructional Recommendation for the End of Kindergarten

The reading risk and health indicators for the end of kindergarten are summarized in Table 8.11. Students scoring in the deficit or at-risk categories are likely to experience reading difficulty without effective intervention. Students scoring in the low risk and established categories are likely to achieve successful reading outcomes with effective core instruction. At the end of kindergarten, the benchmark goal is established phonemic awareness, 35 correct phonemes per minute, on the DIBELS PSF measure. Additional indicators of adequate early literacy progress and low risk at the end of kindergarten are an LNF score of 40 or more and an NWF score of 25 or more. The possible patterns of performance on the DIBELS measures and the percentage of children with the pattern who achieve subsequent early literacy goals are presented in Table 8.12. It is clear from an examination of Table 8.12 that achieving established phonemic awareness without making adequate progress on phonics skills is not enough to be on track for positive reading outcomes. The LNF score also serves as a powerful indicator of difficulty achieving subsequent benchmark goals. Although it is an unusual pattern, students who are on track for phonemic awareness and alphabetic principle but who are at risk on LNF only have even odds of achieving the DORF goal at the end of first grade.

In the DIBELS system, we have focused our instructional recommendations and goals on PSF and NWF scores as kindergarten outcomes and referred to the LNF score as a risk indicator. The problem is that there is ample, strong, and converging support for the importance and causal role of phonemic awareness and phonics skills in early literacy (National Reading Panel, 2000). However, the causal role of fluency with letter names is unclear. That the LNF score is a predictor is clear, but why it is a predictor is less clear. It may be a measure of speed of cognitive processing or rapid automatized naming. Indeed, measures of rapid color naming, rapid shape naming, rapid object naming, and rapid number naming serve almost as well as predictors of risk. Alternatively, fluency with letter names may be an indirect measure of par-

Table 8.11. Descriptive levels of performance at the end of kindergarten as measured by Dynamic Indicators of Basic Early Literacy Skills (DIBELS)

Variable	Performance	Descriptor
LNF	< 29	At risk
	29–39	Some risk
	≥ 40	Low risk
PSF	< 10	Deficit
	10–34	Emerging
	≥ 35	Established
NWF	< 15	At risk
	15–24	Some risk
	≥ 25	Low risk

Key: ISF = Initial Sound Fluency, LNF = Letter Naming Fluency, PSF = Phoneme Segmentation Fluency, NWF = Nonsense Word Fluency

ental involvement. Early parental involvement in reading is manifested by knowledge of letters, while later parental involvement in reading may be manifested in time spent reading, support for reading, availability of reading materials, and so on.

The decision utility of the end of kindergarten instructional recommendations is reported in Table 8.13. Most children with a benchmark instructional recommendation at the end of kindergarten (87%) reach the DORF reading goal of 40 or more words correct at the end of first grade. Few students with a benchmark instructional recommendation (2%) experience severe reading difficulty at the end of first grade.

Reviewing End of Kindergarten Outcomes

The fifth organizing question is, "How do the early literacy skills of kindergarten students in our school at the end of the year compare with students' skills in other schools participating in the DIBELS Data System?" A school-based normative context to evaluate the percentage of students with a benchmark, strategic, or intensive instructional recommendation is provided in Table 8.14. In a typical (median) school, 15% of students have a recommendation for intensive intervention, 17% of students have a recommendation for strategic support, and 65% of students have a recommendation for benchmark instruction. Using Table 8.14, a school's early literacy team can evaluate their end-of-kindergarten outcomes compared with other schools using the DIBELS Data System. Strong kindergarten outcomes would have a high percentile rank for benchmark recommendations and low percentile ranks

Table 8.12. Instructional recommendations for individual patterns of performance on end of kindergarten Dynamic Indicators of Basic Early Literacy Skills (DIBELS) Benchmark Assessment

| LNF | PSF | NWF | Percentile | Percentage of students meeting later goals | | | Incidence | Instructional support recommendation |
				Middle of first grade NWF	End of first grade DORF	Average		
At risk	Deficit	At risk	2	8	19	13	More common	Intensive—substantial intervention
At risk	Emerging	At risk	6	15	24	19	More common	Intensive—substantial intervention
At risk	Established	At risk	10	17	25	21	More common	Intensive—substantial intervention
At risk	Deficit	Some risk	12	21	27	24	Extremely rare	Intensive—substantial intervention
At risk	Established	Some risk	13	27	33	30	More common	Intensive—substantial intervention
At risk	Emerging	Some risk	15	27	37	32	Unusual	Intensive—substantial intervention
Some risk	Deficit	At risk	16	22	43	33	Unusual	Intensive—substantial intervention
At risk	Emerging	Low risk	17	28	39	33	Extremely rare	Strategic—additional intervention
Some risk	Established	At risk	18	26	46	36	Unusual	Strategic—additional intervention
Some risk	Emerging	At risk	20	28	46	37	More common	Strategic—additional intervention
Some risk	Deficit	Some risk	22	24	56	40	Extremely rare	Strategic—additional intervention
Some risk	Emerging	Some risk	23	35	55	45	More common	Strategic—additional intervention
At risk	Established	Low risk	25	40	52	46	Unusual	Strategic—additional intervention

Low risk	Deficit	At risk	26	34	64	49	Extremely rare	Strategic—additional intervention
At risk	Deficit	Low risk	27	36	63	49	Extremely rare	Strategic—additional intervention
Low risk	Emerging	At risk	28	34	65	50	Unusual	Strategic—additional intervention
Some risk	Established	Some risk	30	41	60	50	More common	Strategic—additional intervention
Some risk	Deficit	Low risk	33	41	62	51	Extremely rare	Strategic—additional intervention
Low risk	Deficit	Some risk	33	41	65	53	Extremely rare	Strategic—additional intervention
Some risk	Emerging	Low risk	35	53	65	59	More common	Benchmark—at grade level
Some risk	Established	Low risk	38	56	68	62	More common	Benchmark—at grade level
Low risk	Established	At risk	42	46	81	63	Unusual	Benchmark—at grade level
Low risk	Emerging	Some risk	44	51	79	65	More common	Benchmark—at grade level
Low risk	Established	Some risk	48	52	79	66	More common	Benchmark—at grade level
Low risk	Deficit	Low risk	52	59	80	69	Extremely rare	Benchmark—at grade level
Low risk	Emerging	Low risk	55	68	87	78	More common	Benchmark—at grade level
Low risk	Established	Low risk	79	81	92	87	More common	Benchmark—at grade level

Key: LNF = Letter Naming Fluency, PSF = Phoneme Segmentation Fluency, NWF = Nonsense Word Fluency, DORF = DIBELS Oral Reading Fluency

Note: Percentage of students meeting goal is the conditional percentage of children who meet the end of first grade goal of 40 or more on Oral Reading Fluency. Based on approximately 32,000 students, 638 schools, and 255 school districts.

Table 8.13. Decision utility for end of kindergarten Dynamic Indicators of Basic Early Literacy Skills (DIBELS) benchmark assessment of Oral Reading Fluency to identify reading health and severe reading difficulty at the end of first grade

DIBELS instructional recommendation	Conditional percentage reading 40 or more	Conditional percentage reading less than 20
Intensive—substantial intervention	27	34
Strategic—additional intervention	57	10
Benchmark—at grade level	87	2

for intensive and strategic recommendations. For example, a school with 80% of students at benchmark, 15% needing strategic intervention, and 5% intensive intervention would be at the 75th to 80th percentile compared with other schools in the number of students with benchmark skills, at the 40th percentile compared with other schools in the number of students with strategic recommendation, and at the 15th percentile compared with other schools in the number of students with an intensive intervention recommendation. The 15th percentile in this case would mean that 85% of schools have as many or more students with an intensive intervention recommendation.

Reviewing Core Curriculum Outcomes in the Second Half of Kindergarten

The sixth organizing question addresses the effectiveness of the core curriculum and instruction in supporting students who are on track in the middle of kindergarten to achieve the DIBELS PSF goal by the end of kindergarten. The primary purpose for evaluating end of kindergarten outcomes is to identify areas in which the kindergarten program can be strengthened to improve outcomes. Disappointing end of kindergarten outcomes may be due to 1) low early literacy skills in the middle of kindergarten, 2) core curriculum and instruction that are not providing adequate focus and emphasis on essential components of early literacy, or 3) a system of additional intervention that is not providing adequate support to students who are at risk of difficulty learning to read. If students are on track in the middle of kindergarten, then the core curriculum and instruction should provide sufficient support for the students to achieve end of kindergarten early literacy goals. In other words, all or almost all students who are benchmark in the middle of kindergarten should achieve end of kindergarten early literacy goals if the core curriculum and instruction are adequate.

A normative context in which to evaluate the effectiveness of the core curriculum and instruction is provided in Table 8.15. A typical

Table 8.14. School-based normative context for evaluating the percentage of students in each instructional recommendation category at the end of kindergarten

School-based percentile	Percentage of students in instructional recommendation category		
	Intensive	Strategic	Benchmark
5	2	6	34
10	4	7	38
15	5	8	44
20	7	11	48
25	8	12	52
30	10	13	57
35	11	15	59
40	13	15	62
45	14	16	63
50	15	17	65
55	16	19	67
60	18	20	70
65	20	21	72
70	21	22	75
75	25	24	78
80	27	25	82
85	33	27	84
90	36	29	88
95	42	33	90
>99	50	39	91

Note: Based on 158 schools with at least 40 students in kindergarten in 2000–2001 and end of first grade in 2001–2002.

school at the 50th percentile of effectiveness of core curriculum and instruction supports 90% of students with a benchmark instructional recommendation in the middle of kindergarten to achieve the end of kindergarten PSF goal of 35 correct phonemes per minute. A school with less than 90% of the at-benchmark students achieving the end of kindergarten goal has less effective core curriculum and instruction. Some schools had only 50% or fewer of their at-benchmark students achieving the end of kindergarten PSF goal. Those schools would be at the 5th percentile compared with other schools in the DIBELS Data System in terms of the effectiveness of their core curriculum and instruction.

The school-to-school variability in outcomes for benchmark students is illustrated in Figure 8.3, represented as solid bars. The majority of schools support at least 91% of at-benchmark students to achieve the end of kindergarten PSF goal. Some schools support only 31% to 40%

Table 8.15. School-based normative context for evaluating conditional percent of each instructional recommendation category achieving end of kindergarten Dynamic Indicators of Basic Early Literacy Skills (DIBELS) Phoneme Segmentation Fluency goal

School-based percentile	Percentage of students in instructional recommendation category		
	Intensive	Strategic	Benchmark
5	0	15	50
10	0	24	61
15	0	29	70
20	0	35	76
25	7	40	79
30	11	45	82
35	15	50	84
40	20	54	86
45	23	58	88
50	26	62	90
55	32	65	92
60	33	70	93
65	40	73	94
70	44	78	95
75	50	82	97
80	59	85	98
85	67	88	99
90	81	93	100
95	100	100	100
99	100	100	100

Note: Based on 404 schools with at least 40 students in kindergarten in 2000–2001 and first grade in 2001–2002.

of their at-benchmark students to achieve the end of kindergarten PSF goal. These differences in school outcomes cannot be attributed to the middle of kindergarten skills of the students because all students with a benchmark instructional recommendation have a level of skills in the middle of kindergarten that is predictive of achieving the end-of-kindergarten goal with effective core curriculum and instruction. The most plausible reasons for the poor outcomes are that 1) the core curriculum and instruction do not provide adequate emphasis on phonemic awareness or 2) that the accuracy and integrity of the DIBELS testing has been compromised. The accuracy and integrity of the DIBELS scores can be evaluated with the Assessment Integrity Checklists in the *DIBELS Administration and Scoring Guide* and by retesting a sample of students to ensure that scores are reliable and accurate. When the core curriculum and instruction is determined to need improvement by the

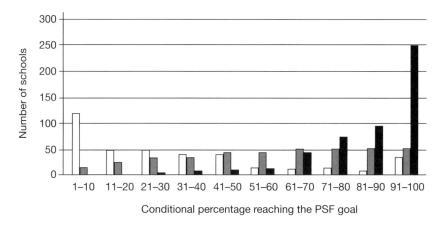

Figure 8.3. Distribution of schools with respect to the conditional percentage of children achieving 35 or more sounds correct per minute on the end of kindergarten Phoneme Segmentation Fluency (PSF) given instructional recommendation category in the middle of kindergarten. *(Key:* □ = Intensive, ■ = Strategic, ■ = Benchmark.)

school's early literacy team, a plan for changing or supplementing the core is indicated.

Reviewing the System of Additional Intervention in the Second Half of Kindergarten

The final organizing question addresses the effectiveness of the system of additional intervention in supporting students who are at risk in the middle of kindergarten for not achieving the DIBELS PSF goal by the end of kindergarten. In addition to effective core curriculum and instruction, a system of additional intervention is necessary for students who require more instructional support to achieve crucial early literacy goals than is available with the core curriculum and instruction. A school-based, normative context to evaluate the effectiveness of the system of additional intervention is also available in Table 8.15. A typical system of additional intervention supported only 26% of children needing intensive intervention to achieve the end of kindergarten PSF goal. The school-to-school variability in effectiveness of systems of additional intervention is illustrated in Figure 8.3. Many schools (approximately 40) were effective in supporting at least 91% of students with intensive intervention needs to achieve the PSF goal in kindergarten. The question becomes, "If those schools can provide intensive additional intervention and support their students to achieve early literacy goals, why not our school?"

DISCUSSION

Beginning reading programs in kindergarten typically include activities for developing phonemic awareness. However, examination of programs indicates great variability in the number and selection of phonological awareness skills to be taught, the extent to which the program targets phonological awareness skills most highly correlated with early reading acquisition, the pace of instruction, and the amount of instructional design and scaffolding of critical skills for students who are at risk (e.g., explicit instruction, systematic review, integration with other key early literacy skills) (Carnine, Silbert, & Kaméenui, 1997; Simmons et al., 2000; Smith, Simmons, et al., 2001).

For example, the National Reading Panel (NRP) report indicated that teaching a few phonological awareness skills that are highly correlated to reading is preferable to teaching many skills. In addition, the NRP report indicated that blending and segmenting instruction had a greater effect on reading development than teaching multiple skills (2000). Moreover, the NRP concluded that the effects of phonemic awareness instruction were greater when the connection between phonological awareness and the sounds of letters was made explicit and integrated. Consequently, teachers need to check core beginning reading programs and supplemental materials at the kindergarten level to evaluate whether sufficient focus is placed on phoneme blending and segmenting and whether there is explicit integration between phonemic awareness instruction and letter sounds. If many skills are taught with apparently equal emphasis, the curriculum is unlikely to be optimally effective. Even teachers who use supplemental programs whose efficacy has been established by empirical research, such as *Ladders to Literacy* and *Phonemic Awareness in Young Children,* may need to modify these highly respected programs to provide intensive intervention for students who need substantial support. When considering the number of phonological awareness skills to teach children with intensive instructional needs, first sound recognition is considered a prerequisite step for segmentation and was the focus of effective preschool and kindergarten intervention studies (Byrne & Fielding-Barnsley, 1989, 1993a, 1993b).

In some instances, effective beginning reading curricula, such as Reading Mastery I (Engelmann & Bruner, 1995) and Read Well (Sprick, Howard, & Fidanque, 1998), are being used at the kindergarten level for all students. However, even in schools with high-quality professional development that includes in-class coaching and highly effective curriculum, we found the percentage of children reaching kindergarten and first-grade benchmarks was not as high as we expected. Our tentative hypothesis is that although these two programs spend some time at the beginning of the year teaching phonological awareness blending and segmenting skills, even more front-end instruction in phonological awareness is needed by some children in order to meet critical benchmarks and progress in a timely manner toward the ultimate outcome of oral reading fluency and comprehension in grade-level materials.

Optimal attention to research findings and a fine-grained response to instructional design principles are critical characteristics of core curricula and supplemental materials for the children who are most at risk. These characteristics are beneficial to all other children, including those who need some additional instructional support or those who require nothing other than effective instruction in effective, research-based materials. Fine-grained modifications of curricular materials are, although highly critical, tedious and time consuming. Such modifications may be beyond the skills and training of the many general classroom teachers and may be appropriate targets for professional development experiences.

Lessons Learned

It seems reasonable to close with some observations from our combined experience with school reform efforts.

1. Teacher perceptions and beliefs are not always accurate—data help.

2. Changes in outcomes at one grade level precipitate changes in the next grade level. That is, changing kindergarten outcomes affects first-grade outcomes the following year.

3. Grade-level data across classrooms indicate much about the general way of doing business within a school.

4. Outcomes are stable and replicable unless big changes in curriculum, instruction, and system of additional intervention are made.

5. Evaluation of student outcome data can be used by schools to change reading outcomes, even when the schools have very different orientations to beginning reading instruction.

REFERENCES

Adams, M.J., Foorman, B.R., Lundberg, I., Beeler, T. (1998). *Phonemic awareness in young children: A classroom curriculum.* Baltimore: Paul. H. Brookes Publishing Co.

Baker, S., & Smith, S. (1999). Starting off on the right foot: The influence of four principles of professional development in improving literacy instruction in two kindergarten programs. *Learning Disabilities Research and Practice, 14*(4), 239–253.

Baker, S., & Smith, S. (2001). Linking school assessments to research-based practices in beginning reading: Improving programs and outcomes for students with and without disabilities. *Teacher Education and Special Education, 24,* 315–322.

Blachmann, B.A., Ball, E.W., Black, R., & Tangel, D.M. (2000). *Road to the code: A phonological awareness program for young children.* Baltimore: Paul H. Brookes Publishing Co.

Bowman, B.T., Donovan, M.S., & Burns, M.S. (2001). *Eager to learn: Educating our preschoolers.* Washington, DC: National Academy Press.

Byrne, B., & Fielding-Barnsley, R. (1989). Phonemic awareness and letter knowledge in the child's acquisition of the alphabetic principle. *Journal of Educational Psychology, 81,* 313–321.

Byrne, B., & Fielding-Barnsley, R. (1993a). Evaluation of a program to teach phonemic awareness to young children: A 1-year follow-up. *Journal of Educational Psychology, 85,* 104–111.

Byrne, B. & Fielding-Barnsley, R. (1993b). *Sound foundation kit.* Artarmon, Australia: Peter Lynden Publishing.

Carnine, D.W., Silbert, J., & Kaméenui, E.J. (1997). *Direct instruction reading* (3rd ed.). Upper Saddle River, NJ: Merrill/Prentice-Hall.

Engelmann, S., & Bruner, E.C. (1995). *Reading Mastery I* (Rainbow ed.). Columbus, OH: SRA/McGraw-Hill.

Good, R.H., Gruba, J., & Kaminski, R.A. (2001). Best practices in using Dynamic Indicators of Basic Early Literacy Skills (DIBELS) in an outcomes-driven model. In A. Thomas & J. Grimes (Eds.), *Best practices in school psychology IV* (pp. 699–720). Bethesda, MD: National Association of School Psychologists.

Good, R.H., & Kaminski, R.A. (Eds.). (2002). *Dynamic Indicators of Basic Early Literacy Skills* (6th ed.). Eugene, OR: Institute for Development of Educational Achievement.

Good, R.H., Kaminski, R.A., Simmons, D., & Kaméenui, E. (2001). Using Dynamic Indicators of Basic Literacy Skills (DIBELS) in an outcomes-driven model: Steps to reading outcomes. *Oregon School Study Council (OSSC) Bulletin, 44*(1), 2–24.

Good, R.H., Simmons, D.C., & Kaméenui, E.J. (2001). The importance and decision-making utility of a continuum of fluency-based indicators of foundational reading skills for third-grade high-stakes outcomes. *Scientific Studies of Reading, 5*(3), 257–288.

National Reading Panel. (2000). *Teaching children to read: An evidence-based assessment of the scientific research literature on reading and its implications for reading instruction.* Bethesda, MD: National Institute of Child Health and Human Development.

Notari-Syverson, A., O'Connor, R.E., & Vadasy, P.F. (1998). *Ladders to literacy: A preschool activity book.* Baltimore: Paul H. Brookes Publishing Co.

O'Connor, R.E, Notari-Syverson, A., & Vadasy, P.F. (1998). *Ladders to Literacy: A kindergarten activity book.* Baltimore: Paul H. Brookes Publishing Co.

Simmons, D.C., Kuykendall, K., King, K., Cornachione, C., & Kaméenui, E.J. (2000). Implementation of a schoolwide reading improvement model: "No one ever told us it would be this hard!" *Learning Disabilities Research & Practice,* *15*(2), 92–100.

Smith, S., Baker, S., & Oudeans, S.M.K. (2001). Making a difference in the classroom with early literacy instruction. *Teaching Exceptional Children, 33*(6), 8–14.

Smith, S.B., Simmons, D.C., Gleason, M.M., Kaméenui, E.J., Baker, S.K., Sprick, M., Gunn, B., Thomas, C.L., Chard, D.J., Plasencia-Peinado, J., & Peinado, R. (2001). An analysis of phonological awareness instruction in four kindergarten basal reading programs. *Reading & Writing Quarterly, 17,* 25–51.

Sprick, M., Howard, L., & Fidanque, A. (1998). *Read well.* Longmont, CO: Sopris West.

Torgesen, J.K., & Bryant, B.T. (1994). *Phonological awareness training for reading.* Austin, TX: PRO-ED.

DIBELS Reviewing Outcomes School Report Directions

1. Using the DIBELS Data System, the tables from this chapter, and the early literacy goals established by the school, complete the intensive, strategic, and benchmark columns of the school report.

2. As a school-based early literacy team, appraise the school performance and judge whether 1) school outcomes are satisfactory, 2) the core curriculum and instruction are satisfactory, and 3) the system of additional intervention is satisfactory.

3. As a school-based early literacy team, plan for changes and enhancements in 1) preschool liaison and community outreach, 2) core curriculum and instruction, and 3) system of additional intervention.

GLOSSARY OF KEY TERMS

Percentage in category: Specifies how many children are in each instructional category. For example, 67% benchmark means that two thirds of the children in the school received an instructional recommendation of benchmark—on track for early literacy outcomes.

Percentile rank of percentage in category: Provides a school-based normative context for percentage in category. For example, 67% benchmark would be at the 85th–90th percentile compared with other schools in the beginning of kindergarten. A school with 67% benchmark would have students with skills as high or higher than 85%–90% of other schools.

Percentage of benchmark achieving goal: Provides a means to evaluate the core curriculum and instruction. Benchmark students should achieve subsequent goals with effective core curriculum and instruction.

Percentile rank of percentage of benchmark achieving goal: Provides a school-based normative context to evaluate the effectiveness of the core curriculum. For example, a percentile rank above 50 indicates that the core curriculum is more effective than a median or typical school.

Percentage of intensive and strategic achieving goal: Provides a means to evaluate the system of additional intervention. With an effective system of additional intervention, more intensive and strategic students should achieve subsequent early literacy goals.

Percentile rank of percentage of intensive and strategic achieving goal: Provides a school-based normative context to evaluate the effectiveness of the system of additional intervention. A percentile rank below 50 indicates that the system of additional intervention is more effective than a median or typical school.

DIBELS Beginning of Kindergarten Reviewing Outcomes Report		
Beginning of kindergarten skills	**School-based Early Literacy Team Appraisal**	
Percentage in each instructional recommendation category	How do current beginning of kindergarten skills of students in our school compare with last year?	
Intensive	Strategic	Benchmark
Current/Last	Current/Last	Current/Last
School-based percentile rank of percentage in each category	How do the beginning of kindergarten skills of students in our school compare with other schools participating in the DIBELS Data System?	
Intensive	Strategic	Benchmark
School-based, desired goal for percentage in each category	How do current beginning of kindergarten skills of students in our school compare with the desired goal level of beginning kindergarten skills?	
Intensive	Strategic	Benchmark
Current/Goal	Current/Goal	Current/Goal

What changes are planned for our system of preschool liason and community outreach prior to the beginning of kindergarten?

Notes

Figure A1. Sample school report for reviewing outcomes at the beginning of kindergarten using the Dynamic Indicators of Basic Early Literacy Skills (DIBELS; Good & Kaminski, 2002).

DIBELS Middle of Kindergarten Reviewing Outcomes Report	
Middle of kindergarten skills	School-based Early Literacy Team Appraisal
Percentage in each instructional recommendation category 	Intensive	Strategic	Benchmark
---	---	---
Current/Last	Current/Last	Current/Last		How do current middle of kindergarten skills of students in our school compare with last year?
School-based percentile rank of percentage in each category 	Intensive	Strategic	Benchmark
---|---|---|	How do the middle of kindergarten skills of students in our school compare with other schools participating in the DIBELS Data System?
School-based desired goal for percentage in each category 	Intensive	Strategic	Benchmark
---	---	---
Current/Goal	Current/Goal	Current/Goal		How do current middle of kindergarten skills of students in our school compare with the desired goal level of middle of kindergarten skills?
Effectiveness of the Core Curriculum in the First Half of Kindergarten	
Percentage of benchmark students in beginning of kindergarten achieving the ISF goal Current/Goal	How does the effectiveness of our school's core curriculum in the first half of kindergarten compare with last year?
School-based percentile rank for percentage of benchmark students achieving the ISF goal Current/Goal	How does the effectiveness of our school's core curriculum in the first half of kindergarten compare with other schools participating in the DIBELS Data System?
School-based desired goal for percentage of benchmark students achieving the ISF goal Current/Goal	How does the effectiveness of our school's core curriculum in the first half of kindergarten compare with the desired goal level of effectiveness?
What systems-level changes are planned for the core curriculum in the first half of kindergarten?	

(continued)

Figure A2. Sample school report for reviewing outcomes at the middle of kindergarten using the Dynamic Indicators of Basic Early Literacy Skills (DIBELS; Good & Kaminski, 2002).

DIBELS Middle of Kindergarten Reviewing Outcomes Report	
Effectiveness of System of Additional Intervention in First Half of Kindergarten	
Percentage of intensive and strategic students in beginning of kindergarten achieving the ISF goal	How does the effectiveness of our school's system of additional intervention in the first half of kindergarten compare with last year?
Intensive / Strategic Current/Last Current/Last	
School-based percentile rank of percentage of intensive and strategic students achieving the ISF goal	How does the effectiveness of our school's system of additional intervention in the first half of kindergarten compare with other schools participating in the DIBELS Data System?
Intensive / Strategic	
School-based, desired goal for percentage of intensive and strategic students achieving the ISF goal	How does the effectiveness of our school's system of additional intervention in the first half of kindergarten compare with the desired goal level of effectiveness?
Intensive / Strategic Current/Goal Current/Goal	
What changes are planned for the system of additional intervention in the first half of kindergarten?	
Notes	

DIBELS End of Kindergarten Reviewing Outcomes Report	
End of kindergarten skills	School-based Early Literacy Team Appraisal
Percentage in each instructional recommendation category	How do current end of kindergarten skills of students in our school compare with last year?
Intensive / Strategic / Benchmark Current/Last / Current/Last / Current/Last	
School-based percentile rank of percentage in each category	How do the end of kindergarten skills of students in our school compare with other schools participating in the DIBELS Data System?
Intensive / Strategic / Benchmark	
School-based desired goal for percentage in each category	How do current end of kindergarten skills of students in our school compare with the desired goal level of end of kindergarten skills?
Intensive / Strategic / Benchmark Current/Goal / Current/Goal / Current/Goal	
Effectiveness of the Core Curriculum in the Second Half of Kindergarten	
Percentage of benchmark students in middle of kindergarten achieving the PSF goal	How does the effectiveness of our school's core curriculum in the second half of kindergarten compare with last year?
Current/Goal	
School-based percentile rank for percentage of benchmark students achieving the PSF goal	How does the effectiveness of our school's core curriculum in the second half of kindergarten compare with other schools participating in the DIBELS Data System?
Current/Goal	
School-based, desired goal for percentage of benchmark students achieving the PSF goal	How does the effectiveness of our school's core curriculum in the second half of kindergarten compare with the desired goal level of effectiveness?
Current/Goal	
What systems-level changes are planned for the core curriculum in the second half of kindergarten?	

(continued)

Figure A3.   Sample school report for reviewing outcomes at the end of kindergarten using the Dynamic Indicators of Basic Early Literacy Skills (DIBELS; Good & Kaminski, 2002).

DIBELS End of Kindergarten Reviewing Outcomes Report	
Effectiveness of System of Additional Intervention in Second Half of Kindergarten	
Percentage of intensive and strategic students in middle of kindergarten achieving the PSF goal	How does the effectiveness of our school's system of additional intervention in the second half of kindergarten compare with last year?
Intensive — Current/Last / Strategic — Current/Last	
School-based percentile rank of percentage of intensive and strategic students achieving the PSF goal	How does the effectiveness of our school's system of additional intervention in the second half of kindergarten compare with other schools participating in the DIBELS Data System?
Intensive / Strategic	
School-based, desired goal for percentage of intensive and strategic students achieving the PSF goal	How does the effectiveness of our school's system of additional intervention in the second half of kindergarten compare with the desired goal level of effectiveness?
Intensive — Current/Goal / Strategic — Current/Goal	
What changes are planned for the system of additional intervention in the second half of kindergarten?	
Notes	

9

Similarities and Differences Between Experienced Teachers and Trained Paraprofessionals

An Observational Analysis

MARCIA L. GREK, PATRICIA G. MATHES, AND JOSEPH K. TORGESEN

There is now widespread recognition that teaching virtually all children to read is possible. However, achieving universal literacy requires that some children receive considerable extra instructional support (Snow, Burns, & Griffin, 1998; Torgesen, 1998). For these children, intensive early instructional intervention is necessary in order to facilitate and maintain grade-level growth in reading. Without such intervention, many of these children will not learn to read adequately early in the primary school experience and may fall increasingly behind as they move through elementary school (Francis, Shaywitz, Stuebing, Shaywitz, & Fletcher, 1996; Torgesen & Burgess, 1998).

Research findings demonstrate that school programs that emphasize early interventions can decrease the number of students with reading difficulties, increase the number of books read by students outside of school, and substantially raise scores on standardized tests (Wolf,

The work presented in this chapter was supported by Grant No. HD30988 from the National Institute of Child Health and Human Development. This article does not necessarily reflect the positions or policies of this funding agency and no official endorsement should be inferred. Requests for information should be addressed to Marcia L. Grek, Ph.D., Florida Center for Reading Research, Florida State University, 227 North Bronough Street, Suite 7250, Tallahassee, FL 32301.

1998). In addition, a number of well-controlled experiments have shown that appropriate early intervention can bring the reading skills of children at risk for reading difficulty solidly into the average range of reading achievement (Mathes, Denton, Fletcher, Anthony, & Francis, 2002; Torgesen et al., 1999; Vellutino et al., 1996). Likewise, once normalized, the reading growth for the vast majority of these children can be maintained through high-quality instruction in the general education classroom (Mathes et al., 2002).

Unfortunately, translating what has been demonstrated in well-controlled and well-funded research studies to everyday practice within public schools has proven to be very difficult (Gersten & Dimino, 2001). Schools that want to provide appropriate and effective early interventions for children who are at risk for reading failure face myriad challenges. For many schools, the largest hurdle to overcome is simply finding the financial resources needed to pay teacher salaries.

A common tactic among schools to minimize the cost of providing additional intervention to struggling readers is to hire paraprofessionals to deliver this instruction. However, because teaching reading to children who experience difficulties with learning to read in the classroom is a very difficult task, even for seasoned teachers (Moats, 1998), it is unclear whether paraprofessionals can deliver instruction for these children as effectively as highly trained teachers.

Presently, studies directly comparing paraprofessionals with teachers have not been conducted; thus, the research base offers little guidance on this topic. However, there is a research base on the use of adult tutors, which allows us to make some inferences about the effectiveness of paraprofessionals. For example, Wasik and Slavin (1993) reviewed five one-to-one adult tutoring interventions and concluded that programs that used highly prepared teachers had a more positive impact on student reading achievement than those that used adult tutors. Also, in the programs that did use tutors effectively, the tutors were highly trained, and they used a highly structured program that included specific manuals, student materials, and training procedures. Wasik and Slavin also reported that in order to be maximally effective, a program must provide continued professional development to the teacher or tutor providing the instruction.

Similarly, Pikulski (1994) reviewed five effective programs delivered either by certified teachers or by trained adult tutors. These school-based early intervention programs were designed primarily for first-grade students who were at risk of school failure because of their difficulty in learning to read. Like Wasik and Slavin (1993), Pikulski concluded that the most successful early intervention programs were those that were taught by highly trained, expert teachers.

More recently, a meta-analysis of the findings related to one-to-one reading interventions delivered by adults for elementary students at risk for reading failure was reported by Elbaum, Vaughn, Hughes, and Moody (2000). This meta-analysis reported that college students and trained, reliable volunteers were able to provide supplemental instruction that significantly helped struggling readers. The researchers noted that these findings indicated that college students and community volunteers can make a significant impact on reading outcomes for many students who are at risk for academic failure when the intervention is one-to-one, supplemental, well-designed, and reliably implemented.

In another review of one-to-one volunteer tutor programs, it was found that little research has documented the effectiveness of using adult volunteers. In fact, the researchers discovered that only two of the 17 programs included in the review provided evaluations using rigorous experimental designs. However, both of these studies supported the effectiveness of one-to-one tutoring using adult volunteers (Wasik, 1998). A study by Allor, Mathes, Torgesen, and Grek (2002), not included in the Wasik (1998) review, reported that adult volunteers have little impact on the academic achievement of struggling readers. However, in this study, tutors received only a short training period and little coaching once in the field.

Although the research reviews reported here and in the meta-analysis reported by Elbaum and colleagues (2000) suggest that adult volunteers can help struggling readers when the intervention is delivered under circumscribed conditions, no studies that directly compare the effectiveness of experienced teachers and well-trained paraprofessionals within the same experimental design have been reported in the literature. Given that schools must make important decisions about how to most effectively spend precious and limited resources, it is critically important to establish whether trained paraprofessionals provide intervention instruction as effectively as experienced teachers do. It is also important to determine whether there are observable differences in the teaching behaviors of these two groups that might help us understand any differences in teaching effectiveness.

This chapter describes the results of an observation instrument that provides quantitative and qualitative information comparing certified teachers with highly trained paraprofessionals. Specifically, we report findings on the similarities and differences between certified, experienced teachers and well-educated, well-trained paraprofessionals in the implementation of a highly prescriptive, first-grade reading intervention designed to prevent reading failure.

We utilized both quantitative and qualitative observational methods in order to provide both reliable evidence and understanding into the instructional process (Ogawa & Malen, 1991). According to Krathwohl, qualitative methods are used when one wants to explore a phenomenon in depth in order to learn more about it and then report it through "thick description and many nuances and details" (1993, p. 352). Thus, qualitative strategies afforded us the opportunity to discern nuances and details about differences between experienced teachers and trained paraprofessionals as they implemented a reading intervention with small groups of struggling readers that might go unnoticed if quantitative observational methods alone were employed.

METHOD

Teachers and paraprofessionals participated in this study, and the intervention was implemented with first-grade students who were identified as most at risk for experiencing difficulty with learning to read. The intervention itself, a highly prescriptive early reading curriculum, was developed specifically for this study. We developed an observation instrument as well, which allowed us to collect quantitative and qualitative data. Observations were conducted at regular intervals, and four stages of qualitative data analysis were used in order to increase the rigor of the study. The following sections address each of these features of our method in more depth.

Participants

This study was conducted across 2 years with two cohorts of first-grade children in five elementary schools serving children of widely varied socioeconomic levels and ethnicities in a southeastern, medium-sized school district. The intervention was implemented with 184 first-grade students most at risk for experiencing reading difficulty. To identify these students, all first-grade students in participating schools (1,020) were screened using a test of letter–sound knowledge. The students who scored in the bottom 35% of the letter–sound knowledge test were screened with the Woodcock Reading Mastery Test–Revised (WRMT-R; Woodcock, 1987), word identification, rapid naming of numbers, and the vocabulary subtest of the Stanford-Binet Intelligence Test, Fourth Edition (Thorndike, Hagen, & Sattler, 1986). Students with an estimated verbal intelligence quotient (IQ) above 70 who scored lowest on a combined index of letter–sound knowledge and rapid naming of numbers were identified. From this group, students at or below the 25th percentile on word identification were included in the study. Verbal IQ ranged from 72 to 122. Students who participated in this study represented 18% of the total population of first-grade students in these five elementary schools.

Teachers   Four certified teachers with varying amounts of previous experience teaching reading to children at risk for reading failure participated in this study. All four teachers participated in both years of the study. Three of the teachers had worked in previous research studies to provide either individual or small-group instruction to first-grade children, and one had served as a research assistant in previous research studies. All four were selected because of their high-level understanding of the principles of effective reading instruction for children in the primary grades.

Paraprofessionals   The paraprofessionals who participated in this study were selected because they demonstrated proficiency in phonemic awareness, alphabetic decoding, and spelling as determined by passing a relatively demanding test. None of the paraprofessionals had any formal training or experience as a teacher. They were also selected because of the warmth of their personalities and their expressed enthusiasm for working with young children.

There were five paraprofessionals during the first year of the study. Two of these continued during the second year of the study, with three new paraprofessionals hired in the second year of the study. The choice to leave the project after the first year was available to all participants, and no one was asked to leave. Six of the eight paraprofessionals had children of their own, and four of them had only recently begun to look for work because all of their children were now in school. Three of the eight were very active in the parent–teacher associations (PTAs) in their schools. One paraprofessional had recently earned a bachelor's degree in psychology and speech pathology; another was a grandmother who had recently retired from a demanding job in private industry. Table 9.1 presents demographic data for both teachers and paraprofessionals.

The Intervention

Teachers and paraprofessionals delivered instruction to small groups of children for 40-minute sessions 5 days per week from October to May. Both teachers and paraprofessionals followed a highly prescriptive early reading curriculum developed specifically for this study. We call this curriculum *Proactive Reading* (Mathes, Torgesen, Menchetti, Wahl, & Grek, 1998).

Table 9.1. Demographic information for teachers and paraprofessionals

	Teacher (n = 4)				Paraprofessional (n = 8)					
	n	Percentage	Mean	Standard deviation	n	Percentage	Mean	Standard deviation	f(1,10)	X^2
Age			47.50	3.80			45.13	10.93	.17	
Teaching certification										
None					8	100%				12.00[b]
Elementary	2	50%								
Special education	2	50%								
Education level										
High school					3	37.5%				
Associate of arts degree					3	37.5%				
Bachelor's degree	1	25%			1	12.5%				6.38[a]
Master's degree	3	75%			1	12.5%				
Years in study										
2 years	4	100%			2	25.0%				6.00[a]

[a]$p < .05$
[b]$p < .01$

Intervention Instructional Design   *Proactive Reading* is a comprehensive reading intervention designed for beginning struggling readers that scaffolds elements of tasks that are initially beyond the learner's capability, permitting the learner to concentrate on and complete only those elements that are within his or her range of competence (Wood, Bruner, & Ross, 1976). Translating the scaffolding of instruction as a deductive process, this intervention provides carefully sequenced teacher-directed instruction designed to assist children in the integrated and fluent use of alphabetic knowledge and comprehension strategies. Lessons were designed to scaffold new information to allow the children to assimilate and integrate this new information into existing schema.

In a typical lesson, the students practiced letter–sound correspondences for previously taught letters, practiced writing these letters, and learned the sound of a new letter that was chosen because it was visually and auditorially dissimilar to other recently presented letter–sound correspondences. Students also played word games designed to promote phonological awareness, practiced sounding out words composed of previously taught letter–sound correspondences, spelled words from dictation based on their letter–sound correspondences, practiced automatic recognition of words that do not conform to alphabetic rules, read and reread connected text composed of phonic elements or sight words that were previously taught, and applied simple comprehension strategies to this text. Over time, the nature of these lessons changed. In the beginning, the bulk of each lesson was devoted to learning to use the alphabetic principle quickly and efficiently, with less focus on connected text and reading for meaning. As students progressed, lessons changed in nature to focus on decoding of multisyllabic and irregular words, fluency building of connected text, and comprehension strategies. Also, as more and more alphabetic elements were mastered and students learned to cope with greater amounts of irregularity within words, the text became increasingly more difficult and more natural, even though it was technically decodable. Likewise, instruction in comprehension strategies included explicit instruction in sequencing, predicting and checking predictions, story grammar, identifying prior knowledge, and identifying main ideas.

Use of Instructional Time   A primary feature of *Proactive Reading* is that it maximized academic engagement (Brophy & Good, 1986; Rosenshine & Berliner, 1978). Lessons were delivered in a fast pace, and there was continuous interchange between the instructor and students. Likewise, teacher talk was kept to a minimum, with phrases and teaching routines used again and again. Students were required to answer many questions simultaneously, thus ensuring that they each practiced all content rather than watching and listening to a peer respond to the teacher. In a typical routine, the teacher asked all students to respond to letters, words, or text in unison, followed by individual turns in which each child was able to demonstrate his or her mastery of the content. Another aspect of the nature of each lesson was that the instructor moved quickly from activity to activity within each lesson. A typical lesson consisted of seven to ten short activities that encompassed multiple strands of content (i.e., phonemic awareness, alphabetic decoding/encoding, text fluency, comprehension strategies). Although time dedicated to each activity varied by the nature of the content to be learned, no activity required more than 7–10 minutes on any given day. By changing activities frequently, children with short attention spans appeared to be able to stay focused on the task at hand.

Teaching Routines Explicit teaching routines for each strategy were an important part of this reading intervention. Teachers followed a highly detailed, prescriptive lesson plan that fully explicated, including exact wording, each aspect of each activity. An overarching teaching routine that was repeated throughout the entire curriculum was composed of the instructor modeling new content, providing guided practice for students, and implementing independent practice for every activity. The specific teaching routines associated with the various activities were also repeated again and again. However, the specific teaching routine changed depending on the skill being taught. Learning the teaching routines were a significant part of the professional development.

Presentation Techniques A crucial part of ensuring the effectiveness of *Proactive Reading* was using the various presentation techniques well. Instruction was delivered to small, homogeneous groups of students who sat in a semicircle around the instructor. This design allowed the instructor the opportunity to give directions, allow think time, and then elicit student responses (Rowe, 1987). Instructors were expected to keep a fast pace for the entire lesson, including making seamless transitions from activity to activity within each lesson. A well-paced lesson moved as quickly as the children within the group were able to move. The objective for the teacher was to help the children develop greater fluency in all aspects of reading and learning, including lexical retrieval, word reading, text reading, and word writing.

Instructors were required to consistently monitor students' responses, provide positive feedback for correct responses, and give corrective feedback if an error occurred. Instructors were asked to maintain a ratio of four positive praise points for every one correction. In terms of errors, instructors were asked to make on-the-spot judgments about why an error occurred and to focus on that aspect of the task when corrective feedback was provided. Likewise, instructors had to establish clear and consistent visual and auditory cues to elicit unison responses from the children when required, and they needed to be able to shift back and forth between asking for group and individual responses throughout the lesson. Instructors were also asked to create a climate of emotional warmth and support and to convey this climate to the students.

To facilitate student enthusiasm for learning, instructors provided immediate positive feedback about each activity as the students demonstrated mastery. Instructors were provided with a mastery sheet that simply listed all of the lessons by number with columns for each activity within the lesson. Instructors placed a checkmark on the mastery sheet at the end of each activity while verbally praising students. Once all of the activities associated with a particular lesson were mastered, a sticker was placed on the mastery sheet for that lesson.

In *Proactive Reading,* mastery was defined as 100% accuracy of each activity by every child every day. A major job for the instructor was judging when mastery had been achieved. Because the curriculum was designed to become more complex gradually and cumulatively, the majority of each lesson was composed of review and generalization work. Each lesson had very little new information. Thus, if mastery had been achieved on previous lessons, children should have experienced little difficulty achieving mastery on new lessons. The expectation was that children would enter each new activity able to achieve at least 80% accuracy on their first try, with 100% mastery being achieved after error corrections and scaffolding had occurred. Children demonstrated mastery during individual turns. If an error occurred during individual turns, the instructor provided additional instruction and group practice, followed by another round of individual turns. This process was repeated until all children were able to perform the task without error. If a particular task proved to be very difficult for a group of children, the instructor was allowed to go on to another activity, returning to the difficult task later in the same lesson or on the following day.

Professional Development   Teachers and paraprofessionals participated in the same professional development over the same period of time. This professional development consisted of two phases. The first phase, initial training, consisted of two full-day and two half-day workshops. During the 2 full days of initial professional development, *Proactive Reading* and its underlying principles were introduced, videotapes of the implementation of *Proactive Reading* were viewed and discussed, modeling by the authors was provided, and practice and feedback was afforded. The days of initial professional development offered the teachers and paraprofessionals the opportunity to practice teaching *Proactive Reading* lessons with each other, ask questions, and receive feedback from the project coordinators.

The second phase of the professional development for *Proactive Reading* consisted of ongoing monthly meetings with teachers and paraprofessionals meeting in their respective groups with project coordinators. During the on-going monthly meetings, a videotaped lesson of one of the instructors was viewed and discussed, concerns were addressed, and more instructional training was conducted. Over time, teaching procedures for *Proactive Reading* activities changed as students became independent readers. During these meetings, teaching procedures were modeled, discussed, and practiced.

As part of the ongoing professional development of the second phase, written and verbal feedback were provided to instructors immediately after a lesson was observed. The project coordinator modeled *Proactive Reading* activities with students as needed. Instructors also had daily access to the project coordinators to answer questions via telephone and e-mail. Finally, *Proactive Reading* instructors were required to view their own videotaped lessons and critique them based on the criteria established for the observation measure, which the following section describes.

The Observation Instrument

For this research study, we developed an observation instrument that allowed us to collect both quantitative and qualitative data in order to determine whether there were observable differences between certified teachers and paraprofessionals, given the same degree of professional development for this intervention. Both of the observers for this research study held at least a master's degree in education, had experience in teaching struggling readers learn to read, and possessed expertise in the design and delivery of the intervention.

As a first step in developing this observation instrument, we reviewed videotaped *Proactive Reading* lessons to discern discrete, observable categories. Identified categories were then discussed with the primary author of the curriculum, and the most critical observable teaching behaviors were determined, including 1) instructional pacing, 2) adherence to the lesson plan, 3) providing independent practice, 4) correcting errors using appropriate scaffolds, 5) teaching until the level of mastery, 6) maintaining student attentiveness, and 7) eliciting student responses. These categories then guided both the quantitative and qualitative data collection.

In addition to the seven categories, observers answer yes or no to several global items, including whether 1) the teacher had materials ready, 2) students could see instructional materials, 3) students were seated appropriately, and 4) the teacher exhibited warmth and enthusiasm for learning. Figure 9.1 presents the first and last pages of the observation instrument illustrating the global items, categories rated for each activity, and how scores for each category were calculated. As illustrated, the general questions are listed first, followed by an observation of each activity rated for the seven critical instructional behaviors. Observers recorded the lesson number, lesson start and end times, and each activity observed on this instrument.

Quantitative Data   Once these categories were identified, the quantitative aspect of the fidelity measure was created. Every *Proactive Reading* lesson encompassed seven to ten activities, so when a lesson was observed, each activity was rated for all seven categories. The primary goal of this observation instrument was to discern how closely *Proactive Reading* instructors implemented the curriculum in the manner in which it was intended. To accomplish this goal, a three-point rating scale was used for each of the seven categories. A score of 3 indicated that the instructor implemented the category in exactly the way it was intended. A score of 2 represented that the category was implemented in an acceptable manner but with some error, and a score of 1 indicated the category was poorly represented.

To conduct an observation utilizing the *Proactive Reading* fidelity measure, the observer needed the observation instrument and the *Proactive Reading* instructor's manual that contained the daily lessons plans. During each observation, the observer sat in an unobtrusive spot and followed along in the teacher's manual as the instructor presented a lesson, but the observer did not interact with the instructor. Instructors were informed prior to each observation which week it would take place, and every observation was videotaped. Each of the seven categories was scored by the observer using very specific guidelines. These guidelines are summarized in Table 9.2.

Data Collection

Observations were conducted approximately every 6 weeks, for a total of 5 observations each year, or 10 across the 2 years of the study. All four teachers and two paraprofessionals were observed across all 10 observations because they participated in both years of the study. Three paraprofessionals were observed six times, and two paraprofessionals

Fidelity Measure for Teachers and Paraprofessionals

This represents excerpts of the observation. Places for recording observations have been compressed. Key: 1 = Poor, 2 = Average, 3 = Excellent.

Date: _____   Instructor: _____

Observer: _____   Start time: _____

Lesson number: _____   End time: _____

Number of students in group: _____   Length of lesson: _____

1. Are the materials ready?	Yes	No
2. Can the students see the materials?	Yes	No
3. Are the students seated properly?	Yes	No
4. Does the instructor exhibit enthusiasm and warmth toward the students?	Yes	No

Activity 1: _____	Numeric evaluation (1–3)
5. Is the pacing appropriate?	
6. Is the lesson plan presented appropriately?	
7. Is the independent practice implemented appropriately?	
8. Are all errors corrected and is scaffolding used appropriately?	
9. Was the activity taught to mastery?	
10. Are the students attentive?	
11. Are all students able to follow the signals and respond in unison?	

Field notes:

Fidelity Measure

Category	Total score/total possible	Average score
Yes/no questions (1–5)		
5. Pacing		
6. Lesson plan adherence		
7. Independent practice		
8. Error corrections/scaffolding		
9. Mastery		
10. Student attentiveness		
11. Signals		

Figure 9.1. First and last pages of the observation instrument.

were observed four times. One paraprofessional was observed only three times because of excessive absences.

Interobserver Reliability   Before collecting the data, interobserver reliability was established through a process of discussing the definitions of each category, reviewing videotape footage of lessons while recording scores on the observation measure, and discussing discrepancies in ratings between observers. Once reliability of 90% was established, observers began to collect observational data of the instructors. Initial observation data were collected by observers and interobserver scores calculated, and discrepancies were discussed and revisions to category definitions were made. Once an acceptable level of interobserver reliability of 85% had been achieved on the revised version, observers collected data independently. However, with each new observation cycle, the process of establishing interobserver reliability was repeated in order to ensure that observer drift was not occurring. In total, interobserver reliability was collected on 47% of all observations. Interrater reliability was calculated for each category of every activity within a lesson by dividing the number of agreements by the total number of agreements and disagreements. Each category across every activity within the lesson was examined to determine whether the observers agreed on the 3-point scale. For example, if a lesson incorporated seven activities, pacing was evaluated activity by activity to determine whether the two observers agreed seven times. If they agreed that each pacing category earned a score of 3 for the first six activities of a lesson but disagreed on the seventh activity (e.g., one observer rated pacing a 3 and the other rated pacing a 2 for the same activity), then 6 divided by 7 was calculated to obtain a reliability score of 86% for pacing for that lesson. With the exception of the category of corrections, reliability observations consistently yielded percentages above 80%, as illustrated in Table 9.3.

Qualitative Data

Four stages of the qualitative data analysis were conducted to increase the rigor of this analysis. The first stage consisted of collecting field notes, which were of primary importance to this study because they were the groundwork for all further analyses. During each observation, the observers recorded field notes for every activity. These field notes were guided by the same categories that were determined as the most critical observable teaching behaviors: 1) adjusting instructional pacing, 2) adhering to the lesson plan, 3) providing independent practice, 4) correcting errors using appropriate scaffolds, 5) teaching until the level of mastery, 6) maintaining student attentiveness, and 7) eliciting

Table 9.2. Guidelines for scoring the seven categories

Category	3: Excellent	2: Average	1: Poor
Instructional pacing	Used quick pace to keep students' attention and increased fluency Did not move so fast that students guessed or made errors Quickly moved from item to item within activity and between activities	Fluctuated between appropriate and too fast or too slow	Consistently moved too fast or too slow
Lesson plan adherence	Used lesson plan as a guide Did not read word for word Followed instructional routines Elicited unison responses before independent practice Provided practice reading connected text the number of times prescribed Led activities when indicated Had students lead activities when indicated Kept extraneous language to a minimum	Did not deliver instruction consistently as prescribed Stopped the lesson in order to study the plan	Obviously was not prepared Presented content in a manner that significantly differed from the lesson plan Consistently participated in the activities with the students
Independent practice	Implemented with each student Made sure that all students could see materials Encouraged all students to practice when it was not their turn Monitored all students	Implemented the lesson plan with only some of the students Did not maintain attention of other students	Did not implement the lesson plan Ignored students while one was engaged in independent practice

Error correction	Corrected all errors immediately using appropriate procedures Implemented scaffolding appropriately No errors occurred	Consistently corrected errors but did implement scaffolding appropriately	Did not consistently correct errors and immediately use error correction procedures and scaffolding
Mastery	Allowed each student to demonstrate his or her ability to complete a task independently with no errors	Did not attend to students consistently Moved on to next activity when current activity was not mastered by every student	Had little regard for ensuring mastery for every student
Student attentiveness	Ensured students' attention before beginning each activity Ensured that students responded appropriately during group work Ensured that students were academically engaged during independent writing	Talked to students more than twice about attending to the activity	Engaged in more discipline than instruction Had no behavior management system in place when it was needed
Eliciting student responses	Used nonverbal or verbal cues predictably and consistently	Used cues that were unclear or unpredictable, resulting in students not answering together	Made no attempt to elicit unison responses Accepted responses from one or two students as unison responses

Table 9.3. Average percentages of interobserver reliability by category for teachers and paraprofessionals

	Number of reliability observations	Pacing	Adherence to lesson plan	Independent practice	Error correction	Mastery	Student attentiveness	Eliciting student responses
Teacher	20%	93%	93%	96%	91%	99%	100%	94%
Paraprofessional	22%	89%	85%	92%	75%	88%	83%	86%

student responses. This preassigned coding system was used to focus the observers' field notes. As they observed each activity across the lesson, the field notes served as the rationale behind the particular quantitative scores earned, especially for ratings of excellent and poor. Incidents, instructor quotes, and behaviors relating to the seven categories were recorded and described.

The second stage of the qualitative data analysis occurred on the same day the observation took place. The observer read the field notes recorded on the observation instrument during that day's lesson and wrote a one-page synthesis report based on those field notes. This synthesis report consisted of specific effective instructional strategies and instructional suggestions and was provided to the instructor as feedback via e-mail on the same day the lesson was observed.

The next stage of the qualitative data analysis was conducted at the end of the study. During this stage, all of the synthesis reports for each instructor were analyzed in terms of each of the seven categories. During this analysis, focus was geared toward one instructor at a time and one category at a time. The synthesis reports were intensely reviewed and patterns for each category emerged until a specific statement (e.g., slow pace) regarding each category could be determined. This statement was recorded on a table. Thus, we created a table for each instructor that contained a succinct statement describing each of the seven categories for every observation. For example, if an instructor was observed six times, then the six synthesis reports were analyzed and six succinct statements for each category were recorded on the table. This systematic method allowed the researchers to organize the salient qualitative observational information of the experienced teachers and trained paraprofessionals.

For the final stage of the qualitative data analysis, the first author compared the tables for each respective group (paraprofessionals and teachers) to determine whether common patterns of behaviors could be detected among the groups. When patterns were found, they were recorded on a matrix. These combined data afforded the researchers the opportunity to compare and contrast the teachers' data and the paraprofessionals' data. Based on this analysis, assertions about similarities and differences between the teachers and paraprofessionals were determined. Videotapes were reviewed to determine the accuracy of these assertions.

Interobserver Reliability   The process for determining interobserver reliability for the qualitative data was stringent. To increase the reliability of the qualitative aspect of this study, the observers remained constant across both years and each held at least a master's degree in education, had experience in teaching struggling readers learn to read, and were very familiar with the project. To guard against observer bias, interobserver reliability for the field notes was collected on 34% of all observations. For each reliability observation, field notes were tallied by activity and by category to determine how many comments the observers had in common. Percentage of agreement for each category was calculated by dividing the number of comments the observers had in common by the total number of comments made by both observers. Field note reliability can be found in Table 9.4.

Academic Measures

Pre- and post-test reading achievement was measured using the Word Attack, Word Identification, and Passage Comprehension subtests of the WMRT–R (Woodcock, 1987). Likewise, end-of-year reading comprehension was measured with the Reading Comprehension subtest of the Stanford Achievement Test 9 (Harcourt Educational, 1996).

RESULTS

Quantitative Data

Quantitative data were analyzed through SPSS for Windows, version 11.0. A 2 between (teacher and paraprofessional) and 1 within (time of observation), repeated measure one-tailed ANOVAs was conducted for each category. The decision to use one-tailed analyses was made before the study began because we expected any differences observed to favor certified teachers. No time by instructor type (i.e. teacher or paraprofessional) interactions or main effects for time of observation were detected for any category. However, main effects for instructor type were observed on several categories. Table 9.5 presents the means, standard deviations, f-values and effect sizes for category averages and total fidelity for the main effects of teacher as compared with paraprofessionals.

Qualitative Analysis

Analysis of field notes indicated that all instructors, with the exception of one paraprofessional, arranged the learning environment appropriately and with minimal environmental distractions. Both the teachers and paraprofessionals exhibited enthusiasm and warmth toward the students. This was demonstrated by the conveyance of verbal and nonverbal positive interactions with the students. Every instructor's

Table 9.4. Consistency of observers on independently collected field notes

	Pacing	Lesson plan adherence	Independent practice	Error correction	Mastery	Student attention	Eliciting responses
Total	43	150	38	115	45	66	85
Observer-common comments	38	110	38	90	40	50	56
Percentage of overlapping comments	88%	73%	100%	78%	89%	76%	66%

Table 9.5. Fidelity to intervention observation average scores for teachers and paraprofessionals

Category	Teachers (n = 4)		Paraprofessionals (n = 8)		f(1,10)	ES
	Mean	Standard deviation	Mean	Standard deviation		
Pacing	95.25	3.59	89.00	6.46	3.64[a]	1.09
Adherence to lesson plan	95.50	3.11	83.50	16.02	1.84	.89
Independent practice	97.75	.95	93.50	7.15	1.31	.71
Correcting errors	99.50	1.00	87.25	10.78	4.83[a]	1.36
Teaching to mastery	98.25	1.25	91.00	10.35	1.79	.84
Student attentiveness	97.75	1.50	87.38	11.08	3.83[a]	1.11
Student responses	97.00	1.63	83.88	13.47	3.48[a]	1.16
Total fidelity	97.29	1.51	87.93	9.61	3.57[a]	1.16

[a]$p \leq .05$

demeanor was pleasant as they all showed genuine interest, concern, and acceptance of all students. The qualitative data also illuminated similarities and differences between teachers and paraprofessionals in regard to the seven categories. These data were consistent with the quantitative data, thus providing triangulation from multiple sources and for a more in-depth understanding of the meaning of the quantitative findings. Table 9.6 presents the average scores for each instructor by each category gathered from the quantitative instrument used to verify observational impressions.

Pacing   In terms of instructional pacing, all certified teachers and five of the eight paraprofessionals were able to consistently maintain an appropriate pace of instruction during lessons. However, three of the eight paraprofessionals found maintaining an appropriate pace very challenging. Evidence of this finding is apparent on the average scores of the teachers and paraprofessionals presented in Table 9.5. Three of the paraprofessionals had scores falling below 90%. Among these three paraprofessionals, pacing was typically too slow, affording the students time to disengage academically and engage in off-task behavior. Conversely, sometimes these paraprofessionals moved through an activity too quickly, skipping elements of the lesson plan and not ensuring student mastery.

Lesson Plan Adherence   Overall, teachers adhered to the lesson plan more closely and more naturally than did the paraprofessionals. Three of the eight paraprofessionals did not always adhere to the lesson plan. This is evident in the average scores of teachers and paraprofessionals as well. Each of the four teachers adhered to the lesson plan

Table 9.6. Means for individual teachers and paraprofessionals by category

	Number of observations	Pacing	Lesson plan adherence	Independent practice	Error correction	Mastery	Student attention	Eliciting responses
Teacher 1	10	90	94	97	100	98	97	95
Teacher 2	10	97	93	97	98	97	96	97
Teacher 3	10	96	95	98	100	98	99	97
Teacher 4	10	98	100	99	100	100	99	99
Teacher average		95	96	98	100	98	98	97
Paraprofessional 1	10	90	96	98	96	97	96	94
Paraprofessional 2	10	98	88	96	93	98	99	97
Paraprofessional 3	6	79	73	96	77	85	67	76
Paraprofessional 4	6	94	96	96	99	100	88	96
Paraprofessional 5	6	93	94	94	94	94	80	85
Paraprofessional 6	4	82	50	76	67	68	80	58
Paraprofessional 7	4	91	93	96	85	92	98	90
Paraprofessional 8	3	85	78	96	87	94	91	75
Paraprofessional average		89	83	93	87	91	87	84

more than 90% of the time, whereas three of the paraprofessionals had a difficult time adhering to the lesson plan, as reflected in averages below 80%. Teachers typically committed minor violations, such as inadvertently omitting a word from a word list, whereas paraprofessionals made major violations including mispronunciation of letter sounds, consistently omitting items within activities, and leading activities when the lesson plan called for the students to lead the activity. Likewise, paraprofessionals were more likely to read directly from the lesson plan, rather than referring to the plan only as a guide and presenting the routine in a natural manner.

Independent Practice   With the exception of one paraprofessional, the quantitative average scores revealed that both teachers and paraprofessionals implemented independent practice. That is, teachers and paraprofessionals implemented independent practice with averages reaching more than 95%. However, the qualitative data revealed specific nuances in the manner in which independent practice was implemented by teachers and paraprofessionals that were somewhat different. On the whole, teachers displayed a greater level of "with-it-ness" by consistently monitoring all students during independent practice, whereas paraprofessionals were more likely to focus all of their attention on the one student who was engaged in independent practice.

Error Correction and Scaffolding   Teachers consistently corrected errors appropriately, whereas four of the paraprofessionals had a more difficult time correcting student errors. As Table 9.5 indicates, the teachers' means for the error correction category were 98% or higher; whereas four of the paraprofessionals had much lower means of 67%, 77%, 85%, and 87%. The qualitative data denoted that the teachers consistently gave immediate corrective feedback to students, implemented the prescribed error correction procedures, and used scaffolding appropriately. However, when a student error occurred, four of the paraprofessionals were more likely to say, "No" or simply provide the answer for the student. For example, during story reading, the paraprofessionals did not consistently follow the prescribed error correction procedure of prompting students to sound out a difficult word; however, the teachers did. An example of a teacher appropriately scaffolding instruction occurred when she assisted the students in arriving at the correct word by having the students analyze the word, using previously mastered letter–sound associations, and then providing other sounds when needed. In similar situations, paraprofessionals were more likely to simply provide the word for the students when they encountered difficulty.

Mastery   With the exception of two paraprofessionals, both teachers and paraprofessionals consistently taught students until they reached mastery. All four teachers had average scores of 97% or better, and six of the eight paraprofessionals had average scores of 90% or better for the mastery category. The qualitative data confirmed that all teachers and six paraprofessionals were mindful of the importance of ensuring that each student mastered every activity, showed patience, allowed struggling students more time to practice, continued to work on a skill when necessary, and did not move to the next activity until each student had mastered the previous one. However, two paraprofessionals consistently continued with the next activity before each student had demonstrated mastery for the previous one. Although these paraprofessionals did provide opportunities for children to demonstrate mastery, the difficulty arose in judging whether mastery had been achieved. In each case, the paraprofessionals consistently accepted partial mastery by correcting the errors but not cycling through group practice and then retesting for mastery.

Student Attentiveness   Overall, teachers held the students' attention more consistently than did paraprofessionals. The quantitative results show that the teachers' average scores in this category were 95% and higher; whereas three of the eight paraprofessionals had average scores of 80% and lower. An important nuance detected through observation was that teachers were more likely than paraprofessionals to gain students' attention before beginning an activity by stating and modeling expectations. For example, a teacher would say, "It is time for stretch and blend," model an example of one item of the stretch and blend activity, and then begin the activity only when she was sure she had each student's attention. In contrast, paraprofessionals did not consistently use any type of transition language between activities or provide a model of what was expected. Paraprofessionals would begin activities even when it was evident that each student was not fully engaged, and they would continue with the activity without full participation from every student.

Eliciting Responses   A consistent observation was that teachers were able to elicit student responses more consistently than were paraprofessionals. This is apparent in the average scores presented in Table 9.5. All four teachers' mean scores were 95% and higher, whereas four of the eight paraprofessionals' mean scores were 58%, 75%, 76%, and 85% for the eliciting responses category. When *Proactive Reading* instruction began, all of the teachers emphasized the importance of the students responding together on signal and provided them time and opportunity to practice this task. Such emphasis did not occur among the four low-scoring paraprofessionals. Likewise, two additional factors impeded these four paraprofessionals in eliciting unison responses. First, visual and auditory signals were not always consistent across activities. Thus, students did not know what to do and when to do it. For example, paraprofessionals said, "Read it" when they wanted students to read a word in one activity and then in the next activity, they simply pointed to the word and expected students to respond. This inconsistency led students to be unsure about when they should respond. Second, paraprofessionals did not always provide enough think time for the students. For example, a cue may have been given at the same time a question was asked, which did not allow the students ample time to determine an answer and then respond at the appropriate time.

Student Achievement Outcomes

In terms of promoting academic growth with students, both the teachers and the paraprofessionals were equally effective in stimulating reading growth in this sample of first-grade children who were at risk for reading difficulties. For both teachers and paraprofessionals, the intervention was very effective. For example, standard scores on a measure of phonemic decoding (Word Attack from the WRMT-R) increased from 86 to 113 for the teachers and from 86 to 111 for the paraprofessionals. Standard scores on the Word Identification subtest increased from 80 to 105 for both teachers and paraprofessionals, and scores on the Passage Comprehension subtest from the WRMT-R test were 99 for both groups. Furthermore, the year-end score on the test of reading comprehension administered by the school (Stanford Achievement Test 9) was at the 50th percentile for the children taught by the teachers, and at the 53rd percentile for students taught by the paraprofessionals. At the end of the year, average words per minute read accurately on first-grade level passages for children taught by the teachers was 57, and for children taught by the paraprofessionals, it was 54.

DISCUSSION

The results of the present study indicate that teachers and paraprofessionals do not deliver instruction equally well. In terms of the quantitative data, reliable differences were detected for these two groups of instructors on instructional pacing, error correction, maintaining student attentiveness, and eliciting student responses. Thus, of seven possible categories, practices in four were significantly different. Therefore, it is not surprising that the overall ratings for teachers and paraprofessionals were also statistically different. In each instance, teachers were rated significantly higher than paraprofessionals were.

Because statistical significance is largely an artifact of sample size and the sample size of the current study was relatively small, we interpreted our results both in terms of p values and effect sizes (Thompson, 1999). The effect size for each of these statistically significant differences ranges from 1.16 to 1.36, suggesting that the magnitude of the observed difference was robust. Likewise, effect sizes for the remaining three categories that were not statistically different had fairly large effect sizes ranging from .71 to .89. In total, effect size information suggests that substantial differences were observed between teachers and paraprofessionals, favoring teachers across all categories.

Qualitative descriptions of instruction provided insight into differences in instructional delivery between teachers and paraprofessionals. These data afford detail descriptions of instructor behavior that explain the quantitative data. This specific information targeted behaviors and could then be utilized as feedback to help improve instruction. It is important to note that three of the eight paraprofessionals had difficulties, in the sense that their quantitative scores were below 80% much of the time.

In terms of the qualitative data, differences were detected between experienced teachers and trained paraprofessionals for each of the seven categories. Overall, teachers were more consistent in implementing instruction the way in which it was intended than were the paraprofessionals. Teachers consistently kept a more appropriate pace of instruction than the paraprofessionals, which assisted in keeping the students' attention. Teachers also provided more scaffolding to the students when an error occurred than did the paraprofessionals. The teachers were better able to elicit student responses through the use of verbal and nonverbal cues. In terms of lesson plan adherence, the teachers were more natural and even though both instructor types implemented independent practice, teachers did so differently.

A Caveat

Given that the findings of this study suggest that the trained paraprofessionals did not deliver instruction as well as the experienced teachers, we predict that academic outcomes of the students would have been affected. However, there were no academic differences detected between students taught by trained paraprofessionals and those taught by experienced teachers. Thus, it would appear that although paraprofessionals and teachers presented instruction in discernibly different ways, these differences were not sufficient to affect the performance levels of the students.

Explaining the Findings

Although we can only speculate about why student outcomes were not different when instructional delivery was different, there are several possible explanations. First, only three of the eight paraprofessionals accounted for the differences between teachers and paraprofessionals. These three paraprofessionals together taught 30 students. Thus, only 16% of the paraprofessional–student sample was affected. Likewise, it is unknown how low fidelity can be before outcomes are affected. Although the average fidelity across paraprofessionals was discernibly lower than that of teachers on four of the seven categories, these scores were still above 83%. Given our results, we must conclude that, for the curriculum being examined in this study, fidelity scores above 83% are adequate to foster academic growth. In other words, both the teachers and paraprofessionals did a good job delivering the instruction, with the teachers doing a reliably better job. In this study, the difference between good and better instructional delivery did not produce a noticeable effect on student outcomes.

It must be recognized that the curriculum itself was designed to promote academic gains, even if instructional delivery was less than perfect. For example, even if an instructor did not correct every error, the curriculum was designed so that the item would appear several more times across several days. Thus, the likelihood that content would never be corrected and that the student would never achieve mastery was greatly reduced. Similarly, the repetitive nature of the lessons provided a safeguard against an instructor's inability to maintain student attentiveness or to ensure that every student masters each task.

Likewise, explicitness of the lessons may have provided adequate structure to allow paraprofessionals to provide reasonably effective instruction. In other words, the way in which the curriculum was organized and lessons were fully explicated ensured student success. The careful design of the curriculum introduced new information and skills only after the students were provided ample practice opportunities to master previously introduced skills. Furthermore, the use of repetitive routines and consistent language facilitated the paraprofessionals' ability to teach hard concepts without confusing students.

It is also important to note that the paraprofessionals in this study were not typical. They were carefully selected based on their skills in phonemic awareness and alphabetic decoding as well as their genuine enthusiasm and dedication to working with young students struggling to learn to read. Twenty-five percent of the paraprofessionals had college educations and could have pursued alternative certification to become certified teachers. Typically, the only qualification for becoming a paraprofessional is having a high school degree. It is unclear if the results observed in the current study would be replicated with a more typical population of paraprofessionals.

Both teachers and paraprofessionals in this study received considerable ongoing support and professional development. It is likely that the fidelity score observed for both teachers and paraprofessionals would be lower in a typical setting. How much lower remains to be seen. We can only speculate that teachers would continue to score higher than paraprofessionals. What we are confident about is that if we had not provided continuous support, the paraprofessionals in this study would have floundered, and teacher fidelity would have been lower.

Finally, all the children in this study were also receiving systematic and explicit instruction in basic reading skills within their regular classrooms for periods ranging from 30 minutes to 2 hours per day. On average, the students received more instruction from the experienced teachers in their classrooms than they did from the intervention teachers and paraprofessionals, and it is clear that effective classroom instruction can produce large gains for children such as those included in this study (Foorman, Francis, Fletcher, Schatschneider, & Mehta, 1998). Thus, student outcomes in the study were the product both of the intervention instruction and of the instruction children received in the classroom. Thus, the differences in instructional delivery between the paraprofessionals and the teachers in the intervention conditions may simply have been overwhelmed by the overall amount of effective instruction students were provided during the period of the study.

In sum, the amalgamation of a carefully planned intervention curriculum, atypical paraprofessionals (carefully selected for phonological and reading skills and enthusiasm for teaching); extensive, ongoing professional development; and effective classroom instruction contributed to the academic success of the students. Given the overall power of the instructional context these children were exposed to in first grade, the differences in instructional delivery observed between the teachers and paraprofessionals in this study were not sufficient to produce differences in student outcomes.

CONCLUSION

We now have evidence that carefully selected paraprofessionals teaching a well-designed reading curriculum and receiving an abundance of professional development can produce similar student outcomes as experienced teachers teaching the same curriculum. However, caution is merited. The conditions of the current study were ideal and may not be easily replicated in typical school settings.

Even further caution is merited in terms of having paraprofessionals provide instruction using curricular materials that are less carefully designed and clearly prescribed. Few instructional materials provide exact phrasing or explain the instructional routines to be followed step by step. Clearly, future research is needed to see if similar outcomes can be found when the curriculum is not as carefully organized and not as much professional development is offered. Furthermore, it is possible that the consistent differences in instructional delivery observed in this study between paraprofessionals and teachers may have been more important for student outcomes if students had not been receiving systematic and explicit instruction in the classroom. It is likely that the quality of the intervention will be increasingly important with the decreasing effectiveness of classroom instruction. Finally, this study raises interesting questions related to the range of fidelity scores that might begin to produce a noticeable impact on student outcomes. Clearly, the answers to these questions are related to other factors in the student's overall instructional experience (e.g., the quality of classroom instruction), but there should be a lower limit beyond which further decreases in fidelity of implementation produce decreasing effectiveness in students' learning.

REFERENCES

Allor, J.H., Mathes, P.G., Torgesen, J.K., & Grek, M.L. (2002). *Using adult volunteers to enhance the effects of peer-assisted literacy strategies with first-grade struggling readers: Research to practice issues.* Unpublished manuscript.

Brophy, J.E., & Good, T.L. (1986). Teacher behavior and student achievement. In M. Wittrock (Ed.), *Third handbook of research on teaching* (pp. 328–375). New York: Macmillan.

Elbaum, B., Vaughn, S., Hughes, M.T., & Moody, S.W. (2000). How effective are one-to-one tutoring programs in reading for elementary students at risk for reading failure? A meta-analysis of the intervention research. *Journal of Educational Psychology, 92*(4), 605–619.

Foorman, B.R., Francis, D.J., Fletcher, J.M., Schatschneider, C., & Mehta, P. (1998). The role of instruction in learning to read: Preventing reading failure in at-risk children. *Journal of Educational Psychology, 90,* 37–55.

Francis, D.J., Shaywitz, S.E., Stuebing, K.K., Shaywitz, B.A., & Fletcher, J.M. (1996). Developmental lag versus deficit models of reading disability: A longitudinal, individual growth curve analysis. *Journal of Educational Psychology, 88*(1), 3–17.

Gersten, R., & Dimino, J. (2001). The realities of translating research into classroom practice. *Learning Disabilities: Research & Practice, 16*(2), 20–30.

Harcourt Educational. (1996). *Stanford Achievement Test Series* (9th ed). San Antonio, TX: Author.

Krathwohl, D.R. (1993). *Methods of educational and social science research.* White Plains, NY: Longman.

Mathes, P.G., Denton, C.A., Fletcher, J.M., Anthony, J., & Francis, D. (2002). *Preventing reading failure in first-grade: A comparison of 3 interventions.* Unpublished manuscript.

Mathes, P.G., Torgesen, J.K., Menchetti, J.C., Wahl, M., & Grek, M.L. (1998). *Proactive Reading: Early reading curriculum for struggling readers, Books A–F.* (Teacher guides, daily lesson materials, and student activity books). Available from P.G. Mathes, Center for Academic and Reading Skills, University of Texas-Houston Medical School, 7000 Fannin, UCT 2443, Houston, TX 77030.

Moats, L.C. (1998). Teaching decoding. *American Educator, 22*(1 & 2), 42–49, 95–96.

Ogawa R.T., & Malen, B. (1991). Towards rigor in reviews of multivocal literatures: Applying the exploratory case study method. *Review of Educational Research, 61*(3), 265–286.

Pikulski, J.J. (1994). Preventing reading failure: A review of five effective programs. *The Reading Teacher, 48*(1), 30–39.

Rosenshine, B.V., & Berliner, D.C. (1978). Academic engaged time. *British Journal of Teacher Education, 4,* 3–16.

Rowe, M. (1987, Spring). Wait time: Slowing down may be a way of speeding up. *American Educator,* 38–43.

Snow, C.E., Burns, M.S., & Griffin, P. (Eds.). (1998). *Preventing reading disabilities in young children.* Washington, DC: National Academy Press.

Thompson, B. (1999). Improving research clarity and usefulness with effect size indices as supplements to statistical significance tests. *Exceptional Children, 65*(3), 329–337.

Thorndike, R.L., Hagen, E.P., & Sattler, J.M. (1986). *Guide for administering and scoring the Stanford-Binet Intelligence Scale* (4th ed.). Chicago: Riverside Publishing.

Torgesen, J.K. (1998) Catch them before they fall. *American Educator, 22*(1 & 2), 32–39.

Torgesen, J.K., & Burgess, S.R. (1998). Consistency of reading-related phonological processes throughout early childhood: Evidence from longitudinal-correlational and instructional studies. In J. Metsala & L. Ehri (Eds.), *Word recognition in beginning reading* (pp. 161–185). Mahwah, NJ: Lawrence Erlbaum and Associates.

Torgesen, J.K., Wagner, R.K., Rashotte, C.A., Rose, E., Lindamood, P., Conway, T., & Garvin, C. (1999). Preventing reading failure in young children with phonological processing disabilities: Group and individual responses to instruction. *Journal of Educational Psychology, 91,* 579–593.

Vellutino, F.R. (1996). Cognitive profiles of difficult-to-remediate and readily remediated poor readers: Early intervention as a vehicle for distinguishing between cognitive and experiential deficits as basic causes of specific reading disability. *Journal of Educational Psychology, 88*(4), 601–638.

Wasik, B.A. (1998). Volunteer tutoring programs in reading: A review. *Reading Research Quarterly, 33*(3), 266–292.

Wasik, B.A., & Slavin, R.E. (1993). Preventing early reading failure with one-to-one tutoring: A review of five programs. *Reading Research Quarterly, 28*(2), 178–200.

Wolf, J.M. (1998). Just read. *Educational Leadership, 55*(8), 61–63.

Wood, D., Bruner, J.S., & Ross, G. (1976). The role of tutoring in problem solving. *Journal of Child Psychology, 17,* 89–100.

Woodcock, R. (1987). *Woodcock Reading Mastery Tests.* Circle Pines, MN: American Guidance Service.

Index

Page numbers followed by *f* or *t* indicate figures or tables, respectively.